Keep thumbs and fingers close to the needle tips, so that they have to move only short distances

In flat knitting, keep the work reasonably gathered towards the working ends. It will feel lighter than if spread evenly along the needles

If you suffer from wrist problems, you might find circular needles less of a strain

Knit in good light, so you don't strain your eyes. If working with dark colours, place a white cloth on your lap – the stitches show better

Relax. Don't clutch the needles as if your life depended on them

Make both hands share equally in the work

Keep the stitches as close to the needle tips as they will go without dropping off, so as not to stretch the work

Circular needles are the best option for knitting in public – they are more portable, and you won't poke your fellow passengers in the eye!

Keep yarn and equipment away from pets and small children

Sit comfortably, without slumping

Wash your hands before you start!

It's okay to drink and knit – but your rows might go wonky

Sitting pretty 11

I've got the book – now what?!

You're probably itching to get started now. For the moment, put that gorgeous knitting pattern to one side – it will probably look dauntingly complicated and written in impenetrable code. Start off slowly, build your skills one at a time, and before you know it you'll be sporting your latest creation. This chapter gives you a bit of orientation to the craft. If you really can't wait to get started, the next chapters will take you through all the techniques and skills you need to become an accomplished knitter, and you'll soon have something simply fabulous on your needles.

Can't wait?

If you have never knitted before and can't wait to get started, here's some advice:

✔ **Choose something straightforward** for your first knit. You're likely to make mistakes, which is absolutely fine – it's the best way to learn. But you might want to put aside your ideas for the Audrey Hepburn-style cashmere sweater just for the moment. Start off simple – try a granny square or a scarf.

✔ **Get a practice ball** of thick, plain yarn. Wool is probably the best choice for your first try. It is easy to handle, feels nice in your hands and knits smoothly. You will also be able to see your stitches clearly. Something fluffy like mohair or an eyelash yarn (a fake-fur type of fibre), is trickier to handle and it's not so easy to tell if you are making mistakes.

✔ **Get some needles.** You're best off starting with medium-large needles, say, between sizes 10 and 11 (6 and 8mm). Sizes larger than that can be a little awkward to handle until you have some prowess. Sizes smaller than that can be fiddly for a beginner, and your knitting grows slowly. You will want to see results soon.

✔ **Follow the basic instructions.** See the panel right to cast on, knit and bind off.

✔ **Admire what you've made.** If you have only made a square, that's a good start. Use it as a woolly beer coaster. Make another one, sew them together, and you've got the start of a very small bag. Make a couple, and you're on the way to making a blanket. Now, buy some more yarn and try something new…

Need more help?

Read these sections if you need a bit more help as you try to get started.
✔ **Read the introductions** to **Getting it on and off!** (pages 36–47).
✔ **Knit and purl** (pages 48–51) explains the two fundamental stitch patterns.
✔ **Joining in yarn** (page 31) shows how to finish off and start yarn ends.
✔ **If things go wrong,** don't panic! See **Common problems** (pages 20–21) and **Sort it out…** (pages 150–152).

Be in-the-know and look out for...

Classy clickers…
Smart, must-have advice you can't live without

Style secrets
Be inspired by these creative ideas

Knit it now…
Practise your moves step-by-step

So what is knitting?

To understand knitting, let's first address the basics – how are the stitches formed? It might help to think of knitting as a succession of yarn 'waves' that have been made to interlock. The 'trough' of a new wave is interlocked with the 'crest' of the previous wave, leaving the crest of the new wave free. To keep this in position, a needle is used. A second needle helps to interlock the following wave.

The knitted stitch

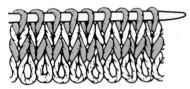

(See also **Needle know-how**, **Working it!** and **Yummy yarns**)

Each loop that is, or has been, on a needle is a stitch. A basic stitch has two sides: the knit side (**Fig 1**), smooth, looking rather like a V; and the purl side (**Fig 2**), rugged, clearly showing how the two waves interlock. If the waves are in different colours or textures, the dividing line is a broken one.

Fig 1

Fig 2

When interlocking (that is, knitting), you decide which side of the stitch you want to show. You can interlock two or more stitches with one new loop to decrease the number of stitches, and two or more new loops into one stitch to increase the number of stitches.

You can make new loops without interlocking them with a previous stitch (yarnovers), and do various other things. This all creates thousands of stitch patterns, used to make fabrics.

Stitch patterns have two sides:
• the right side; the one you want to show.
• the wrong side; the one you do not want to show.
Some patterns look good from both sides, and can be used for reversible fabrics.

Whilst working, you may be turning the knitting. Either side of the stitch pattern can then be:
• at front of work, if you see it. Or,
• at back of work, if you do not see it.
You then have:
• right-side rows – lines of stitches made whilst the right side is at front of work.
• wrong-side rows – lines of stitches made with the wrong side at front of work.

This will only occur when you knit flat pieces. If you make tubes (in circular knitting), the rows will become rounds and you will never turn the work. All rounds will be either right-side or wrong-side – usually the former.

Stitch and needle

Although there are exceptions, the normal position of a stitch on the needle is with its right arm at front of work (**Fig 3**). If the right arm is at the back of work (**Fig 4**), the stitch will become twisted when you interlock it.

Normal work progresses from right to left, with the yarn hanging from the right needle. The left needle merely holds the stitches from the previous row. If the last stitch made is a knit, the yarn hangs at back of work; if purl, it hangs at front of work.

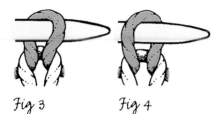

Fig 3   *Fig 4*

Classy clickers… *straighten a stitch going the wrong way, drop it and insert the needle from the other side; or pass it onto the other needle and return it straight; or work into back arm instead of front arm (which, in either case, is the right-hand arm).*

Stitch size

The size of a stitch is the direct result of yarn thickness and needle size (**Fig 5**), influenced by stitch pattern. If the needles are too fine for the yarn, working is difficult. The resulting fabric is stiff, has no 'give' and tends to felt – it is tight. If the needles are too thick, the fabric is loose. It may look appealingly soft, but it has no hold. It grows and grows and never recovers its original shape. It may also be uneven. If the needles are correct, the fabric is elastic and keeps its shape. It is not stiff, nor sloppy, but nicely firm. And it looks and feels more even.

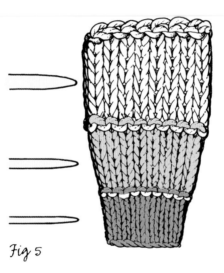

Fig 5

❀ *Knit it now…*

Take a good selection of needles and a ball of medium-thick yarn. Cast on 15 or 20 stitches on the finest needles and work your way up the sizes, allowing 10 or 12 rows on each. Work in stockinette (stocking) stitch with a purl row at each needle change (see page 50). Pull each section around and feel the differences between them.

Which needles?

No two knitters work alike, but we all think of ourselves as 'average', and take the needle size as mentioned on ball bands or in instructions as 'the' one for us. This is not always the case.

The size of the stitches you get with a pair of needles depends on:

1) yarn tension, or how much you pull the yarn. You may be a tight knitter (perhaps so tight that knitting is hard work and the stitches take some persuading to glide down the needles), or a slack knitter (perhaps so slack that the stitches keep dropping off the needles).

2) length of yarn drawn through. We may think our stitches go all the way round the needle as in the previous illustrations, when in fact they only go half-way round (as a result of a tight yarn tension, of keeping the finger feeding the yarn too high, or of not pulling the needle far enough when drawing the new stitch). **Fig 6.**

Fig 6

If a pair of needles gives you a looser fabric than desired, you need thinner needles. If they give you a tighter fabric, you need thicker needles. Sometimes you can successfully work certain areas with thinner or thicker needles than the rest, either for texture or for shaping. What you should never do is change the size of an entire project by altering needle size, instead of altering number of stitches and rows, because fabric quality and performance will be drastically affected.

Having established what needles give you the best fabric with a certain yarn, keep in mind that changing stitch pattern can alter stitch size and/or shape (see **Stitch patterns** on page 16).

Do not be surprised if, as a result, you need a very different needle size.

Occasionally, you may choose the 'wrong' needle size intentionally – if you want something very stiff and sturdy that can be achieved only with fine needles, or you want to make use of the holes left by large needles when working lace. In this case you should block the fabric (see pages 122–124) well stretched, so no further stretching is likely to occur.

Gauge

The stitch size of a fabric is measured by the number of stitches and rows to a given square, normally 4 x 4in (10 x 10cm). (Note that metric and imperial are not identical, and should not be interchanged.) In the US, this is referred to as gauge. In Britain, it is tension (not to be confused with yarn tension).

Samples

Before you start a project, whether following instructions or designing your own, you must make sure that the fabric will be neither tight nor loose. Work a sample to measure the gauge.

For good results, the sample must be:
• off the needles – bound off or with a length of yarn securing the free loops.
• larger than 4in (10cm), or other intended measurement, so that you can check away from the distorted edges. If you are told to achieve, say, 28 stitches in 4in (10cm), your sample should have at least 32.

If the sample feels tight, try again with thicker needles; if it feels loose, try again with finer needles. It should be:
• pinned flat to reach its natural size, or blocked; stretched if the fabric is to be stretched. Wash if you want to perform a shrinkage test (see also **Handle** and **Resilience** on page 28).
• worked in the same yarn colour and quality as the final fabric will be, and in the same stitch pattern.

• worked flat or circular, but always as the intended project. To work a 'circular' sample, with circular or double-pointed needles, cut yarn at end of each row and then, without turning, slide the sample to the right end of the needle and join in the yarn again.

Work one sample for each stitch pattern and each yarn involved.

When trying to achieve gauges stated in instructions, it may be impossible to achieve both stitch and row counts. Concentrate on the stitches and, if the row difference is large, avoid projects where the numbers of rows are crucial. In projects where length is checked with a tape measure rather than by counting rows, remember you will probably need a different amount of yarn than the instructions say.

If you are designing, and do not need to know the row count from the start, you may only need to check the stitches. A 2–3in (5–7cm) deep sample is then usually enough. Check row count later, over the part-knitted project.

To measure the sample (Fig 7):

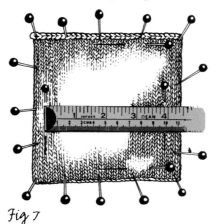

Fig 7

✿ *Knit it now...*

a Place edge of tape measure or ruler at least two stitches away from left edge, and mark with a pin.
b Keeping the tape totally horizontal, place another pin at 4in (10cm). With very fine yarns, you could make a smaller sample and measure only 2in

(5cm). With extremely thick yarns you may need 6 or 8in (15 or 20cm).
c Count the number of stitches. When following instructions, having more stitches than you should means that your stitches are too small – try again with thicker needles. Having fewer stitches means that they are too large – try again with finer needles.

Repeat vertically to check rows. ***Do not dismiss half, or even quarter, stitches or rows.***

Another way of checking is with a knit gauge tool (tension gauge). You may be asked to mark a certain number of rows or stitches on the sample. Placing the graduated tool over the sample tells you how many there would be in 4in (10cm). This helps when stitches are too small to be seen properly, or when the stitch pattern makes them difficult to count.

A way of counting complex stitch patterns is to measure one or more complete repeats. Knowing, as you do, the number of stitches in each repeat (the stitch pattern instructions will tell you this), you can work out the number of stitches in 4in (10cm):

$$\frac{\text{stitches in repeat x 4 (10)}}{\text{width or length of repeat}}$$

Calculating stitches and rows

Once you know the number of stitches in 4in (10cm), it is very easy to find out how many are required for a certain width. Simply divide:

$$\frac{\text{stitches in 4in (10cm)}}{4(10)}$$

To obtain the stitches in 1in (1cm), multiply by the total number of inches (centimetres) required, to obtain the total number of stitches. This is all there is to it, but if you would like to work from a table instead, look on pages 155–156. You can also work directly from the width of one single repeat.

Stitch patterns

Together with yarn texture, stitch patterns are the means of obtaining fabric texture. Yarn and pattern go hand in hand:

• Smooth yarn emphasizes a smooth pattern, and counters a rugged one.
• Delicate motifs look even more delicate in a soft, lightweight yarn, but positively coarse in a heavy, oiled yarn.
• Lace patterns look light and airy in a very fine yarn, heavy in a chunky yarn.
• Bouclé yarns make a knobbly fabric if the pattern has many purl stitches, but have little impact in a fabric with many knit stitches, because the 'bumps' will naturally stay on the purl side.
• Shiny yarns look shinier on knit and lose some sheen on purl.

Classy clickers...
help identify a pattern repeat by attaching a safety pin to the stitch before the start of the repeat to be measured, and another to the last stitch of the repeat.

Style secrets
Choice of yarn affects the character of stitch patterns. Never decide on a pattern without first knitting up a sample swatch in the yarn you intend to use to check you like the look of it.

Fabric character

Character is determined by the structure of the stitch pattern. A knitted stitch pulls in a certain way. When all the stitches show the same side (knit or purl), the original pull is magnified; if some of the stitches show the other side, the pull is countered around those stitches. If you work a very small sample in single rib and pull the needle to free the loops, you will see how clearly the knit stitches come to the front and the purl stitches go to the back. (See also the **Knitted stitch**, page 13; **Knit and purl,** pages 48–51; **Slipping away,** pages 52–53; **A colourful life,** pages 86–95; **In a twist,** pages 108–111; **Getting a raise**, pages 112–113; and **All sorts,** pages 114–115.)

Interlocking in unusual or combined ways adds new dimensions to the interaction of knit and purl stitches. Even taking the yarn to the other side of work between a knit and a purl stitch has an effect. Not only is the pull reversed, but more yarn is used.

Fabrics can be roughly classified as:

• wide or narrow, depending on the number of stitches. Cables, cross stitches and slip stitches make fabrics narrower. Double stitch makes fabrics wider.
• long or short, depending on the number of rows. Slip stitches, consecutive knit or purl rows (garter stitch), double stitch, and pull-up stitch make fabrics shorter. Elongated stitch makes fabrics longer.
• flat or curly. Fabrics with a stockinette stitch base are curly, an effect often emphasized by slip stitches. Fabrics with a garter-stitch base, and fabrics with close, balanced arrangements of knit and purl stitches (such as seed/moss stitch or ribbings) are flat.
• thin or thick, irrespective of yarn thickness. Narrow and short fabrics tend to be thick. So do ribbings,

brioches, jacquard, mosaic, and all the embossed and raised-motif fabrics.
• elastic or inelastic. Vertical arrangements of knit and purl stitches (such as ribbings) and brioches are very elastic. Fabrics with a slip-stitch or cross-stitch base are very inelastic. Most of the remainder fall in between.

All of these can, of course, be used in combination. In general, narrow, short or thick fabrics take a longer time to knit, and require more yarn.

Measuring knitting

Length and width are totally interconnected. If you look only at one you can usually get any measurement you want.

For good results:

• Use a flat surface. Pin work down if necessary, or ask someone to keep it in place.
• Measure width at least 1in (2.5cm) below the needles, away from ribbings and other gatherings.
• Measure for length on a vertical line, away from edges.
• Half-stretch ribbings, to how they will be in use.
• Measure on the true vertical, or the true horizontal.
• Measure work often, especially if prone to uneven gauge.
• With large, heavy pieces that may sag, stop short of the required length and leave to hang for a couple of days before deciding how much more to knit.
• DO NOT CHEAT. To unravel half-way up is distressing; to discover that you have finished something useless is maddening.

To measure:

a If working flat, stop work at mid-row.

b Spread knitting on needle(s) until the last row is quite flat. With a circular needle and with short straight needles you will have to place some of the stitches on holders or spare needles.

c Spread the rest of the work to the required width (**Fig 8**) without pulling (unless you intend stretching). If it is noticeably wider or narrower, admit that something has gone wrong. If it cannot be corrected, perhaps by altering the width of an adjoining piece, unravel.

d Keeping the work spread at full width, measure length from under the needle to the cast-on, or other appropriate place. Use fabric markers to highlight critical rows, such as the armhole in **Fig 9**.

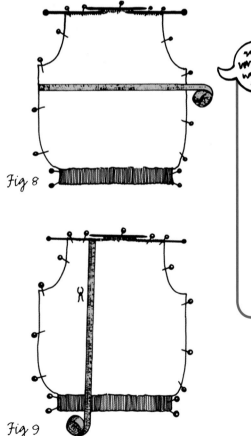

Fig 8

Fig 9

Identical pieces

When matching the length of identical pieces, count rows instead of using a tape measure. (Two identical pieces, flat or circular, can be worked together to save you counting) Some stitch patterns are easy to count because they have very clear repeats. You just count the repeats, then multiply by the number of rows in each one. With other stitch patterns, you have to count every row. This is easier to do if you point at each row with something short and sharp like a sewing or a cable needle – when your eyes start seeing double, push the needle into the fabric and take a rest. If your eyesight is poor, or if you want to count the rows at a glance, work in a string of bead markers.

Stockinette stitch is easy to count if you see each stitch as a V; however, some people prefer to count ridges on the purl side.

Classy clickers... know that although you should usually measure knitting flat, there are some times when it's better to measure a piece upright hanging off the needles – when you're making something that is likely to drop (that is, stretch vertically). Some stitch patterns are prone to dropping, as are some yarns, particularly ribbon yarns, heavy yarns, and yarns with a lot of drape, such as linen blends.

Problem fabrics

Slanted fabrics

This may be caused by a very high twist in the yarn, by continuously twisting or plaiting the stitches, by some other type of fabric construction that somehow stresses the fabric, or by a combination of these. It cannot be corrected, but you should be able to spot it on the gauge sample, when there is time to prevent it.

• If it is a fabric problem, use a different stitch pattern.

• If it is a yarn problem, look for a pattern that slants in the opposite direction (perhaps twisted or plaited stockinette stitch).

Uneven fabrics

Something has gone wrong with the gauge. Perhaps you changed it unwittingly because the weather made your hands numb or sticky, or you were distracted while watching TV!

Alternatively, perhaps the yarn was not evenly spun, or you kept poor control over yarn and needles. Someone helping you might be another cause, because no two knitters work alike. If the problem is that the last stitch of a group of two or more knit stitches in a rib or a cable pattern is consistently larger than the others (**Fig 10**), try this next time:

• on the right-side row, knit-back the offending stitch (see **Fig 2**, page 48);

• on the return row, purl the stitch wrapping the yarn under the needle (see **Fig 7**, page 49).

Fig 10

So what is knitting? / 7

needle know-how

It's important to learn how to handle your needles properly. The way you hold the needles and your body has a direct effect on your knitting, comfort and enjoyment. Poor posture can be a real pain! If you are learning to knit, read on carefully and practise one of the recommended methods. If you learnt a long time ago, a quick read will do you no harm, and could help. Some ways are easy to learn; other ways make it hard to work evenly. There are two basic knitting positions: yarn in right hand, and yarn in left hand. Both make stitches in exactly the same way, but because the yarn is held at a different angle they appear somewhat different while you're making the stitch. You will soon find out which method suits you best.

See also 'Holding the yarns' under **A colourful life**

Yarn in right hand

Knitters from many countries hold the yarn in the right hand, but the yarn can be wound around the right hand in a number of possible ways, a few of which are shown in **Fig 1**. Use whichever you find more comfortable to get a steady flow of yarn. My favourite is the first one.

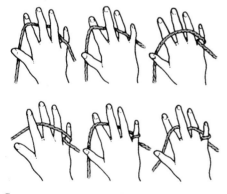

Fig 1

Fixed needle

An excellent way of keeping control of your work. The right hand is free to concentrate on wrapping the yarn, using the right needle merely as a rest. The shuttle movement of this hand automatically helps the new stitches to glide over the needle.

You need double-pointed needles or standard needles not shorter than 14in (35cm) – which are not very convenient if you want to knit on a train or on the bus to work.

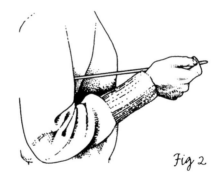

Fig 2

✿ *Knit it now …*

a Tuck needle under right arm (**Fig 2**) or under a loose, narrow belt (see also **Double-pointed needles**, page 23).

b Wrap yarn around right hand and place hand on top of needle.

c Take needle with stitches in left hand.

d Push first stitch to tip of needle with left thumb and, at same time, flick left needle so that right needle gets inserted into the stitch.

e Wrap yarn, moving right hand as little as possible (**Fig 3**).

f Flick left needle with left hand to pass the old stitch over the new wrap and, at same time, push tip of right needle back through the old stitch with left thumb (purl) or left index finger (knit). Take care not to tighten the right arm too much against the body.

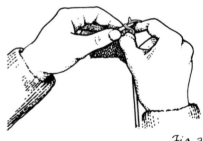

Fig 3

Needle as pen

✿ *Knit it now…*

Work as before, but omit step **a** and hold right needle as in **Fig 4**. Use the shortest needles that will accommodate all the stitches, either standard or circular.

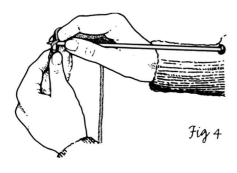

Fig 4

One problem with this method is that many knitters try to make the right hand do all the work, and there are so many things to be done that mastering them all is not easy, especially if the right thumb is bent up against its natural inclination.

Another problem is that, after a few stitches, a lot of fabric gathers at the crook of the right thumb. If you carry on gathering fabric, the stitches on the right needle may start to drop off.

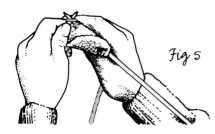

Fig 5

So, you then put the thumb under the fabric (**Fig 5**), which does nothing to improve needle control. In either case, with so much pawing, the fabric may look grubby before you even finish, control over needles and yarn is lost and the work tends to be uneven.

Beware not to move your elbows about and not to bend your right thumb up as this can quickly cause cramp.

Hand on top

Half-way between fixed needle and needle as pen. Control is not quite as good, but better than in needle as pen.

✿ *Knit it now…*

Work as for fixed needle but omit step **a**. Work with standard or circular needles. Beware not to stick your elbows out and not to clutch the right needle.

Yarn or needle

This is the slowest, most awkward, most tiring and least even way of knitting. After inserting the right needle into the stitch, the needle is dropped and forgotten. The yarn is then picked up, wrapped (**Fig 6**) and dropped, leaving the hand free to go back to the needle and draw the loop through.

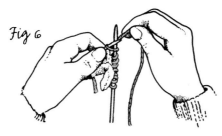

Fig 6

Yarn in left hand

This is also called German or continental knitting (somewhat misleadingly, as many European countries do not use this method). Using circular or standard needles, just long enough to hold the work, it is a very fast method to knit, but not so much to purl. Purl stitches too large (see page 20) are fairly common.

✿ *Knit it now …*

a Wind yarn around left hand in one of the ways shown in **Fig 7**.

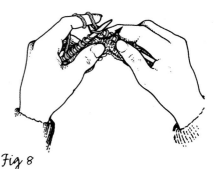

Fig 7

b Take needle with stitches in left hand and empty needle in right hand. Both hands should be on top of needles.

c Push first stitch to tip of needle with left thumb and insert right needle into it.

d 'Hook' yarn with right needle and pull through the stitch. To hook the yarn to knit is very straightforward (**Fig 8**).

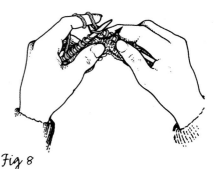

Fig 8

To purl, it is less so (**Fig 9**), unless you work a plaited purl stitch (**Fig 10**). However, as explained on page 20, the new stitch needs to be untwisted on the next row.

Take care not to move your right arm more than necessary.

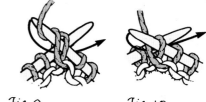

Fig 9   *Fig 10*

Left-handed knitters

Left-handed knitters are often given the advice to hold illustrations next to a mirror, and follow their reflection, and to reverse any non-symmetrical instructions. However, I think this is a convoluted and off-putting method. I advise you simply to think of knitting as the two-handed craft it really is. Use either the fixed needle or the yarn-in-left-hand approach, whichever you prefer, and forget that the instructions are for right-handed knitters. Beginner knitters, whether left- or right-handed, have to train both hands to do something completely new. (See also 'From left to right' under **Picking it up**, page 71.)

Common problems — solved!

No matter what the problem, there is always a solution to your knitting woes. Here are some basic problems that all beginner experience (you are never alone!), plus handy hints for getting yourself out of those tight spots.

Does your knitting grow very slowly?

You might be:
- making your fingers travel too far to make each stitch?
- keeping the working stitches too far from the tips of the needles?
- not keeping the needles under full control?
- trying to keep one needle still whilst the other does all the work?
- using needles with very long, very blunt tips?

Do you keep dropping stitches?

You might be:
- keeping the working stitches too close to the tips of the needles?
- a slack knitter?
- not keeping both needles in your hands all the time?
- holding the right needle like a pen, with the work tightly gathered into the crook of the thumb?

(See also **Flat knitting**, page 22.)

Is the left edge too long?

This problem creates havoc when trying to sew two edges together. The main cause is lack of control when starting to purl. Are you holding the yarn in your right hand but not fixing the right needle? Try tightening the yarn more on the first purl stitches. It is not as easy as with knit stitches, but quite possible. If that fails, try a double-chain selvedge (see page 69) on the over-long edge.

Are the edges stretching?

You probably have problems both when starting to purl and to knit, perhaps made worse by a slippery yarn. Apply the solutions for 'left edge too long' to both edges.

Are your purl stitches too large?

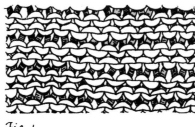

Fig 1

This gives a stripy look to stockinette stitch (**Fig 1**). It is a fairly common problem amongst yarn-in-left-hand knitters, but can also happen to others.

Try these solutions:
- Practise tightening the purl stitches and loosening the knit stitches (see **Which needles?**, page 14).
- Purl with a finer needle than you knit. This only works with stockinette stitch.
- When purling, wrap yarn under needle as in plaited purl stitch (**Fig 2**). On the next row, knit-back the resulting stitches (**Fig 3**) to straighten them up. Again, this works only for stockinette stitch and a limited number of stitch patterns.
- Adapt to circular knitting and avoid stitch patterns with groups of purl stitches on the right side – the odd one is not likely to be a problem.

Fig 2

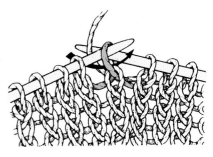

Fig 3

Is your work uneven?

Fig 4

This is invariably caused by poor control (**Fig 4**). Do you:
- hold the right needle like a pen?
- drop the yarn or any of the needles regularly?
- keep the yarn quite long between the work and the finger that wraps it around the needle?
- work some stitches well away from the tip of the needles, and others very close?
- hold the needles at a longish distance from the tip?
- use needles with very long tips?

Why the aches and pains?

If knitting gives you arm or hand cramps, stiff shoulders, neck ache, or backache, look at the way you arrange yourself and use your muscles. Do you:
- keep your head permanently bent forward, or to one side?
- let your body slump in a heap?
- sit on something that does not give support to your back?
- get all tensed up?
- clutch needles or yarn?
- stick your elbows out?
- keep your two arms in constant movement?
- bend your right thumb up to hold the needle?

Ouch! Knitting isn't supposed to be a pain in the neck!

Working it!

Almost all knitting is done from right to left, building up a fabric in rows. But going from left to right without changing yarn position is equally possible. In fact, it has some very interesting and potentially creative applications.

Flat or circular?

Whichever direction you work in, you can produce either an open flat fabric, or a tube. Each has advantages and limitations. Your choice is likely to be a result of the sort of things you knit. If you are interested in odd-row stripes, round mats, seamless garments, gloves, hats, socks, or jacquard, or if you hate sewing (or find it difficult because of eyesight problems), then circular knitting may be for you. If you love intarsia, open collars, edgings, wall hangings, shawls, bedspreads, pieces that require very accurate blocking, or if you hate transcribing instructions and do not want to design your own work, then go for flat knitting. If you want to add a round yoke or border to something worked flat, use first one method and then the other. When changing methods, gauge (tension) may be altered – check beforehand. Having made your decision, you have a further choice between straight (standard or double-pointed) and circular needles.

Try the different methods and decide which one works best for you. Don't let anyone tell you that one way of knitting is better than the others.

Flat knitting

In flat knitting, you use a pair of standard needles or one circular needle.

Each line of stitches is called a row. At the end of a row, the left needle is empty and the right needle full. Turn the work, so that if you were first seeing the right side, you now see the wrong side. Swap hands and start again.

To knit flat using a circular needle, work in exactly the same way.

Identical pieces

In flat knitting, it is easy to work two symmetrical or identical pieces (such as two sleeves or two jacket fronts) at the same time, using two balls of yarn (**Fig 1**). This saves much time checking shapings, and ensures identical results. If your gauge is not very stable, this is a good way of compensating for it – If the two pieces were worked separately, one might end up much longer than the other.

Fig 1

Circular knitting

Each circle of stitches is a round. Rounds are arranged like a spiral, worked without breaks. As a result, a 'step' forms on the pattern when changing from round to round. Use a needle marker to see where the rounds start. (See also **Casting on circles**, page 43.)

Because the work is never turned, you are always facing the same side. This is usually the right side. If you want to work from the wrong side, your hands will be at the far end of the circle.

Circular knitting can be done on a circular needle or a set of double-pointed needles. The sets can be used for any size of circle, from glove fingers to huge round rugs, although it is not too comfortable to work very small circles with the longer needles; if the stitches grow too crowded, extra needles can be added. Circular needles must be smaller than the circle, otherwise the stitches are stretched out of shape and work is slow and awkward; if the project changes width, you might need to change needle length.

The shortest circular needle usually available is 16in (40cm) long; shorter ones are very difficult to work with. Smaller circles, therefore, cannot be worked adequately with circular needles. If changing from sets to circular needles, your gauge may alter; check it.

Classy clickers... *when using a circular needle for flat knitting, think of each point as a separate needle – forget that they are joined (**Fig 1**).*

Style secrets

With circular knitting, you can produce totally seamless projects, including whole sweaters. These are appealing garments that are also deeply rooted in tradition. Many knitters love making jumpers and vest tops with circular needles because you can create shapely, well-fitting items with no tedious side seams to sew up at the end. These garments can look really elegant and professional. And most knitters much prefer knitting to sewing, anyway...

Circular needle

Simply work round and round (**Fig 2**). Measuring might require additional needles, if it is impossible to lay the work flat.

Circular needles – the good points:

• The stitches can be slipped onto the cord so that they do not drop when you put the work away, or set into a slant if left for any length of time.
• They are good for working in a tight space.
• You can make very wide flat pieces that would not fit on standard needles.
• You can never lose the 'other' needle.

And the bad points:

• They are not so easy to store as straight needles.
• There is no size indication on the needle itself, so you will need to label them yourself, or use a needle gauge (see page 27).
• They are difficult to keep dead straight when spreading the work for measuring.
• The work gets heavy if you knit as you walk.
• The stitches have to be pushed more often because not many can be crowded on the stiff points, and the ones on the connecting cord keep slipping back. If working in circles, you also have to make the stitches go all the way round.

Beware...

Creative types may find that circular needles:

• are heavy and cumbersome in their final stages;
• show a step at the start of the rounds;
• restrict shape experimentation;
• make certain types of blocking awkward, if not impossible;
• are better than badly-put-together, 'homemade' flat knitting, but not necessarily better than good flat knitting;
• are not so easy to adjust as garments worked in pieces if something goes wrong with the sizing.

But are circular needles good to work with? If you hold the yarn in left hand, yes, they are excellent. You have no right needle swinging around, which can be quite heavy if full of stitches. If you hold the yarn in your right hand, circular needles do not give nearly the same control as a straight fixed needle, although people used to working with hand on top find them quite satisfactory. The fact that the weight of the fabric is now on the lap will not impress fixed-needle knitters much, because they have already taken care of the weight problem. In fact, they might get worried about having to bend their neck because their hands are now much lower. Non-fixed-needle knitters, though, might welcome resting the work on their lap.

Double-pointed needles

Double-pointed needles come in sets of four or five. One needle is kept free, and the stitches divided amongst the other needles, equally if possible. Having worked the stitches off one needle with the free needle, a new needle is released. If the needles are crowded, use stops.

Use as many needles as make sense for a particular shape. Trying to work a square on three needles is nonsense, as you will not see how work progresses, and the join stitches will get distorted; you need to use four needles.

It is essential to keep an even yarn tension when changing needles. Loose stitches often appear but are easily avoided – always start a new needle on top of the old one (**Fig 2**); pull the first stitch tight. Changing needle position by two or three stitches each time is only partly helpful. You could end up with a spiral of loose stitches instead of a vertical line of them, and unless you have many needles it could be awkward.

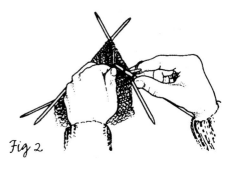

Fig 2

Identical pieces

Although two identical tubes (such as sleeves or socks) are generally worked independently, it is possible to work them at the same time, one inside the other. The advantages would be those outlined in **Flat knitting**, above.

✿ Knit it now...

With two balls of yarn:

a Cast on, alternately, one stitch from each ball, until you have enough stitches for both tubes. Make sure that the two yarns do not get tangled.

b Work each stitch with the yarn it was cast on with. You can either work all rounds with two yarns (use second or third methods of holding yarns explained in **Jacquard**, page 92), or work one round with one yarn and the next with the other – each time slip purl-wise the stitches not being worked. If the two tubes are in stockinette stitch, knitting the outside tube and purling the inside one helps to differentiate the two layers. Gauge is likely to be looser than in one-layer work. Check it, and use finer needles if necessary.

> *Classy clickers... when working two identical pieces, with two balls of yarn, turn the work clockwise at the end of one row anti-clockwise at the end of the next row to prevent the two yarns twisting.*

Adapting instructions for circular knitting

Most instructions, including those in this book, are intended for flat knitting. When adapting them to circular knitting, whether you are working from row-by-row instructions or from charts, the stitch pattern must flow continuously. That is, you need complete pattern repeats, which in written instructions are the stitches between asterisks. If the number of odd stitches at either side of the asterisks varies, a repeat is probably split between the two ends. Chart the pattern, or knit a sample with at least two repeats, to find out the relevant stitches. Then, reverse all wrong-side rows:

• Read them from the end, in order to reverse the sequence.

• Work knit for purl and purl for knit. Rows instructing 'knit the knit stitches and purl the purl stitches' take care of themselves.

• Work increases and decreases from the other side. The instructions in this book mention shapings on knit or on purl – either of which can be the right or wrong sides. If a wrong-side row has an increase on knit (purl), work the same increase on purl (knit) when you are working rounds.

• Work with yarn in front instead of with yarn at back, and vice versa. To avoid mistakes, it is best to transcribe the instructions before starting to work. If there are armholes or other openings, divide work and shape as required. Either change to flat knitting, or make a bridge and continue in circles.

From left to right

This is a way of working flat without actually turning the work. Some people use the method to work large pieces knitting back and forth from end to end. Even if you do not want to go this far, you will find it useful for some raised patterns (which, of course, can also appear in circular knitting).

✿ Knit it now...

Keep yarn in right hand. To knit:

a Insert left needle into back of stitch.

b Wrap yarn down front and up back of needle (**Fig 3**).

c Draw new stitch through.

Fig 3

To purl:

a Insert left needle into back of stitch.

b Wrap yarn up back and down front of needle (**Fig 4**).

c Draw new stitch through.

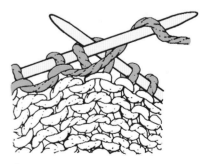

Fig 4

Tools of the trade

Once you get into knitting, you may find yourself yearning after all sort of fancy equipment. Knitting is a dream for the gadget lover. But you really don't need expensive items of kit – if you're thrifty, you can often find cheap alternatives.

There are three types of needles: standard, circular and double-pointed. **Standard needles** (or pins) are only used for flat knitting. Choose the length according to how you hold the work.

Circular needles can be used for flat or circular knitting, and consist of two very short needles connected by a strong, flexible cord. The short, stiff ends must be long enough to span your closed hand for a good grip. Before buying, inspect the joint between needle and cord; it must be absolutely smooth or your knitting will snag.

Double-pointed needles are used for circular knitting (these were the only choice until the invention of circular needles). They come in sets of four or five. Two of them with a stop at one end can be used for flat knitting. (See also **Needle know-how**, pages 18–21, and **Working it!** pages 22–24.)

Needle tips should taper to a blunt point (keep your needles well protected when not in use). If the tapering is very long and/or the point is too blunt, knitting will be slow and awkward.

Modern needles are most commonly made out of bamboo, aluminium, plastic or wood. In the past, you could find steel, tortoiseshell, celluloid, bone, ivory, and even silver. The more polished the surface, the faster the stitches glide. Some needles are rigid, while others gradually bend as the knitter works. Length varies tremendously, reflecting a wide range of uses and different ways of holding the work.

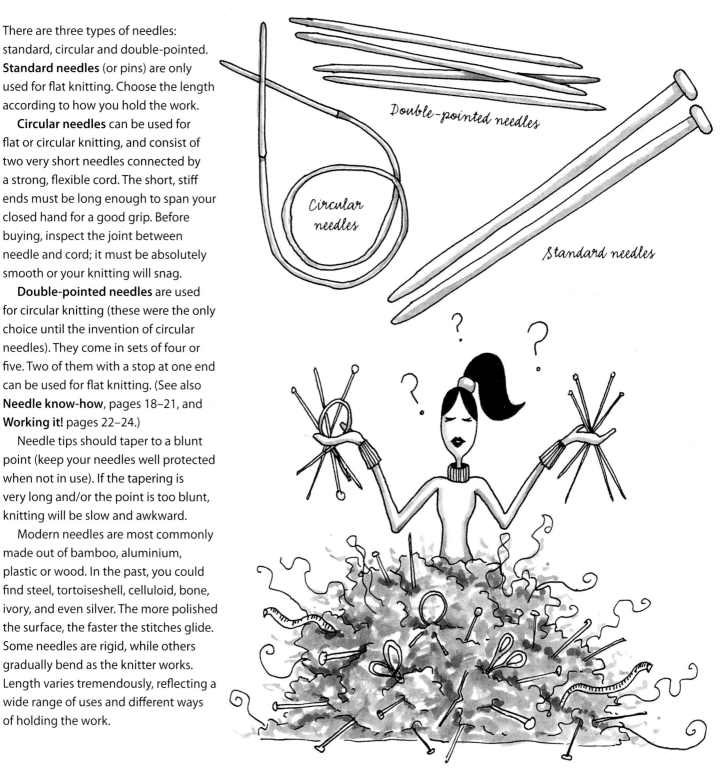

Double-pointed needles

Circular needles

Standard needles

The thickness varies between countries. The finest needles were used for the most delicate work: lace knitting. Today it is difficult to find really fine needles, finer than size 0 (2mm), though they used to be the norm. To have as wide a selection as possible, shop for knitting needles when you travel abroad. The following table shows approximate equivalents between ranges. Metric equivalents to American sizes vary – not surprisingly, since American needles often fall between the sizes of the other two ranges.

Needle size converter

US	Metric
0	2mm
1	2.25mm
2	2.75mm
	3mm
3	3.25mm
4	3.5mm
5	3.75mm
6	4mm
7	4.5mm
8	5mm
9	5.5mm
10	6mm
10½	6.5mm
	7mm
	7.5mm
11	8mm
13	9mm
15	10mm
19	15mm
35	20mm

Classy clickers... *beware of slippery yarns on high-gloss needles – whole rows could drop off.*

Style secrets

It might seem unlikely that a useful knitting gadget could also double up as an accessory, but many of the stitch markers available now are truly beautiful items. Some have been specially designed so that you can wear them as pendants or earrings when they're not on your needles.

Essential accessories

Stitch markers

Stitch markers are closed or coil rings slipped around the needle to highlight things such as changes in stitch pattern, the start of rounds in circular knitting, lines of increases or decreases or pattern repeats.

Alternatively, if you're in a thrifty mood, you could use loops of contrast yarn, safety pins or paper clips.

The same items can be attached to the knitting itself to make fabric markers to pinpoint increases or decreases, row 1 of pattern and so on.

Sewing needles

These are also known as 'yarn', 'knitter's', 'heavy embroidery', or 'tapestry' needles. They must have a blunt point, to prevent splitting the yarn. Use the size most appropriate to the yarn, as this can be ruined if forced through too small a needle.

Scissors

If you are using conventional yarn, these do not need to be very big, but they must be sharp.

Sewing needles
Choose the correct size for your yarn. Use jumbo needles for decorative work.

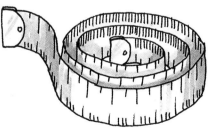

Tape measure
An absolute essential for every knitter's work bag.

Stitch markers
Stitch markers come in all shapes and sizes, including gorgeous beaded versions – think of them as jewellery for your work!

Scissors
They don't have to be very big, so are ideal for knitting on the go!

Tape measure

Use an accurate dressmaker's tape, or a rigid ruler. It is important to take all measurements consistently in either inches or centimetres.

Blocking board

Use anything large, flat and able to take pins. Ironing boards are usually too small. Covering with a checked cloth will help you keep straight lines.

Sprayer

For blocking, use a steam iron, or an ordinary plant sprayer giving a fine mist.

Work bag

Any large bag or basket can be used for storing your knitting in progress. The best are easy to carry, with a flat base so that they can be left on the floor without falling on one side, large enough to hold the nearly finished work, and with organizer pockets for small pieces of equipment. There are many specially designed and glamorous-looking tote bags for knitting available now – they're the ideal thing if you want to transport your knitting projects round town while still looking stylish. They are generally large enough and have enough useful compartments in them to double up as a shoulder bag to contain all the essential items that you'd usually carry round with you.

Useful accessories

Needle gauge

Used to check needle size, especially of circular or double-pointed needles that have no indication of size. The needle is the size of the smallest hole it can go through.

Cable needles

These are available in straight or angled versions (so that the stitches do not drop off). Straight ones look like very short double-pointed needles. Apart from their obvious use for cables, they are good for poking stitches into place when blocking or counting stitches.

Stitch holders

These keep stitches from unravelling when they are not needed. They come in various shapes; buy the ones least likely to unfasten when knocked about. Alternatively, use spare needles with stops at both ends, safety pins or a length of contrast yarn.

Stops

These are used to protect the point of the needles, or to prevent crowded stitches from dropping off.

You could also use corks, wooden beads or elastic bands wrapped over and over. Avoid sticky products used for fixing posters – they can stain.

Crochet hooks

Apart from being used in a number of techniques, these are very good for picking up dropped stitches. Keep at least one or two to hand.

Knit gauge tool (tension gauge)

A graduated ruler that, placed over a certain number of stitches or rows, gives an immediate reading of the gauge (tension) in 4in (10cm). You can also use a tape measure (or ruler) and calculator.

Row counter

These little gadgets fit onto the end of your knitting needles; use them to keep track of rows and repeats. Alternatively, use a pocket abacus, strokes and dashes on a piece of paper, or pencil marks by each row.

Stitch holders
Often an essential item when knitting garments.

Knitting gauge
Combine your needle and knit gauge with one handy tool.

Crochet hook
Useful in an emergency-dropped-stitch situation!

Cable needles
If you're into cables, these could be your best friend.

Point protectors
Available in fab designs and colours to decorate your needles.

Row counter
A very useful gadget. Buy a couple if you're likely to have more than one project on the go.

Yummy yarns

The range of yarns available now is hugely varied – you won't be able to resist. Not all yarns suit the same designs, even if they knit to the same stitch size. So, if you are following a pattern, and decide to use a yarn other than the recommended one, take great care. Always knit a selection of samples and compare the different effects.

Fibres

There are basically two types: natural fibres and manmade. Natural can be animal (wool, mohair, angora, cashmere, alpaca, llama, vicuña, silk) or vegetal (cotton, linen, raffia, bamboo). Manmade fibres are made from regenerated natural fibres (viscose, rayon, acetates) or synthetic (polyamides, polyesters, acrylics).

Each fibre has its own characteristic handle, resilience, strength, inflammability, resistance to dirt and/or moths and mildew and resistance to heat and water. In general, manmade fibres are easier and cheaper to produce, attract fewer pests, and are easier to clean than untreated natural fibres. These fibres do not shrink, although they can stretch in a hot wash. Natural fibres generally breathe and are absorbent; they are still comfortable in the rain or heat. They pill less, if at all, take dyes better and attract less dirt.

Many blends try to make the most of both natural and manmade fibres by mixing them.

Classy clickers... *understand a cheap mohair blend may only have 10 or 15 per cent mohair. Even if the name 'mohair' appears prominently on the label, the yarn will have little in common with 85 per cent mohair blends, and even less with pure mohair.*

Cotton, linen and wool may shrink, even when washed at low temperatures. Wool can be treated to make it shrink-resistant and/or machine washable. This needs to be worked slightly tighter than ordinary wool, and it has a different handle.

Shrinkage test

❋ *Knit it now...*

a Work a sample.
b Cut a piece of paper to the exact shape of the sample, or take a photocopy
c Wash the sample.
d Block and, when dry, compare with original shape.

Handle

The way a yarn 'feels' to the touch is its handle. Very smooth and shiny yarns tend to be slippery, so they glide through your hands and along the needles. This makes for easy work, but also easy unravelling and easily dropped stitches, especially when worked loosely. This can be an advantage in techniques such as provisional cast-on where a contrast yarn is used as a foundation to be unpicked at a later stage. Spun silk is possibly the most slippery of all yarns, followed by mercerized cotton and some types of viscose.

Classy clickers... *watch out for slippery yarns that make your knitting sag, especially if it is heavy.*

Resilience

This is the elasticity or 'give'. Some yarns (such as wool), will immediately recover their original length if stretched and released. Others (silk, some manmades and all vegetal fibres) either cannot be stretched, or remain stretched if pulled. Elastic stitch patterns such as ribbings can only be knitted successfully with resilient yarns. In, for example, silk or cotton, they widen and widen until they are totally useless.

Classy clickers... *have learnt that silk or cotton knitting should never have ribbings as borders – it doesn't have enough resilience.*

Twist

Totally untwisted yarns are very warm, because air is trapped between the fibres, but they are weak and break easily. High-twist yarns are strong and give a much clearer stitch pattern definition, but they are not so warm.

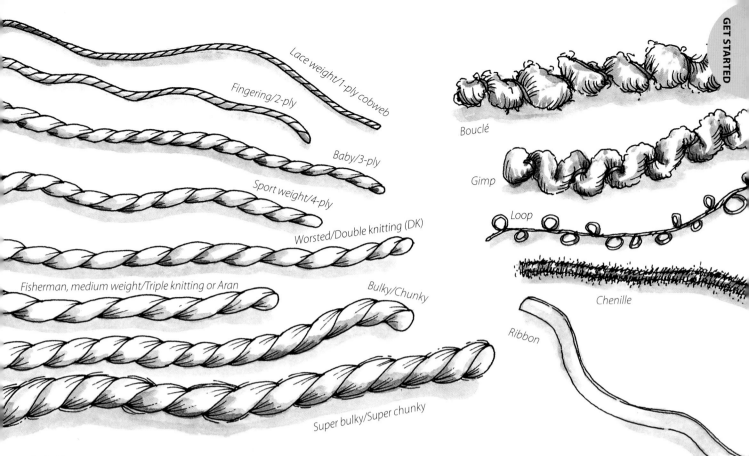

Lace weight/1-ply cobweb

Fingering/2-ply

Baby/3-ply

Sport weight/4-ply

Worsted/Double knitting (DK)

Fisherman, medium weight/Triple knitting or Aran

Bulky/Chunky

Super bulky/Super chunky

Bouclé

Gimp

Loop

Chenille

Ribbon

Thickness

There are various terms for thickness. Britain, for example, uses the term 'ply' (a ply is one of the twisted strands that make a yarn). The more plies there are, the thicker the yarn. The US uses other terms.

Thickness within each category also varies; not all worsted or double knitting yarns are the same by any means. Keep this in mind when substituting yarns. Consult a yarn substitution guide. Check the ball band on a ball of yarn for the suggested gauge (see page 30).

Colour introduces another factor. Dark colours use more dye, making the yarn both thinner and heavier. Two large, identical items, knitted in a very light and a very dark colour of exactly the same yarn, might require different needles, different stitch sizes and different amounts of yarn.

Texture

Match yarn texture to stitch pattern. (See also **The knitted stitch**, page 13 and **Stitch patterns**, page 16.)

• The knit side of the stitch is smooth. If teamed with a smooth yarn, the effect will be emphasized. With a highly textured yarn, one will counter the other.

• The purl side of the stitch is rugged. Any bumps or loops in the yarn will naturally stay on that side, and stand out far better than from the knit side.

• Complex stitch patterns in highly textured yarns are a waste of time, because they do not show.

• Some yarn textures make certain techniques awkward. Brushed and hairy yarns get caught when passing one stitch on top of another, as in basic bind (cast) off and certain decreases.

Brushed yarns (such as most mohair) and hairy yarns (such as angora) may shed hairs and cause choking, especially in young children. Work these yarns loosely, letting the hairs fill the gaps, or work tightly for a furry effect. Brushing after making up gives extra lift to the hairs. Projects in plain yarn can also be brushed, either in parts or all over, to achieve a brushed-yarn effect.

Bouclé (or poodle yarn) can refer to three types of yarn: real bouclé, gimp and loop.

Chenille is a velvety yarn with a deep pile surrounding a central core.

Classy clickers... place hairy yarns such as mohair and angora in the fridge (in a plastic bag) for a couple of hours to reduce shredding.

Ribbons give extraordinary depth to purl stitches. They require special treatment if they are to be knitted without any twists. Try threading a knitting needle or similar object first through one side of a box, then through the ball or spool of ribbon, and then through the other side of the box. In flat knitting, working the return rows from left to right helps to keep ribbon untwisted.

Colour

Yarns can be dyed in many ways, apart from in solid colours. Heather mixtures are very subtle combinations of fibres – dyed and blended before spinning. Twists are combinations of strands of different colours. Ombré or space-dyed yarns have different shades of the same colour appearing at regular, or irregular, intervals. (See also **Thickness**, above.)

Yummy yarns   29

Buying yarn

Addresses of Internet or mail-order yarn retailers can be found in knitting magazines or via an Internet search. Some offer superb qualities that are not viable for the mass market, or more ordinary yarns at a reduced price because they are selling direct.

Yarn is dyed in batches, called dye-lots. Colours may differ subtly between dye-lots. Mixing dye-lots can add depth to colour knitting, but is best avoided. If you have no option but to mix, change dye-lots every couple of rows, to give an all-over effect.

Labelling

Yarn bought from shops (except sometimes yarn on special offer), always carries a label or a ball band. Information on the label will include some, or all, of the following:

- Fibre content
- Weight
- Cleaning instructions
- Approximate length in yards and metres
- Suggested needle size and tension

Symbols such as those of **Fig 1** should be read:

'The manufacturers recommend a tension of 24 stitches and 32 rows in stockinette stitch; an average knitter will obtain this with size 5 (4mm) needles, then use size 4 (3.5mm) needles for the ribbings. Use size 5 (4mm) needles to work your first gauge sample, and assess how average you are; if necessary, change needles until the correct gauge is achieved. For patterns other than stockinette stitch you could need a totally different gauge and possibly different needles too.'

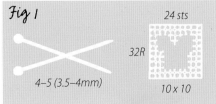

Fig 1

24 sts

32R

4–5 (3.5–4mm)

10 x 10

Using yarn

Keep yarn clean inside the work bag or in a yarn box. Slippery yarns should always be kept in a yarn box. Most handknitting yarn comes in balls, but some is sold in skeins (hanks). There are also occasional spools and, if you want to use machine-knitting or industrial yarns, cones.

Commercial balls are easier to start from the outside, but it is better to start them from the inside to avoid twists.

Instructions always tell you how much yarn you need, but if you change tension, stitch pattern, style or indeed yarn, you will need more or less.

Skeins

These need to be wound into a soft ball (tight balls put the yarn permanently under stress). Stretch the skein over a chair back or ask someone to hold it for you (**Fig 2**). Undo the tie and start winding the end that hangs from the outside. Wind carefully and slowly.

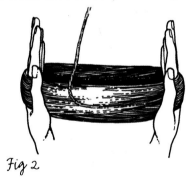

Fig 2

a Leaving an end at least 8in (20cm) long, wrap yarn around thumb and little finger of left hand in a figure of eight, say 10 to 20 times (**Fig 3**).

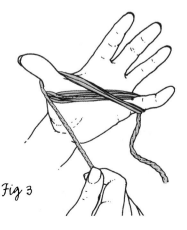

Fig 3

A good excuse to shop!

b Slip the little hank off your fingers, without disturbing it, and fold in half.

c Keeping the free end to the left, place the hank against the left fingers and wind the yarn over both the hank and the fingers, some 20 to 30 times (**Fig 4**).

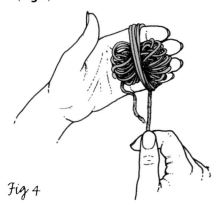

Fig 4

d Turn the ball and wind 20 or 30 times more over ball and left fingers, at right angles from **c**.

e Wind again between **c** and **d**. Always keeping the free end loose, repeat **c** to **e** until the skein runs out.

f Tuck the end of the skein into the ball. You now have a ball of yarn that can be started from the centre (**Fig 5**).

Fig 5

If you want a ball that starts from the outside, wind the start of the skein around the fingers of the left hand, instead of **a** and **b**. Do not leave a tail.

Joining in yarn

In flat knitting, unless you are desperately short of yarn, or cannot face unpicking a nearly finished row, try to join yarn only at seam edges. Otherwise,

join in at mid-row but NOT at a free edge unless extraordinary circumstances force you to do so. Darning the yarn ends could easily spoil the edge.

When joining at mid-row, try doing it at a change in stitch pattern, near a solid area in lace patterns, or at any other place that will make darning easy. If the two tails can lie on the wrong side, so much the better.

Always treat knots and imperfections in the yarn as if they were breaks. Cut them and rejoin.

To find out if you have enough yarn for one row, make the slip knot one-fourth of the length away from the needle, and see whether you can knit a quarter of a row.

If a join leaves you with a long length of yarn that could be used for seaming, do not cut it. To stop it from getting in the way, tie it into a little bundle:

a Starting with the free end, wrap yarn around a couple of fingers, until a short distance away from the work.

b Make a loop and place wrapped yarn inside it (**Fig 6**).

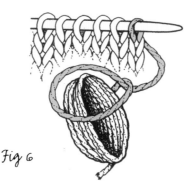

Fig 6

c Pull to fasten loop.

When nearing the end of a ball, to find out if you have enough yarn to complete two rows:

a Fold what is left of the yarn in half.

b Make a slip knot.

c Knit first row. If you have reached the knot before the end of the row, there is not enough left for the second row.

Knots

Knots are best avoided, but if you do need them, make them properly. The ordinary, 'granny', knot can come undone. When joining yarns of the same thickness, use a reef or square knot (**Fig 7**). This is best when you can control exactly where you want it (see **Drop and take**, below); if done in advance you may have difficulties passing it through a stitch. Work as for granny knot, but tie first left over right, then right over left.

For yarns of different thickness, use a weaver's knot (**Fig 8**). This has to be done in advance.

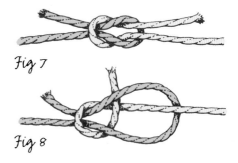

Fig 7

Fig 8

Drop and take

Best for self-coloured knitting. Drop the old yarn, take the new yarn, and continue knitting. Leave tails not shorter than 6in (15cm), and darn them later (or tie into a square knot). If you find it difficult to keep an even yarn tension on the next row, work the first stitch after the join with the two yarns. Unpick one of the two strands before darning.

Woven join

Good for colour knitting. Weave in the old tail for not less than ten stitches when you start knitting with the new yarn, as in jacquard (see pages 90–91). On the next row, weave in the new tail in the opposite direction. In circular knitting, weave in the two tails together. Cut tails after blocking.

With slippery yarns and chenille, it is safer to weave in the tails on two rows, changing direction, or to weave them in for a longer length.

Loving care...

Once you've put your new-found skills into action and knitted yourself some gorgeous new garments and accessories, you will need to keep them looking as good as the day you made them. Coming up is indispensable advice and clever tips to keep your woolies in tip-top condition forever... or for as long as they're in fashion!

Keep your knits looking simply fabulous

• **Dust** is a great destroyer of textiles. Closed wardrobes and drawers make better storage areas than open shelves.

• Act swiftly on **stains**; once set they are often impossible to shift. Washing without treating them first, or trying to remove them with the wrong agent, may cause them to set. Dab, sponge or soak with cold water, but do not rub. Avoid water on oil-based stains such as paint, ballpoint ink, grease and lipstick; these should be treated with a solvent – applied from the wrong side to drive the stain out of the fabric and onto a clean white cloth placed against the right side.

• Never cut **snags**. If possible, ease the yarn back where it belongs with a cable needle or a blunt sewing needle. Otherwise, take the loop to the wrong side with a crochet hook.

• Knitwear stays **fresher** if you change it often. To give it a chance to 'breathe', don't put it away as soon as you take it off. Instead, leave flat on a chair overnight. If it has taken on a smell (perfume, tobacco smoke, cooking) air it outdoors for a little while, away from direct sun. Fold and put away. DO NOT HANG.

• **Moths** love animal fibres, oiled yarns, food particles and human perspiration; this is why only clean knitting should be stored for any length of time.

Moth deterrents work best in enclosed environments, such as sealed boxes or bags. Many things are said to repel moths: cedar wood (it might lose its effectiveness after a few years), lavender, scented soap, and many others.

Cleaning

Look at the yarn label for instructions. Cleaning instructions often adopt the symbols of the International Textile Care Labelling Code:

- Hand wash only
- Machine wash at stated programme
- Do not wash at all
- Chlorine bleach may be used
- Chlorine bleach must not be used
- May be tumble dried
- Do not tumble dry
- Cool iron
- Warm iron
- Hot iron
- Do not iron
- May be dry cleaned (Letter indicates to dry cleaner which solvent to use.)
- Do not dry-clean

Washing

Use a washing machine only when specifically mentioned in the label. Only machine-washable or shrink-resistant wool should be put into a machine, and then only on a wool program. Non-washable trimmings, such as untreated wooden or leather buttons, should be removed or tightly covered with aluminium foil.

When hand washing, use soap or detergent for delicate fabrics. Squeeze the fabric gently to release dirt. Do not rub. If you lift the knitting from the water, do not let it hang; support it with both hands. Squeeze as much water as you can, but do not wring. Place the wet knitting flat over a dry, clean towel and roll the two together to absorb as much water as possible. Repeat if necessary. Natural fibres may be spin dried on a short cycle.

Drying

The best way to dry knitting is flat. Do not tumble-dry natural fibres, especially wool. Yarns that 'plump up' when washed, such as Shetland wool, need stretching into shape. Shake the knitting and gently pull small areas of fabric to open up the fibres and re-trap the air that has been expelled. Do not tumble-dry.

Ironing

Knitting should NOT be ironed, but pressing is often recommended. There is a difference! When you are ironing you move the iron up and down the fabric, but when pressing you rest it gently on the surface, then lift it, then rest it again. Pressing is done wrong side up, on a well-padded surface. Despite the name, pressure should not be applied. Steam, though, is essential. Do not press ribbings or elastic fabrics.

Personally, I never let an iron get anywhere near knitting, hand or machine. Drying flat gives the best results and avoids accidental scorching or flattening.

 Classy clickers... *when tumble drying manmade fibres, take them out before they are quite dry and leave them flat to finish drying.*

Cracking the code

Once you start exploring the world of knitting magazines and books – and you'll find a lot of irresistible designs around these days – you'll need to learn how to read patterns. Many of the instructions are abbreviated into what looks like secret code. Don't be put off, however – you'll soon know your wyabs from your pssos! The rest of this book will be using some of these terms, so we've listed them here.

k	knit
k2 tog	knit two stitches together
k-b	knit-back (insert needle through back of loop)
k-b2 tog	knit-back two stitches together
kwise	knitwise
p	purl
p2 tog	purl two stitches together
p-b	purl-back (insert needle through back of loop)
p-b2 tog	purl-back two stitches together
psso	pass slip stitch(es) over
pwise	purlwise
sl	slip
sl st	slip stitch
ssk	slip, slip, knit (see knit decrease)
st, sts	stitch, stitches
st st	stockinette (stocking stitch)
wyab	with yarn at back
wyif	with yarn in front
yb	yarn back
yf or yfwd	yarn forward
yo	yarn over or over
yrn	yarn round needle
(...)	Repeat instructions inside brackets as many times as indicated after brackets
...	Repeat instructions between asterisks to end of row

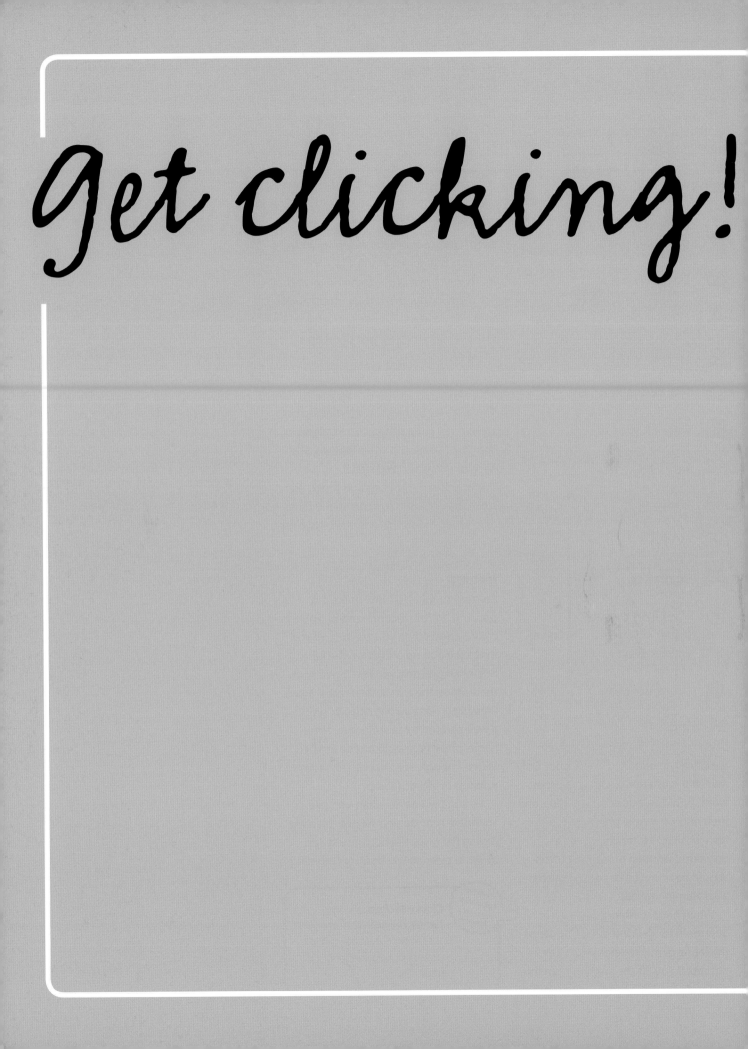

get clicking!

Right, this is where the fun really begins. We're now going to start taking you through the techniques you need to actually get some knitting on your needles. We've been pretty comprehensive here, but don't be daunted. We've covered the basics, too, and there are clear instructions that take you step by step through each skill. You can go a long way just knowing the basic stitches and a few ways of increasing and decreasing. But for truly fabulous knitting, you will probably want to know more.

Getting it on and off!

When it comes to starting (casting on) or finishing (binding off) a piece of knitting, it is very tempting to learn one method and then stick to it whatever the circumstances. You can go a long way with a basic cast-on, and many knitters choose one method and stick to it. But if you want to get simply fabulous results, it is often worth thinking carefully about using a specific cast-on and bind-off method to produce the most stylish and professional-looking finish. Any knitted edge (cast-on, bound-off or selvedge) is as important to the end result as the main fabric. Choosing one or another method might be the deciding factor as to whether you cherish that garment when it's off the needles or whether it languishes in the fashion graveyard at the back of your wardrobe.

Casting on

A cast-on is a foundation row of stitches – without it, you cannot knit. Samples are a must. A cast-on may have a stitch size far greater or far smaller than that of the pattern to follow. If necessary, cast on a different number of stitches than required by the pattern, and adjust on the first row. Alternatively, consider using different needle sizes.

Do not take anything for granted. One side of the cast-on may blend in better with the pattern than the other side. Make two very small samples, starting one with a right-side row, and the other with a wrong-side.

Always leave at least a 6in (15cm) tail of yarn. Shorter tails are difficult to darn. If it can be used for seaming, make the tail much longer and tie it up into a little bundle.

When binding on many stitches, a needle marker after every tenth stitch (or after the stitches required for each pattern repeat) helps with the counting. (See also **On the edge**, pages 66–69 and **Getting seamy**, pages 129–135; extra stitches may have to be allowed for these.)

Style secrets
Experiment with colour:
• use a contrast yarn to cast on, or
• in methods requiring two strands, use two colours instead of one, or
• cast on one stitch in one colour and the next in a second colour.

Slip knot

The slip knot is the starting point (**Fig 1**).
a Loop the yarn into a full circle.
b Draw the short end through the circle with a needle.
c Tighten first the long end, then the short one.

Classy clickers... watch their tension. A tight cast-on will not make a firmer edge – just the opposite. An edge that pulls will soon snap. To avoid this, try one of the following:
• pull the yarn less
• cast on with thicker needle(s)
• cast on a few extra stitches and decrease evenly on the first row
• cast on the stitches on two needles held together.

Conversely, a loose cast-on will crinkle and look awful. To avoid it, try one of these:
• pull yarn tighter
• cast on with finer needle(s)
• cast on a few stitches less than necessary and increase evenly on first row.

Don't feel daunted by the number of cast-on methods. Learn one or two that work for you, and as you progress, you can add more to your repertoire. Think of choosing the right cast-on method for your garment as a stylish finishing touch.

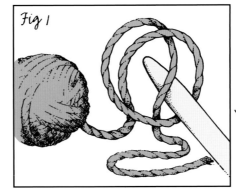

Fig 1

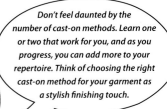

ORDINARY EDGES
two-strand
twisted two-strand
cable

BUTTONHOLES
See *end of rows*,
right

END OF ROWS
For firm edges:
double-twist loop
buttonhole
For lace and soft edges:
loop (*for softest results*)
twisted loop
alternate loop
chain

REINFORCED EDGES
twisted two-strand
double two-strand
Channel Islands

DECORATIVE EDGES
*Use either for contrast or to
blend in with the main pattern:*
alternate loop
twisted two-strand
double two-strand
Channel Islands
bind-off
tubular

MEDALLIONS
If worked in short rows:
provisional (when a medallion
is to be grafted. If it's to be
sewn, use any cast-on that will
make a bold line, or blend with
the pattern after sewing – see
decorative edges, above right).
If worked from the centre out:
pinhole
centre line

LACE AND SUPPLE EDGES
loop (*for softest results*)
twisted loop
alternate loop
chain
edging
two-strand (*as a last resort
and probably on a
thicker needle*)

HEMS
loop
twisted loop
chain

RIBBINGS
two-strand (*starting pattern
with a wrong-side row*)
Channel Islands
tubular
provisional (*for single rib
only – once unravelled, the
work will not ladder*)

FRINGED EDGES
chain
provisional

CROCHET EDGINGS
(*to be added*)
bind-off

TUBULAR FABRICS
For an open end:
cast on half the stitches on one
double-pointed needle and half on
another needle. Use appropriate cast-on
for fabric. Fold, so that the last stitch faces
the first one (**Fig 2**, below). On first row,
work one stitch from each cast-on needle.
For a closed end:
two-strand
Channel Islands
tubular

TEMPORARY EDGES
*Eventually to be unravelled,
so that another piece of work can be
grafted on. To avoid errors, cast on
with a contrast colour. For greater
ease use a slippery yarn.*
loop
twisted loop
double-twist loop
provisional
(See also *two-way
edges*, right)

TWO-WAY EDGES
*After completing work in
one direction, pick up stitches
from the cast-on and work in
the opposite direction. Check
the number of stitches
after picking up.*
loop
chain

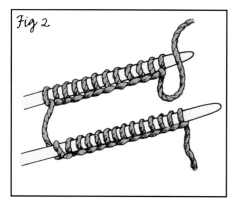

Fig 2

Choosing a cast-on

It is amazing how, with so many cast-ons to choose from, the selection offered to knitters is usually poor. I suggest you start with a good all-rounder: two-strand cast-on.

Follow with three methods to improve common situations: one for

adding on stitches – double-twist loop or buttonhole; one for single rib – tubular or Channel Islands; and one for lace – chain or twisted loop.

Several other methods are covered in the following pages. Choose the most appropriate one using the options above.

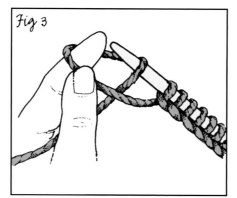

Fig 3

Loop cast-on

One needle; one strand (**Fig 3**). Very easy. The first row can be tricky because the stitches sometimes drop off the needle.

This method gives a very understated and soft edge, without much strength. For extra softness, it can be worked on two needles held together. One needle is removed before the first row. This makes it easier to work the loops – but even easier to drop them.

✿ *Knit it now...*

a Make a slip knot.
b Lift yarn with left index finger, moving away from you.
c Catch strand behind index finger, as shown in illustration.
d Tighten loop.

Twisted loop cast-on

One needle; one strand (**Fig 4**).
Slightly firmer than loop cast-on, but just as easy.

Work first row through front of loops, even if the stitches seem to ask to be worked through the back. This is what gives the twist to this method.

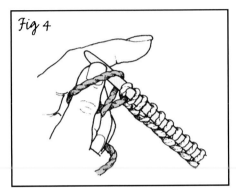

Fig 4

✿ Knit it now...

a Make a slip knot.
b Lift yarn from behind with left thumb, moving from left to right.
c Catch strand in front of thumb, as shown in illustration.
d Tighten loop.

Alternate loop cast-on

One needle; one strand (**Fig 5**).
A soft, decorative edge.

• Alternate one stitch from loop cast-on with one stitch from twisted loop cast-on.

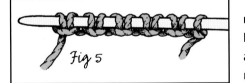

Fig 5

Double-twist loop cast-on

One needle; one strand (**Fig 6**). Very easy. Somewhat firmer than twisted loop cast-on. Easier to knit first row.

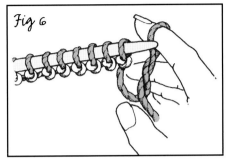

Fig 6

✿ Knit it now...

a Make a slip knot and take needle in left hand.
b Lift yarn from behind with right index finger.
c Twist yarn twice with your finger and place on needle.
d Tighten loop.

Two-strand cast-on

Generally one needle; two strands. Strong, elastic and the most versatile of all methods. Structure like loop cast-on (it may face the other way) plus a first knit row, but performance radically altered by the base loops being tightened. A variation has a purl, rather than a knit, row. Another alternates k1 and p1.

In flat knitting, it is best to start most patterns with a wrong-side row. Exceptions are reverse stockinette stitch and other patterns with purl rows on the right side.

There are many versions. The thumb cast-on is popular, but beginners may find Italian cast-on (and, even more, simplified cast-on) easier and less painful – no thumb prodding. Yarn-in-left-hand knitters are likely to prefer German cast-on.

All versions start with:

a Make a slip knot, leaving a tail at least 3 times the width to be bound on.

Thumb cast-on (Fig 7)

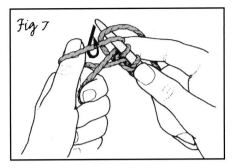

Fig 7

✿ Knit it now...

b Take needle and long strand in right hand.
c Holding short strand in left hand, catch a loop with left thumb, moving clockwise.
d Catch loop around thumb with needle.
e Wrap long strand under needle.
f Pass loop over tip of needle and pull short strand.
g Tighten long strand.

Italian cast-on (Fig 8)

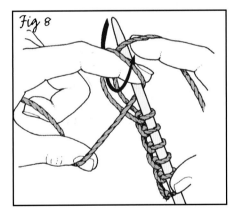

Fig 8

✿ Knit it now...

b Take needle and long strand in right hand.
c Holding short strand in left hand, catch yarn from underneath with both thumb and index finger.
d Catch yarn with needle, from left to right. This makes a loop around index finger.
e Wrap long strand under needle.
f Pass loop over tip of needle and pull short strand.
g Tighten long strand.

Simplified cast-on (Fig 9)

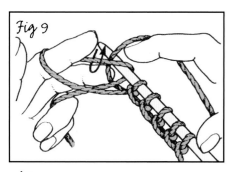

Fig 9

✿ *Knit it now...*

b Take needle and long strand in right hand.

c Holding short strand in left hand, catch yarn with index finger moving backwards.

d Catch yarn behind index finger with needle. This creates a loop.

e Wrap long strand under needle.

f Pass loop over tip of needle and pull short strand.

g Tighten long strand.

German cast-on (Fig 10)

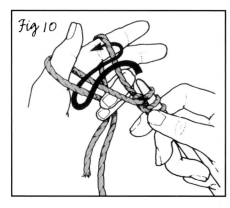

Fig 10

✿ *Knit it now...*

b Take both strands in left hand and needle in right hand.

c Catch short strand with left thumb, moving clockwise.

d Lift long strand with index finger.

e Catch loop around thumb with needle.

f Catch strand going to index finger with needle and draw through thumb loop.

g Let go thumb and pull short strand.

h Tighten long strand if necessary.

Twisted two-strand cast-on

Giving an extra twist to the two-strand cast-on results in an edge of great strength and elasticity. The Italian version is the better known.

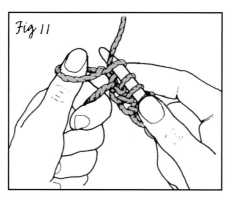

Fig 11

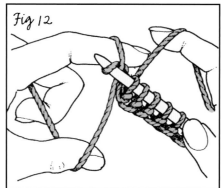

Fig 12

Twisted thumb cast-on

Fig 11. Like thumb cast-on but:

d Pass needle in front of short strand and catch back of loop around thumb, from behind.

Twisted Italian cast-on

Fig 12. Like Italian cast-on but:

d Catch back of strand around index finger, from behind.

Double two-strand cast-on

Fig 13. To strengthen a two-strand cast-on:

• Wrap yarn twice around thumb (thumb and German) or index finger (Italian and simplified), and insert needle into the double loop.

The same idea can be applied to twisted two-strand cast-on.

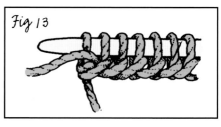

Fig 13

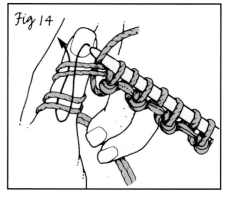

Fig 14

Channel Islands cast-on

Strong and very well suited to single rib. Knit the overs and purl the stitches on first row.

Work a two-strand cast-on but:

• use two strands of yarn in left hand (one strand for a softer edge).

• wrap the two strands twice around thumb or index finger – in the usual way if using simplified method, the other way round if using thumb, Italian or German methods.

• after each stitch, wrap yarn under and up the front of needle to make another stitch (**Fig 14**).

Chain cast-on

Chain cast-on (knitted or crochet) gives a loose cast-on, good for soft edges. It can be made firmer by working the first row twisted. Another way is to twist the loops before placing them on the needle (knitted version) or picking them up with the needle (crochet version). But even these tricks fail to make it ideal for firm patterns.

The knitted version, popular in several countries, is often used for the wrong purpose. The crochet version is much faster if you can handle a hook (not that difficult). Always work the first stitch of the first row, whatever the selvedge.

Knitted chain cast-on

Two needles; one strand.

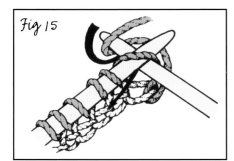

Fig 15

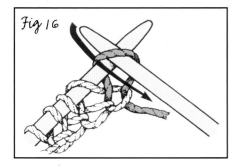

Fig 16

❀ Knit it now...

a Make a slip knot.

b Take needle with slip knot in left hand, and free needle in right hand.

c K into slip knot (**Fig 15**) and place new st onto left needle (**Fig 16**). Repeat **c**, always knitting into the last made st.

Crochet cast-on

One thick hook; one strand.

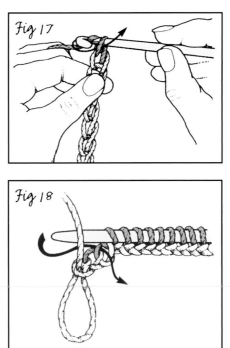

Fig 17

Fig 18

❀ Knit it now...

a Crochet a very loose chain (**Fig 17**), 1 link for each st required.

b Draw a long last loop to stop any unravelling.

c Turn the chain back to front with the last loop to the left.

d Pick up top of each link with a knitting needle, from back to front, starting with the 1st link (**Fig 18**).

e Place last loop on needle and tighten it.

Bind-off cast-on

Another chain method, popular in Japan, but this time it is the back of the link that makes the stitch. Looks exactly like chain bind-off. If the loops are not taken off the hook and reversed, the resulting chain is twisted.

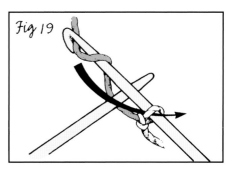

Fig 19

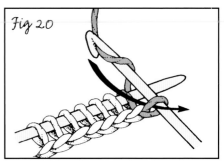

Fig 20

❀ Knit it now...

a Take needle in left hand and crochet hook with slip knot in right hand.

b Place needle over long strand, held in left hand.

c With hook, draw a loop over needle and through slip knot (**Fig 19**).

d Place yarn again under needle.

e Remove hook from its loop and insert it again from the other side.

Repeat **c** to **e** (**Fig 20**) until 1 st short of number required. Transfer last loop from hook to needle after **d**.

Style secrets
Stockinette stitch will show no break if bound on at mid-height, but most patterns will. Provisional cast-on is best used at a change-of-pattern line.

Buttonhole cast-on

One needle: one strand (**Fig 21**).
Like a series of slip knots worked
from one single end. Best used for
buttonholes and for adding stitches at
the end of rows in firm fabrics.
Avoid gaps between knots. The
instructions give the hand position that
minimizes gaps.

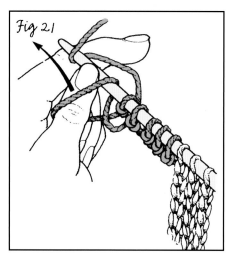

✺ *Knit it now...*

a With yarn in right hand, lift yarn from
   behind with left thumb, moving
   clockwise.
b Catch strand in front of thumb with
   needle, as in twisted loop cast-on.
c With right hand pass yarn under and
   up front of needle.
d Pass left-thumb loop over tip of
   needle.
e Remove thumb from loop and place
   on top of needle, securing new st.
f Pull yarn with right hand to tighten st.
   Make sure that final loop goes all the
   way around needle.

Classy clickers... *know that
looping is the fastest method
for provisional cast-on. Two-
strand will give neat results
first time without having to
learn extra tricks. Crochet is
very cunning, faster than two-
strand and very easy if you
can crochet a chain (**Fig 17**).*

Provisional cast-on

Sometimes called invisible. There are
three methods, all using a contrast,
preferably with a slippery yarn as
foundation. This is later unravelled to
free the loops for grafting or picking up
– either for a fringe, for an edging bind-
off, or to work in the opposite direction.
One stitch may need to be increased in
the last case.

   The looping method sometimes uses
the main yarn as foundation; this can
later be pulled to gather the edge if
desired. In the other two methods, if the
edge is to be gathered with the same
colour yarn, this has to be threaded later
– leave a long end.

Two-strand provisional cast-on

Cast on in a contrast yarn. Continue
in main yarn and main pattern. When
appropriate, snip the cast-on, stitch by
stitch, and pull to free the loops.

Crochet provisional cast-on

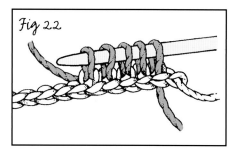

This is popular in Japan.

✺ *Knit it now...*

a With contrast yarn, crochet a chain
   – 1 link for each st required plus 1. Cut
   yarn and pull last loop.
b With main yarn, pick up a st from each
   link. This must be done from the loop
   at the back of the link. Do not pick up
   any sts from last link made (**Fig 22**).
   One k row made.
When required, pull back of last link.
Chain will unravel, leaving loops free.

Looping provisional cast-on

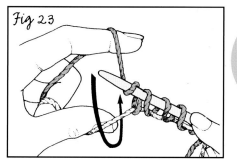

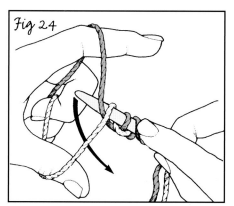

✺ *Knit it now...*

a Make a slip knot at one end of a
   foundation yarn, of a length over
   twice the required width.
b Make another slip knot in main yarn.
   Leave a long end only if of use later.
c Take needle in right hand and yarn
   in left hand as in German two-strand
   cast-on, with the foundation yarn
   around thumb. Taking one strand in
   each hand is possible but slower.
d With a flick of right wrist, catch main
   yarn from underneath, working from
   centre out (**Fig 23**, before arrow
   movement).
e With another flick of the wrist, go
   under foundation yarn, from the front
   (still **Fig 23**); catch main yarn from
   the top and bring it up from under
   foundation yarn (**Fig 24**).
Repeat **d** and **e**. The main yarn must
make a full loop around needle. If it only
goes halfway, use a thicker needle or
two needles held together.
Drop the contrast slip knot at end of 1st
row. Tie the 2 foundation ends.

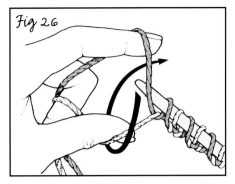

Fig 26

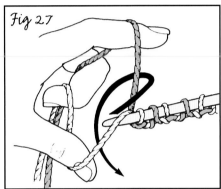

Fig 27

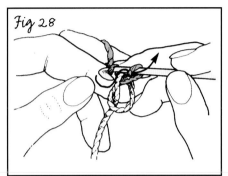

Fig 28

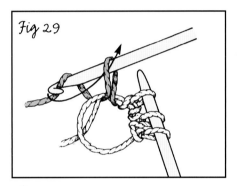

Fig 29

Tubular cast-on (two-strand)

Sometimes called invisible, tubular cast-on can be applied to a wide range of patterns, but is best known for the beautifully rounded edge it gives to tubular stockinette (tubular stocking) stitch and single rib (**Fig 25**). The two-strand version given here is the fastest

One needle; two strands. The wrist movements are NOT as in looping provisional cast-on.

Fig 25

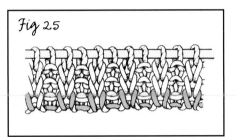

❋ Knit it now...

a Make a slip knot, leaving a free end 4 times the desired width (shown here in white for clarity).

b Keep both yarns in left hand, as in German two-strand cast-on, with the free end around thumb. Taking one strand in each hand is possible but slower.

Style secrets

In edges expected to stretch and recover (such as cuffs or waistbands) tubular cast-on may tend to gape. Always work with needles two or three sizes finer than for the pattern to follow, but do not work it too tight. Try a sample first.

c With a flick of right wrist, go over and behind the long strand, catch free end from the top and bring it up from under long strand (**Fig 26**).

d With another flick of the wrist, go over and in front of free end, catch long strand from the top and bring it up from under free end (**Fig 27**).

Repeat **c** and **d**, making sure the sts go all the way around the needle.

e Tie the 2 strands under the needle after the last st.

f Work 2 or 4 rows in tubular st st – k the k sts, sl the p sts pwise wyif. The 1st st of the 1st row will be k if last cast-on st was a **c**, it will be sl if last cast-on st was a **d**. On 1st row only, k-b k sts.

g Continue in chosen pattern, with ordinary size needles.

For softest results, single rib can be started directly after **e**.

Pinhole cast-on

For any work that starts from one central point. Avoid binding on directly on a set of needles. It is too awkward for good results. Crochet-hook methods are best.

Tiniest hole cast-on

❋ Knit it now...

a Wrap yarn around index finger of left hand.

b Draw through a loop with hook.

c Remove finger from circle. Secure circle between finger and thumb.

d Draw a new loop through loop on hook (**Fig 28**).

Repeat **b** and **d** until you have enough sts for 1st needle. Transfer sts from hook to needle.

Continue on sts for 2nd needle (**Fig 29**). When work is completed, pull free end tight and darn.

Larger hole cast-on

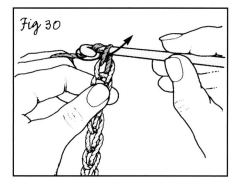

Fig 30

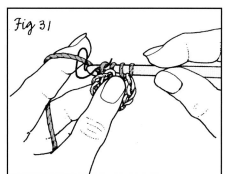

Fig 31

❋ Knit it now...

a Make a crochet chain, 1 link for each st (**Fig 30**).

b Close chain by drawing a loop through 1st link.

c Draw a loop through each link until you have enough for 1st needle (**Fig 31**).

d Transfer sts from hook to 1st needle and repeat **c** for each of the other needles.

To tighten up hole, sew inside edge of links with the yarn tail using a running stitch. Pull, then darn free end.

Centre line cast-on

Oval and rectangular work often starts from a line across the centre. There are two solutions, using whatever cast-on blends in best with the pattern – either by disappearing or by creating a bold line.

Sewn cast-on

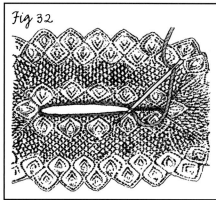

Fig 32

❋ Knit it now...

a With a circular needle, or a set of needles, cast on twice the number of sts required for the centre line.

b Close the circle and work in rounds. Bind off.

c Spread the work flat and seam the 2 sides of the cast-on (**Fig 32**).

Two-way cast-on

More fiddly, but easier to check progress.

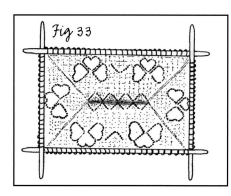

Fig 33

❋ Knit it now...

a Cast on the centre-line sts, plus 1, on the 1st needle of a set of 5.

b Pick up the same number of sts from the cast-on edge, with the 2nd needle.

c Work in rounds. The short sides are worked on the other 2 needles, from the extra cast-on st (**Fig 33**).

Casting on circles

The first stitch of the first round will close the circle. Before working it, check that the cast-on is not spiralling over the needle(s) as happens in **Fig 34**.

If the first round has any decreases, try to work one of them over the first and last cast-on stitches, either at the start or end of the round.

With a circular needle, slip a marker around the needle before closing the circle.

With sets of double-pointed needles, distribute the stitches evenly on the holding needles. Pull yarn firmly when changing to a new needle. If in trouble, cast on with straight needle(s), then slip or work the stitches onto the set.

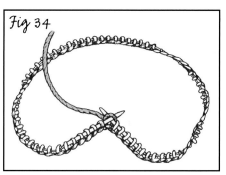

Fig 34

Classy clickers... know that if your circle joins are untidy you can:
• pull yarn firmly at the join, or
• cast on an extra stitch and decrease, or
• cast on an extra stitch and decrease over the first and second cast-on stitches.

Binding off

A bind-off (or cast-off) is the row that closes the free loops, so that they cannot unravel. Most of the comments on casting on apply, with obvious adaptations, to binding off. Gauge samples are not so essential. Check the bind-off as you go along, and unravel if it pulls or crinkles. But samples may still be needed to compare methods and decide whether to bind off on the right or the wrong side. If increases or decreases are necessary, work them discreetly and evenly on the actual bind-off row. If the last few stitches tend to be untidy, watch the way you hold the needles. You may be stretching these stitches by moving the left needle too much. Before trimming the yarn, check that the bind-off does not pull and make sure that the work has no major errors. Leave a yarn tail long enough for darning or sewing.

Style secrets
Work double crochet bind-off with a contrast yarn to create a decorative effect on the wrong side of a garment.

Choosing a bind-off

Chain bind-off is essential. Provisional and diagonal are both easy and very useful. Tubular requires some effort, but is worth it. Several others are covered in the following pages. Choose the most appropriate one from those listed below.

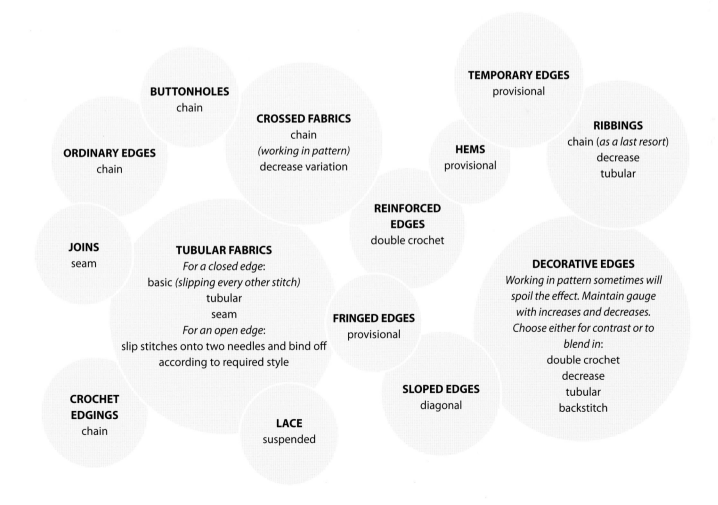

TEMPORARY EDGES
provisional

RIBBINGS
chain *(as a last resort)*
decrease
tubular

BUTTONHOLES
chain

CROSSED FABRICS
chain
(working in pattern)
decrease variation

HEMS
provisional

ORDINARY EDGES
chain

REINFORCED EDGES
double crochet

JOINS
seam

TUBULAR FABRICS
For a closed edge:
basic *(slipping every other stitch)*
tubular
seam
For an open edge:
slip stitches onto two needles and bind off
according to required style

DECORATIVE EDGES
Working in pattern sometimes will spoil the effect. Maintain gauge with increases and decreases. Choose either for contrast or to blend in:
double crochet
decrease
tubular
backstitch

FRINGED EDGES
provisional

CROCHET EDGINGS
chain

LACE
suspended

SLOPED EDGES
diagonal

Chain bind-off

The most widely used bind-off (for a perfect match, see bind-off cast-on). It is often knitted too tight. For best results, the working loop should be loosened up each time; this is preferable to using a thicker needle or hook. Always bind off in pattern, following knit, purl, slip stitches, overs, decreases etc. Bind off free edges of stockinette stitch and garter stitch on the wrong side, to hide the chain (**Fig 35**).

This bind-off can be worked in three ways. Use basic unless you prefer to crochet rather than knit. Use suspended if the yarn is not resilient, or you cannot loosen the tension enough.

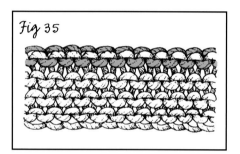

Fig 35

Classy clickers... *if instructed to bind off a certain number of stitches, count the times that they pull a stitch over another stitch.*

Basic bind-off

Fig 36

✿ *Knit it now...*

a Work 2 sts.

b With left needle pull the 1st st over 2nd st and off the needle (**Fig 36**).

c Work another st and pull previous one over it. Repeat **c** to the last st. Trim yarn and pull last loop.

If binding off purl stitches, either lift the stitch from the other side of the needle, or take yarn to back of work before lifting the stitch. The loop on the right needle after binding off a group of stitches is not considered bound off. If you next have to 'pattern 5', that loop is the first of the five. Lace patterns might not follow this convention.

Crochet bind-off

Hold yarn in left hand and keep at back.

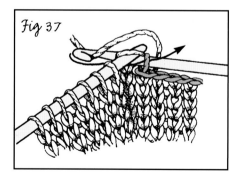

Fig 37

✿ *Knit it now...*

a Sl 1st st pwise onto hook.

b Insert hook into next st and drop the st from left needle.

c Catch yarn with hook and draw through the 2 sts (**Fig 37**). Repeat **b** and **c**.

Suspended bind-off

Work as for basic, but keep lifted stitch on left needle. Work the next stitch on left needle (**Fig 38**) and drop them both together.

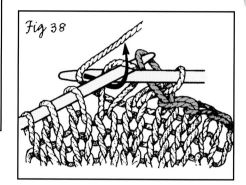

Fig 38

Double crochet bind-off

A variation of crochet chain – a row of double crochet is worked directly onto the free loops. Strong and elastic. Good base for crochet edgings (but not necessarily for crab stitch). Hold yarn in left hand and keep at back.

Fig 39

✿ *Knit it now...*

a K 1st st with hook: insert hook into st, catch yarn from underneath and draw it through the st.

b Drop st from left needle.

c K next st with hook and drop from needle.

d Catch yarn with hook and draw through the 2 sts on hook (**Fig 39**). Repeat **c** and **d**.

Decrease bind-off

Decorative. Much better than chain for ribbings, but not as good as tubular. Try alternating knit with purl: k if 2nd st on left needle is a k st, p if it is a p st.

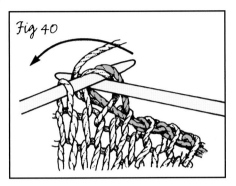

Fig 40

✿ Knit it now...

a K2 tog, through front.
b Sl new st back onto left needle without twisting.
Repeat **a** and **b** (**Fig 40**).
Variation: k-b the 2 sts to give a chain bind-off with a twisted last row.

Provisional bind-off

The easiest of them all. Use for gathering, or when stitches are to be left in waiting for any reason, such as grafting, fringing or measuring.

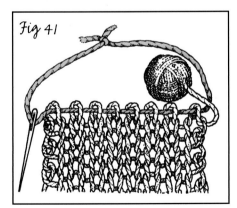

Fig 41

• With a sewing needle, thread a piece of yarn through all the stitches, dropping them off the knitting needle (**Fig 41**).

Classy clickers... *use the main yarn if they want to gather the work using provisional bind-off. Otherwise a contrasting, slippery yarn is best. Use a long piece that can be tied in a huge loop without drawing in the knitting.*

Tubular bind-off

Also called invisible. A sewn bind-off that makes a perfect match for tubular cast-on (**Fig 25**).
Learn knit grafting before you tackle it.

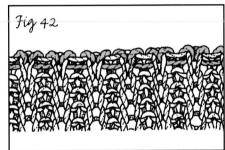

Fig 42

✿ Knit it now...

a Work at least 2 rows in tubular st st. In single rib this is not strictly necessary, but it makes life easier. Remember that 2 tubular rows equal 1 ordinary row.
b With working yarn trimmed to about 4 times the length to be bound off, graft the front (1 row deep) layer of st st to the back layer.
To practise, slip the front stitches onto a double-pointed needle. Do the same with the back stitches. Graft with a contrast yarn. You should obtain a series of Vs on the top edge.

Style secrets
Tubular bind-off is ideal for neckline ribbings, but work very loosely or your head will not go through!

When confident, try the one-needle approach. Starting with a front (k) stitch:

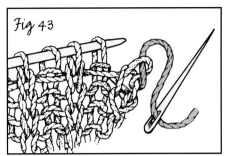

Fig 43

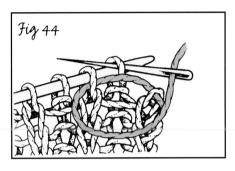

Fig 44

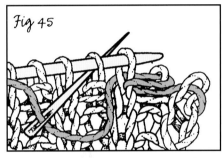

Fig 45

✿ Knit it now...

a Insert sewing needle kwise into 1st st. Drop st (**Fig 43**).
b Insert sewing needle pwise into 3rd (k) st. Do not drop st. Pull yarn through, not too tight.
c Insert sewing needle pwise into 2nd (p) st. Drop st (**Fig 44**).
d Working round the back of the st, insert sewing needle kwise into 4th (p) st. Do not drop st. Pull yarn through (**Fig 45**).
Repeat **a** to **d**.
With practice, all four stitches can be dropped as soon as the sewing needle has gone through them, and the process can be cut down to two movements: **a** and **b**; **c** and **d**.

Backstitch bind-off

A subtle, decorative method also achieved with a sewing needle (**Fig 46**). Also called sewn bind-off or cast-on bind-off.

Use a length of yarn 4 to 5 times the width.

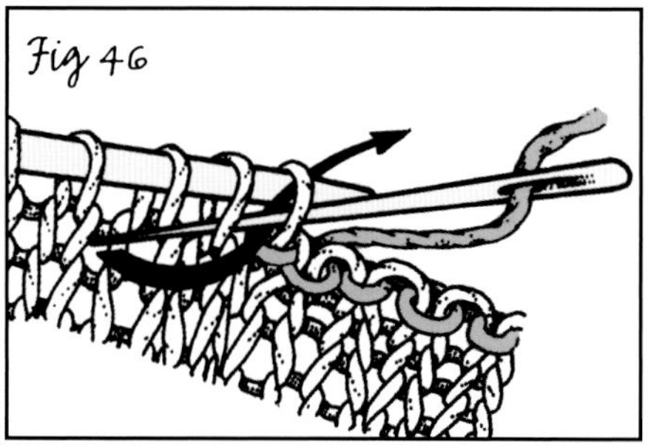
Fig 46

Knit it now...

a Insert needle into 1st 2 sts pwise. Pull yarn.

b Insert needle into 1st st kwise. Drop st and pull yarn.

Repeat **a** and **b**.

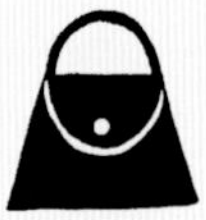

Style secrets
Backstitch bind-off will stretch the edge of fabrics that draw in, such as ribbing. This is used to advantage in a related technique: free-loop backstitch seam.

Diagonal bind-off

For sloping edges, such as sweater shoulders.

Bind off the stitches in groups, every other row. For 2 symmetrical slopes, bind off the right slope on the right side and the left slope on the wrong side.

Two ways of avoiding 'steps'. Work a dart and bind off all the stitches in one go. Or, be cunning:

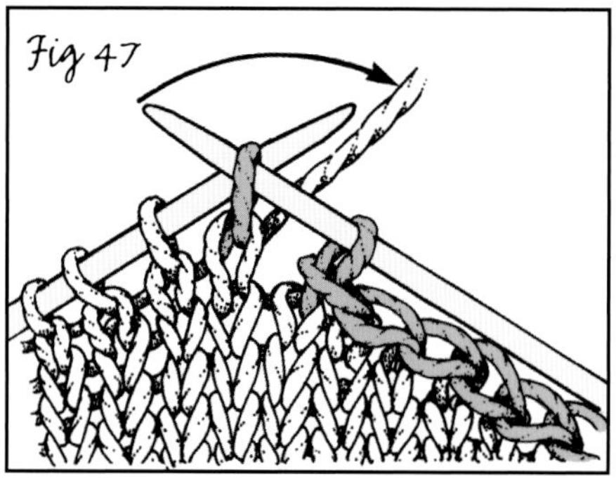
Fig 47

Knit it now...

a Having bound off 1st group, do not work last st of return row. Turn work, 1 st on right needle.

b Sl 1st st on left needle pwise (**Fig 47**).

c Pass 1st st on right needle over sl st. First st of the new group is now bound off. Continue in usual way.

Adapt this method if using a bind-off other than chain.

Seam bind-off

For tubular fabrics or to join two pieces with out sewing them up.

Done from the wrong side (the two right sides facing), or from the right side (wrong sides facing). Two symmetrical bind-offs (for example, shoulders) must be started from the same end if worked on the right side. Tubular fabrics must be divided onto two needles. (See also **The hard graft**, pages 126–128, and **The seamy side**, pages 129–135.)

- Proceed as for basic bind-off, but keep working together 1 stitch from each needle (**Fig 48**). If you want the bound-off chain to sit astride the top edges, and look the same from both sides, work in single rib (k tog the 1st st from each needle, p tog the 2nd st from each needle).

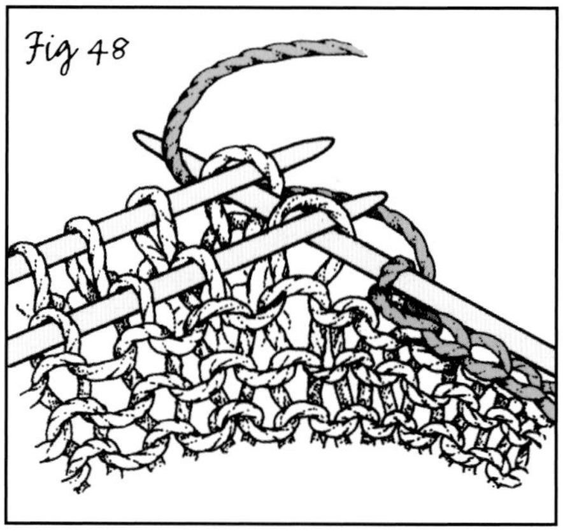
Fig 48

Many of the other binding-off methods explained could be adapted.

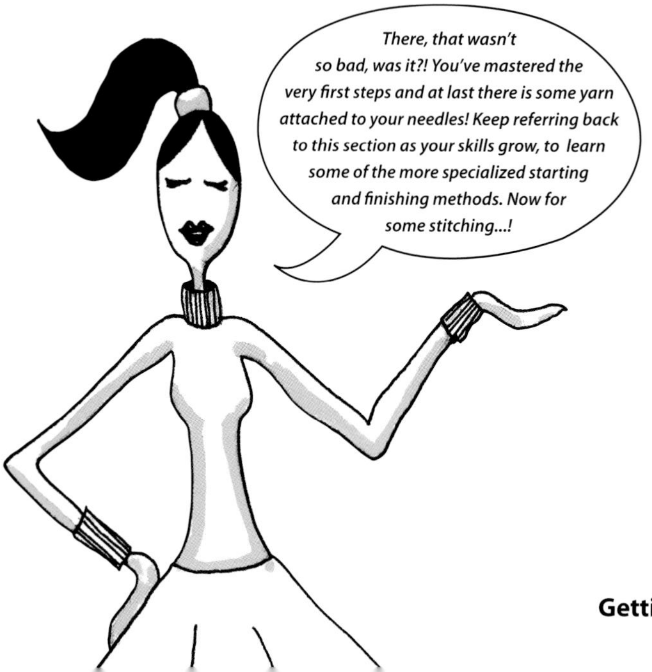
There, that wasn't so bad, was it?! You've mastered the very first steps and at last there is some yarn attached to your needles! Keep referring back to this section as your skills grow, to learn some of the more specialized starting and finishing methods. Now for some stitching...!

Knit and purl

If you've only ever heard of a few knitting terms, they will probably include 'knit' and 'purl', and the phrase 'knit one, purl one' might come into your head. The knit stitch and the purl stitch are the two fundamental building blocks of knitting. If you knit one row and purl the next row, you create what is the standard knitted fabric – stockinette stitch (also known as stocking stitch). You can see this for yourself even on machine-made, shop-bought knitwear. Once you know knit and purl, you can start getting interesting; the combination of these stitches in various ways can be used to create all sorts of funky patterns and beautiful textures. Let's look at the basics first.

Knit stitch

The basic knitted stitch worked from the smooth side. **Fig 1** shows the most popular (plain) version (k):

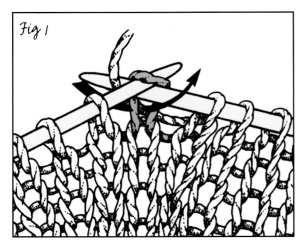

Fig 1

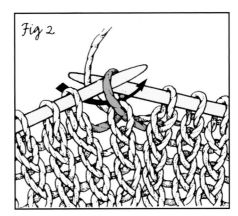

Fig 3

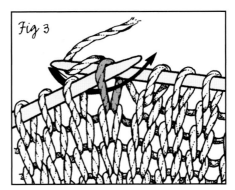

Fig 2

If, instead, the needle is inserted through the back of the loop (knit-back or k-b), the original stitch becomes twisted (**Fig 2**). That is, unless the yarn is wrapped over the needle rather than under it, as in the second version of the plain stitch (**Fig 3**). Inserting the needle through the front of the loop will now produce a plaited stitch (**Fig 4**). This is like a twisted stitch going the other way.

❀ *Knit it now...*

a With yarn at back, insert right needle into 1st st on left needle, from front to back.
b Pass yarn under and up the front of right needle.
c Draw yarn through st with right needle.
d Drop original st from left needle.

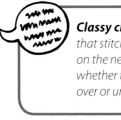 *Classy clickers...* know that stitches look different on the needles depending on whether the yarn is wrapped over or under.

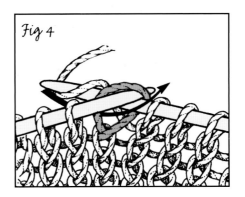

Fig 4

Purl stitch

The basic knitted stitch worked from the rugged side. The common version (p) is shown in **Fig 5**:

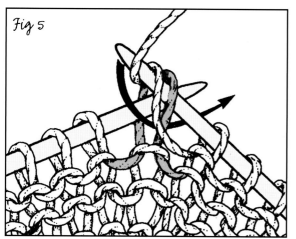

 Knit it now...

a With yarn in front, insert right needle into 1st st on left needle, from back to front.

b Pass yarn over, down the back and under needle.

c Draw yarn through st with right needle.

d Drop original st from left needle.

For a twisted stitch (**Fig 6**), insert needle through the back of the loop (purl-back or p-b).

Wrapping the yarn under the needle gives an untwisted stitch if the loop is worked from the back (**Fig 7**), and a plaited stitch if worked from the front (**Fig 8**).

Style secrets

Once you know the knit and purl stitches, you can combine them to create motifs in your knitted fabric; the bumpy purl stitches will stand out against the smooth surface of the knit background. Create something cute and kitschy like a heart or a flower shape; fun animal shapes for a kid's jumper; or sophisticated abstract shapes to add pattern to a knitted cushion cover.

Knit and purl can be combined into a huge range of stitch patterns and fabrics. Some of the characteristics of these stitches are set out here:

From knit and purl to fabulous fabrics

• Knit stitches are smooth; the yarn is at the back.

• Purl stitches are bumpy; the yarn is at the front.

• To knit after purling, or vice versa, take yarn to the other side under the needles (see yarn under).

• Knit stands up from purl in vertical arrangements. It recedes in horizontal ones.

• Fabrics may 'draw in' (ribbings), 'draw up' (welts), look embossed (damasks) or even ripple all over, depending on how knit and purl stitches are combined.

• Fabrics may curl in or out. They may also be flat.

• A firm tension gives best results.

• Twisting or plaiting increases elasticity, texture and firmness. If extra firmness is not required, use thicker needles.

• Non-twisted stitches are easier to work.

• To work in rounds, read knit for purl, and purl for knit, on wrong-side rows.

Garter stitch

A flat, slow-growing fabric (**Fig 9**). It 'draws up' so much that one stitch and two rows can sometimes produce a perfect square. Often used for borders.

Each bump equals two rows. Both sides are alike: a succession of horizontal ridges with vertical elasticity. Worked sideways, garter stitch can sometimes replace single rib.

All rows: k (or p).

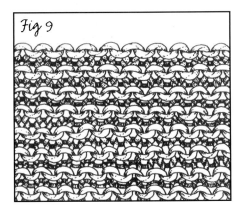

Fig 9

Stockinette stitch

'The' knitted fabric; taken as norm when assessing width and height of other fabrics. Top and bottom curl out. Sides curl in. The knit side (st st) is smooth (**Fig 10**). The purl side (reverse st st) is very lumpy (**Fig 11**) and curls in the opposite way. On the knit side, each V is a row.

Row 1: k. Row 2: p.

Yarn-in-left-hand knitters sometimes knit back then wrap the yarn under the needle when purling. This makes the work easier and more even (see also page 20).

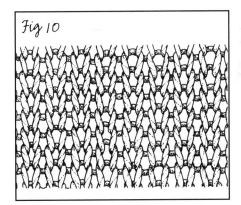

Fig 10

Fig 11

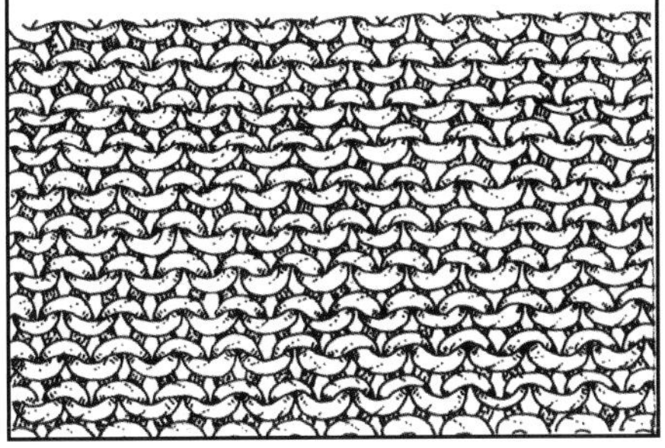

Classy clickers... *know that half-twisted and half-plaited stockinette stitch keep every other row straight and are less prone to slant.*

Knitting as in **Fig 2** and purling as in Fig 7 gives twisted st st (**Fig 2**).

Knitting as in **Fig 4** but purling in the ordinary way gives half-twisted st st – one row is twisted and the next not.

Knitting as in **Fig 4** and purling as in **Fig 8** gives plaited st st (**Fig 4**).

Knitting as in **Fig 4** and purling as in **Fig 7** gives half-plaited st st – one row is plaited and the next not.

Twisted and plaited st st sometimes slants to right or left. If this happens, it cannot be totally corrected, but slanting the other way when blocking might help.

Seed (moss) stitch

A flat, thickish fabric that grows fairly slowly (**Fig 12**). Good for borders.

Row 1: *k1, p1* to end.
Row 2: k the p sts, p the k sts.

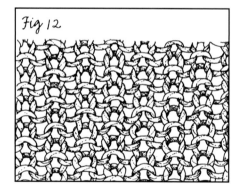

Fig 12

Style secrets
Make ribbings firmer and more elastic by twisting or plaiting. Yarns with little resilience such as cotton or silk make poor ribbings.

Ribbings

Vertical combinations of knit and purl; also called ribs. Very strong 'drawing in' tendency. Ideal for cuffs and waistbands because of their great elasticity. (See also **Choosing a cast on**, page 37; **Choosing a bind-off**, page 44; and **Planning for seams**, page 130)

Work tightly. Needles one, two, or even more, sizes finer than for stockinette stitch are standard practice, because the vertical arrangement of yarn unders increases the stitch size (see **Fabric character**, page 16). Knitted-in borders will often require you to pull the yarn firmly in order to increase the yarn tension, or to place the border stitches on short double-pointed needles of the appropriate thickness; change from border needles to main needles as for circular knitting (see **Fig 2**, page 23).

Ribbings can be regular (same number of stitches are first knitted, then purled) or irregular (more, or fewer, stitches are knitted than purled). If the last stitch of a group of two or more knit stitches looks too large, see page 20 for advice.

• Two rows. The 1st sets the sequence. The 2nd is always: k the k sts, p the p sts.

Single (1 x 1) rib

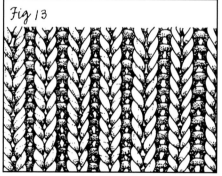

Fig 13

Row 1: *k1, p1* to end.
Row 2: see above.

Double (2 x 2) rib

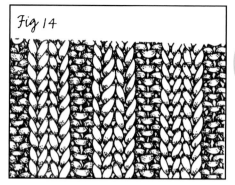

Fig 14

'Draws in' more than single rib.
Row 1: *k2, p2* to end.
Row 2: see above.

Style secrets
Reverse stockinette stitch welts have deep furrows. Do not try to block them flat! You'll ruin the look of the pattern.

Welts

Combinations of knit rows and purl rows, resulting in garter stitch or reverse stockinette stitch raised stripes on a stockinette stitch background. Strong tendency to 'draw up'.

Any combination of rows is possible. **Fig 15** shows:

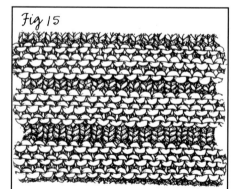

Fig 15

Rows 1, 3, 5, 6 and 8: k.
Rows 2, 4 and 7: p.

Slipping away

Once you have knit and purl under your belt, you can try a few fancier things. Slip stitch (sl st), for example, is a stitch that is passed from left to right needle without being worked. The result is an elongated stitch with a bar across it on the side the yarn is held. Many techniques use slipped stitches, especially slip-stitch knitting and tubular knitting. If the instructions do not say 'with yarn in front' (wyif), or 'with yarn at back' (wyab), leave the yarn where it is. There are two ways of slipping stitches. Unless otherwise instructed, do it purlwise but without changing yarn position.

Purlwise (pwise)

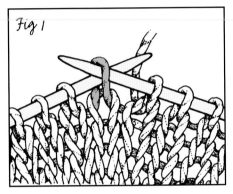

Fig 1

❀ Knit it now...

a Insert right needle into st as if to p it.
b Drop st from left needle.
c Work next st without pulling yarn too tight.

Note (**Fig 1**) that the stitch does not become twisted.

Knitwise (kwise)

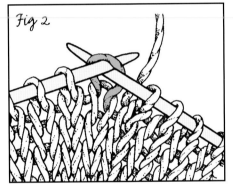

Fig 2

❀ Knit it now...

a Insert right needle into st as if to k.
b Drop st from left needle.
c Work next st without pulling yarn too tight.

Note (**Fig 2**) that the stitch is twisted by the action.

Slip-stitch knitting

(See also **multicolour slip stitch**, page 95.)
Fabrics emphasize the elongated loop (**Fig 3**, 'heel stitch' – row 1: *k1, sl1* to end; row 2: p), sometimes slipping it over several rows, or the bar across the loop. Across one stitch, a bar can produce intriguing 'woven' effects (**Fig 4**, 'slip-stitch honeycomb' – rows 1 and 3: k; row 2: *k1 sl1* to end; row 4: *sl1, k1* to end). Across several stitches, bars become quite dramatic (**Fig 5**), but are prone to snagging.

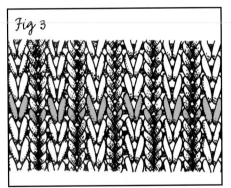

Fig 3

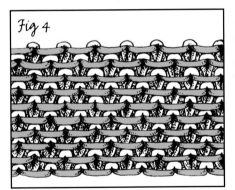

Fig 4

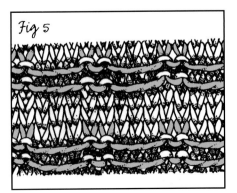

Fig 5

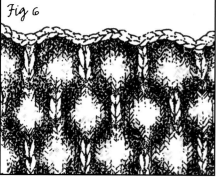

Fig 6

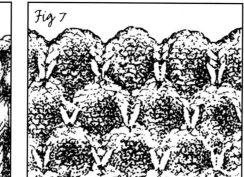

Fig 7

Classy clickers... *know that slip-stitch knitting has the following qualities:*
- **Thickness** *tends to increase.*
- **Elasticity** *tends to decrease.*
- **Fabric** *width may decrease; more stitches may be needed.*
- **Fabric** *length may decrease, more rows may be needed.*
- **On** *a st st base, tendency to curl increases, especially if slipping over several rows.*
- **Curling** *is only partially corrected by blocking.*
- **Slipping** *for several rows can create deep three-dimensional textures, of interest from both sides of work (**Figs 6** and **7**).*
- **Unless** *specified, yarn should not be pulled tightly after slipping.*

Tubular knitting

(See also **Double-sided jacquard**, page 95.)

By slipping every other stitch, two layers of fabric can be worked at the same time. The instructions below are for stockinette stitch, which gives a firm, thick and flat fabric. Many other patterns are possible, even different ones on each layer. Pull yarn tight after slipping and/or use fine needles.

Top and lower edges can be closed or open. See **Choosing a cast-on**, page 37, and **Choosing a bind-off**, page 44.

For closed sides, on an even number of stitches:

Row 1: *K1, slip 1 pwise wyif*, to end.
Row 2: k the sl sts, sl the k sts from previous row.
Repeat row 2.

For open sides, use two balls of yarn:
Row 1: with 1st ball, *k1, slip 1 pwise wyif*, to end.
Row 2: with 1st ball, p the k sts of row 1 and sl the sl sts pwise wyab.

Row 3: with 2nd ball, p the sl sts of rows 1 and 2 and sl the others pwise wyab.
Row 4: with 2nd ball, k the p sts of row 3 and sl the sl sts pwise wyif.
Repeat rows 1 to 4.

Alternatively, use double-pointed needles, and work row 1, row 3, row 4 and row 2, in this order. Because two independent layers result, this work cannot strictly be called tubular. The sides, though, can be closed by twisting one yarn around the other every two rows if working with double-pointed needles. It is then possible to work the two layers of a truly tubular piece in two colours (**Fig 8**).

Tubular bands placed horizontally on ordinary knitting may or may not need exactly twice the number of stitches. Try samples.

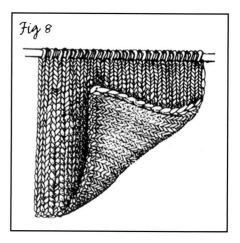

Fig 8

The ins and outs

Knitting is shaped by adding or subtracting stitches (increases and decreases), usually one or two at a time. Unless you intend on only knitting square and rectangular pieces for the rest of your life, you should learn to increase and decrease. This will help you create shapely garments, for example, that nip in at the waist and curve out in all the right places.

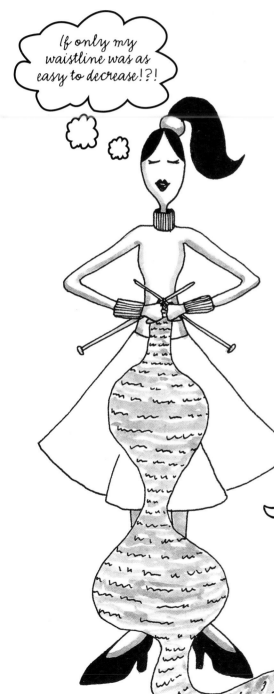

If only my waistline was as easy to decrease!?!

Increasing and decreasing is also a way of creating texture – in which case the stitches increased in one place have to be decreased in another. To add or subtract three or more stitches at the start or the end of a row, cast on or bind off. Increases and decreases are instantly spotted when a fabric marker is placed next to each one. Fabric markers are essential when working the shapings every so many rows, together with a needle marker next to the guide stitch – the stitch that aligns the shapings vertically.

Some shapings pull the fabric. One may be immaterial; ten in line may not. Shaped edges travel diagonally and are longer than the ordinary vertical ones. Work them loosely, checking that they do not pull.

Classy clickers... use needle markers at the start and end of the block of complete repeats to keep a pattern correct whilst shaping. You can move marker(s) a whole repeat in or out as required.

Choosing shapings

The first increase to learn is strand (either left or right); the first decrease is knit (if not looking for symmetrical decreases, learn only k2 tog). Otherwise, choice depends on fabric and whether you want a decorative effect. Knit some samples to see the effects.

Points to remember:
- Most methods of shaping show a slant. This is especially clear in decreases.
- Two similar methods, pointing in opposite directions, make a pair. Use pairs for symmetrical shapings.
- Unless pattern suggests otherwise, use only one type of slant when working many shapings along a row.
- Shapings slanting with the fabric blend in (**Fig 1**).
- The same shapings slanting against the fabric stand out (**Fig 2**). Try knitting some samples.
- Double shapings are shown in central positions. They could also be

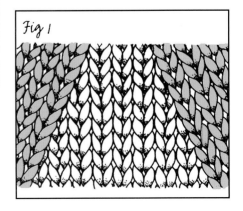

Fig 1

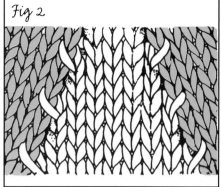

Fig 2

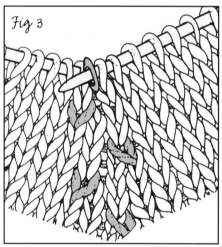

Fig 3

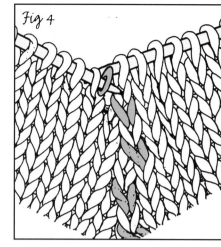

Fig 4

Calculating shapings

Suppose you have to add 10 stitches in 60 rows. A straight division tells you to increase 1 stitch every 6 rows. Had the result been 5.8 rows, you would have had a choice: work the first or last increase only 4 rows away from the edge, or add 2 more rows to the total. If using double or paired increases, halve the number of rows first. Decreases are calculated the same way.

Notes

Instructions are given for both knit and purl situations, so that shapings can be an odd number of rows apart. However, only the knit side is shown because this is where differences really show. On wrong-side rows the left shaping is worked first. Unless otherwise instructed, needle markers are slipped as follows:
RIGHT
On knit: before shaping. On purl: after shaping.
LEFT
On knit: after shaping. On purl: before shaping.

Paired single increases

Work right-hand increases after the guide stitch, and left-hand increases before the guide stitch.

Pinhole increase

The simplest, but leaves a hole (**Fig 5**). (See **Strand increase**, page 56, for ways to avoid the hole.)

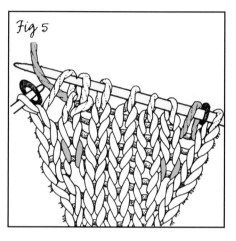

Fig 5

RIGHT
On knit: k into horizontal strand between last st and next st.
On purl: p strand.
LEFT
On knit: k strand.
On purl: p strand.

Style secrets
Whereabouts in a row you work your shapings will affect the look of your garment. It is usually best to work shapings one or two stitches in from the edge. This creates a nice sleek line that looks smarter and is easier to seam. (See also **Shaped edges**, page 66.)

worked at the edges. The marker(s) should then always be kept to one side.
• To adapt single shapings to central positions, alternate one shaping before marker and one shaping with opposite slant after marker (**Fig 3**). To maintain the slant (**Fig 4**), always shape before marker to decrease or after marker to increase; move marker one stitch to left after 1st, 3rd, 5th, etc shapings. The effect will be slightly off-centre – try some samples before deciding on the best marker position.
• For other ways to adapt single shapings to central positions, see **Double increases**, page 57 and **Double decreases**, page 60.
• Do not feel restricted to using knit shapings only on knit fabrics. Try them on purl, or any other fabric.
• Double shapings can be chosen for their decorative value: five doubles instead of ten singles make a bigger impact.

Eyelet increase

Very decorative (**Fig 6**). Structure similar to pinhole, but leaves a larger hole one row later.

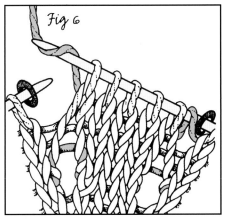

RIGHT

On knit: front-to-back yo. On purl: back-to-front yo.

LEFT

On knit: back-to-front yo. On purl: front-to-back yo.

DO NOT twist the overs on next row. Work them through back of loop if necessary.

Strand increase

Same principle as pinhole, but twisting the strand to avoid the hole (**Fig 7**).

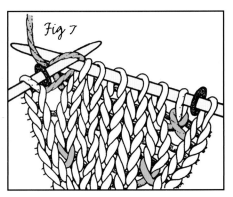

RIGHT

On knit: with left needle, pick up horizontal strand between last st and next st, from the front, and k-b.

On purl: pick up strand from the front and p-b.

LEFT

On knit: pick up strand from the back and k. On purl: pick up strand from the back and p.

Closed eyelet increase

To avoid the hole in eyelet (**Fig 8**). Same structure as strand but looser and one row later.

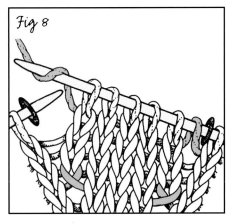

RIGHT

On knit: front-to-back yo.
On purl: front-to-back yo.
LEFT (sometimes called garter increase)
On knit: back-to-front yo.
On purl: back-to-front yo.
Twist the overs on next row.

Cast-on increase

Also same structure as strand, but even more loose than closed eyelet (**Fig 9**).

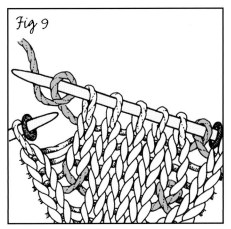

RIGHT

On knit: loop cast-on 1.
On purl: loop cast-on 1.
LEFT
On knit: twisted-loop cast-on 1. P-b on next row.
On purl: twisted-loop cast-on 1. K-b on next row.

Row below increase

Very neat (**Fig 10**). The new stitch must be loose enough not to pull.

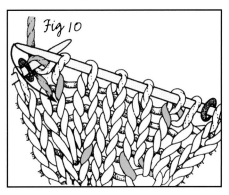

RIGHT

On knit: k first into st below, then into st.
On purl: p1 but do not drop; p into st below.
LEFT
On knit: k1 but do not drop; k into st below.
On purl: p first into st below, then into st.

Lifted increase

Also very neat (**Fig 11**). Unless worked loosely, the increases will pull the fabric if placed one on top of another.

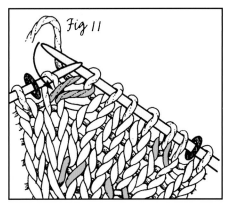

RIGHT

On knit: k the back head of st below next st; k1.
On purl: p1; with left needle pick up head of st below st just taken off needle, from the back; p-b.
LEFT
On knit: k1; with left needle pick up side loop of st below st just taken off left needle, from the back; k-b.
On purl: p head of st below next st; p1.

Bar increase

Tightens slightly the stitch over which it is worked (**Fig 12**).

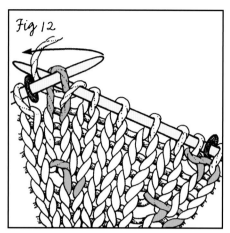

Fig 12

RIGHT

On knit: k a st first through front and then through back. If using markers: sl pwise st before marker; drop marker; return st to left needle; k but do not drop; place marker on right needle; k-b st.

On purl: p through front and back.

LEFT

On knit: k through front and back.

On purl: p through front and back. If using markers: sl pwise st before marker; drop marker; return st to left needle; p but do not drop; place marker on right needle; p-b st.

Double increases

Two ways of adding two stitches:

FIRST METHOD Place 2 single increases side by side, perhaps with 1 (or more) guide stitch(es) in between. Place marker(s) to pinpoint centre line or to define the guide stitch(es).

Fig 13 shows a pair of lifted increases next to each other, order maintained.

Fig 14 shows them in reverse order, divided by one guide stitch.

SECOND METHOD Use a true double increase: similar principles as single increases but 2 extra stitches are made each time. If using markers, place one at each side of the guide stitch. When increasing only on one side of work, or if the increases do not have a centre stitch, one marker is enough. Markers will need repositioning each time.

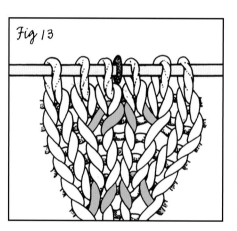

Fig 13

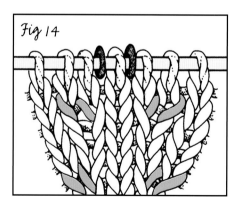

Fig 14

Double eyelet increase

A nice, bold hole (**Fig 15**).

On knit or purl: work a double over – front to back and round again. Slip marker between 1st and 2nd wrap. On next row, work 2nd wrap (the 1st made) twisted.

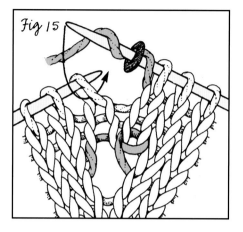

Fig 15

Double cast-on increase

A smaller hole (**Fig 16**). Alternate loop and twisted-loop cast-ons for a subtle criss-cross effect.

On knit or purl: either loop or twisted-loop cast-on 2 sts. Place marker between the 2.

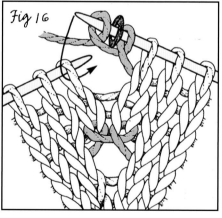

Fig 16

Over increase

No single increase counterpart (**Fig 17**).

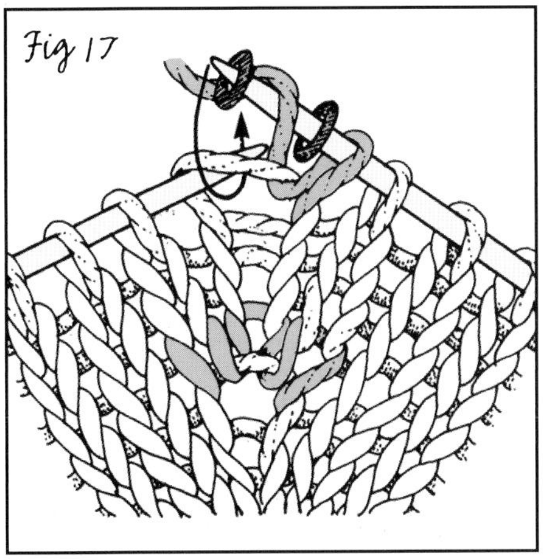

Double row-below increase

Decorative (**Fig 18**). Make sure that the stitch worked on the row below does not pull.

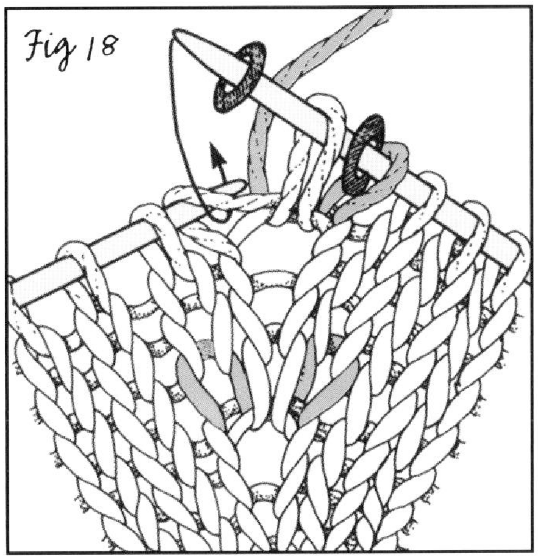

Double lifted increase

Work very loosely or it will pull (**Fig 19**).

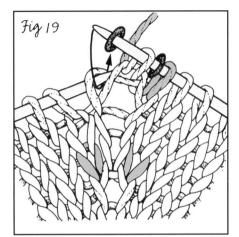

Fig 17

Fig 18

Fig 19

❀ Knit it now...

On knit:

a K1, but do not drop from left needle.

b Front-to-back yo.

c K same st again.

On purl:

a P1 but do not drop.

b Yo as before.

c P again.

DO NOT twist the over when working next row. Re-position marker(s) next to the over.

❀ Knit it now...

On knit:

a K1 but do not drop from left needle.

b K into st below.

c K again original st.

On purl:

a P1 but do not drop.

b P into st below.

c P again original st.

❀ Knit it now...

On knit:

a K the back head of st below next st.

b K next st.

c With left needle pick up side loop of st below st just worked, and k-b.

On purl:

a P head of st below next st.

b P next st.

c With left needle pick up head of st below st just worked, and p-b.

Reposition marker(s) next to the ordinary st.

Multiple increases

A development of double increases, mostly worked as part of a pattern. Wrap the yarn around the needle to make the extra stitches.

Paired single decreases

Two stitches are involved. Work right-hand decreases after the guide stitch and left-hand decreases on the two stitches before the guide stitch. If decreasing at the very edge, use a decrease with a right slant on the left edge, and vice versa. Read carefully even if you are an experienced knitter! Changing the order of knit, slip and twist decreases from right to left will give more decorative results (**Fig 2**, page 55).

Knit decrease

The right-slant decrease is often paired with the left-slant of either slip decrease or twist decrease. **Fig 20** shows correct pairing.

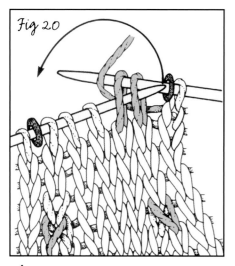

Fig 20

✱ Knit it now...

RIGHT (slant to left)
On knit (ssk – slip, slip, knit):
a (slip 1 kwise) twice.
b insert left needle into front of these two sts, from left, and k2 tog.
On purl:
a (slip 1 kwise) twice.
b Return the 2 sts to left needle in this twisted way.
c Insert right needle, from the back, first into 2nd st then into 1st st, and p-b2 tog.
LEFT (slant to right)
On knit (k2 tog):
a Insert right needle into front of next 2

sts, from left to right.
b K2 tog.
On purl (p2 tog):
a Insert right needle into front of next 2 sts, from right to left.
b P2 tog.

Slip decrease

More obvious than knit decrease (**Fig 21**).

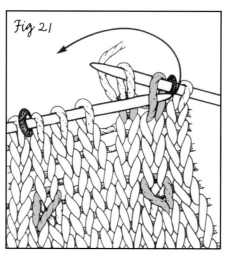

Fig 21

RIGHT (slant to left)
On knit (slip 1-k 1-psso):
a Slip 1 kwise.
b K1.
c With left needle pass sl st over st just worked, as in basic bind-off.
On purl:
a P1.
b Slip 1 kwise and return to left needle in this twisted way.
c Return p st (from **a**) to left needle.
d With right needle pass twisted st over p st and off needle.
e Sl p st pwise.
LEFT (slant to right)
On knit:
a K1.
b Sl k st back onto left needle, without twisting it.
c With right needle pass 2nd st on left needle over k st and off needle.
d Sl k st pwise.
On purl (slip 1 – pl-psso):
a Slip 1 pwise.
b P1.
c With left needle pass sl st over st just worked and off needle.

Twist decrease

For projects making use of other twisted stitches (**Fig 22**).

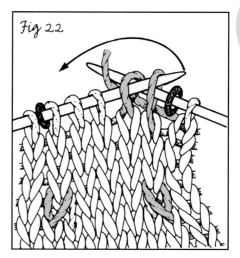

Fig 22

RIGHT (slant to left)
On knit (k-b2 tog):
a Insert right needle into back of next 2 sts.
b K2 tog.
On purl (p-b2 tog):
a Insert right needle, from back, first into 2nd st then into 1st st on left needle.
b P2 tog.
LEFT (slant to right)
On knit:
a (Slip 1 kwise) twice.
b Return the 2 sts to left needle in this twisted way.
c Insert right needle, from front, first into 2nd st then into 1st st.
d K2 tog.
On purl:
a (Slip 1 kwise) twice.
b Return the 2 sts to left needle in this twisted way.
c P2 tog.

Double decreases

See comments on double increases. Double decreases with a slant are shown forming criss-cross patterns. They need not do so: simply work them all with the same slant instead of alternating one of each. If using markers, keep one at each side of the three (or four) centre stitches.

Double knit decrease

Just as knit decrease but on three stitches (**Fig 23**). Reposition marker(s).

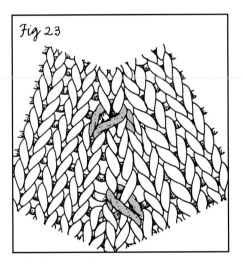

Fig 23

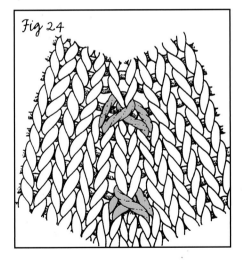

Fig 24

Double slip decrease

Fig 24. Similar to slip decrease, with the following changes:
SLANT TO LEFT
On knit (slip 1-k2 tog-psso):
b K2 tog.
On purl:
a P2 tog.
SLANT TO RIGHT
On knit:
a Ssk.
On purl:
b P-b2 tog.
Reposition marker(s).

Double twist decrease

Work twist decrease over 3 sts (**Fig 25**). Reposition marker(s).

Straight decrease

A clean, vertical line (**Fig 26**). No single decrease counterpart.
On knit (sl2 tog-kl-psso):

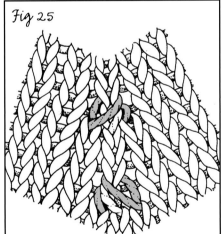

Fig 25

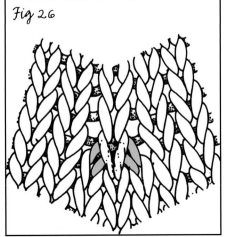

Fig 26

a Insert right needle into front of next 2 sts, from left to right.
b Sl the 2 sts together off left needle.
c K1.
d With left needle pass the 2 sl sts over st just made and off needle.
On purl (sl-b2 tog – p1– psso):
a (Slip 1 kwise) twice.
b Return the 2 sts to left needle in this twisted way.
c Insert right needle, from back, first into 2nd st then into 1st st.
d Sl the 2 sts together off left needle.
e P1.
f With left needle pass the 2 sl sts over st just made and off needle.
Reposition marker(s).

Multiple decreases

A development of double decreases, over several stitches, mostly worked as part of a pattern. If you find it difficult to draw the yarn through a large number of stitches, try using a crochet hook.

Horizontal gathers

Widely used, for instance to give fullness to the top of a waistband or cuff. The most popular device, often combined with a pattern change, is to work single increases or decreases at regular intervals along one row – easier on plain knit or purl rows.

- To calculate, divide the stitches on the needle by the number of shapings. If the result is 7 and you are increasing, add a new stitch after every 7 original stitches. If you are decreasing, every 7th stitch must be removed. Adjust to fit in with pattern if it makes sense: say, one shaping after 3 stitches and the next after 11 stitches.

In flat knitting, work only half the key number of stitches before the first shaping (4 sts in the example). The other half (3 sts) will find their way to the other end of the row.

In general, do not shape across borders.

Ruching

Narrow bands of heavy gathers. First, the original stitches are doubled by increasing on every stitch. After a few rows, they are decreased to the original number. Extra heavy ruching (**Fig 27**) repeats the increase row to double the stitches again. Decreasing is also done in two rows.

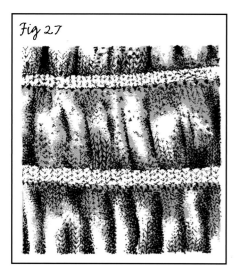

Fig 27

Style secrets
Darts have a practical function – to increase or decrease the knitted fabric. However, you can also turn them into decorative features, by working a central narrow strip in a contrast pattern.

Vertical darts

A series of increases or decreases, one on top of the other, to make the fabric steadily wider or narrower (see **Calculating shapings**, page 55). Strictly speaking, darts are placed away from the edges.

Use slanted shapings and keep marker position if one of the sides is vertical (**Fig 28**). Use double, central shapings and reposition marker if both sides are diagonal (**Fig 29**). For single shapings, see also **Figs 3** and **4**, page 55.

Fig 28

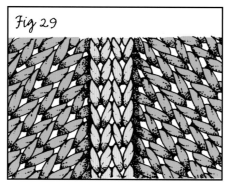

Fig 29

Mitred corners

(See also **Short rows**, pages 100–103.) Mitred corners can be shaped with a double vertical dart, a technique often used in neckline bands. The exact shaping sequence depends on the pattern and the type of angle required. In rib corners, double increases or decreases are usually worked every:
  • row or round for acute angles (V-necks);
  • two rows or rounds for right angles (square necks);
  • three or more rows or rounds for obtuse angles.
Very acute angles may require extra shapings. Short fabrics require fewer shapings. Straight decrease blends in well with single rib (**Fig 30**). Symmetrical knit decreases separated by two knit stitches blend in well with double rib (**Fig 31**).

Fig 30

Fig 31

Bias knitting

Increasing at one end and decreasing at the other end, on alternate rows, makes the fabric slant whilst maintaining its width. The slant is:
• to the right, if starting with a decrease (**Fig 32**);
• to the left, if starting with an increase. All rows, including cast-on and bound-off edges, show the same slant. Row direction is at right angles to work progress. Any pattern can be adapted. Choose shapings to fit in with the pattern. Work them right at the edge, or inside a selvedge or border.

Double or multiple shapings, or shaping on every row, will increase the slant. A tight increase, or an increase into a stitch two rows below, will make the work curve (**Fig 33**). A two-step slant is achieved by adding short rows to one of the sides (**Fig 34**).

GET CLICKING

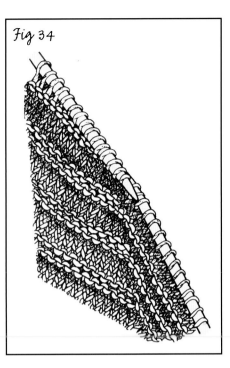

Fig 34

Diagonal fabrics

Bias knitting turns diagonal bands of pattern into horizontal bands (**Fig 35**).
To work a bias square:
a Cast on 3 sts for 1st corner.
b Increase regularly at sides.
c When 2nd and 3rd corners are reached, decrease towards last corner.
See also **Calculating shapings**, page 55. If working a rectangle, calculate narrow and long sides separately. Shape sides at different intervals.

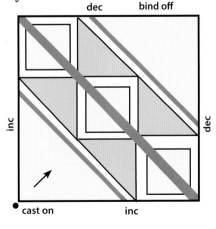

Fig 35

Chevrons

Two diagonal fabrics, side by side, moving in opposite directions. **Figs 36** and **37** show row direction and shapings on a square. Work progress is at right angles to row direction – horizontal stripes emphasize the effect while vertical lines appear perpendicular to the rows.

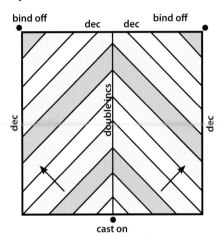

Fig 36

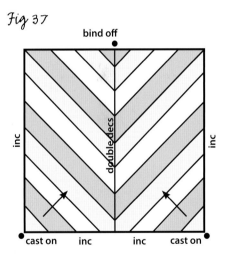

Fig 37

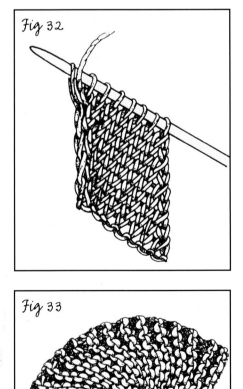

Fig 32

Fig 33

Zigzags

Many chevrons, one next to the other. Welts and rows in several colours emphasize the effect (**Fig 38**).

• Edge shapings are single. All the others are double, alternating increases and decreases. Generally, the diagonal sections are narrow, and all the stitches are cast on at the same time. Cast on and bind off loosely at the meeting points, or they will pull.

If only every other section is on the bias (all slanting in the same direction), and the rest are straight, the result will both zigzag and slant at right angles to the bias. In circular knitting, a spiral will form (**Fig 39**).

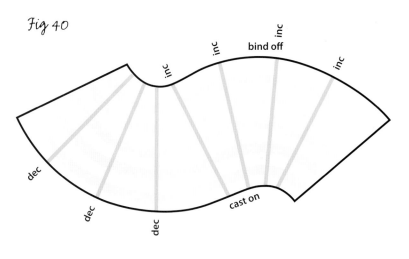

Fig 40

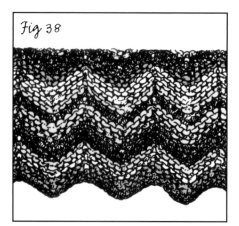

Fig 38

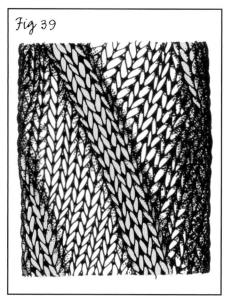

Fig 39

Curves

(See also **Short rows**, pages 100–103.) If darts are placed in a regular sequence, a curve will form (**Fig 40**). Skirts and yokes are often shaped with many darts. In decorative knitting, the scope is very wide.

• Calculate the number of stitches needed at start and end of the curve, and the number of rows involved. Supposing you need 30 stitches more at the start than at the end, you could have 3 darts with 5 double decreases, 3 darts with 10 single decreases, 5 darts with 3 double decreases, or 5 darts with 6 single decreases. Choice depends on fabric, effect desired and how well each option fits in with the row total (see also **Calculating shapings**, page 55). The more darts involved in decreasing a given number of stitches, the smoother the curve.

Darts with increases are worked out similarly.

Medallions

Individual geometric shapes. Many small ones can be sewn together into large patchwork projects. Medallions worked on two needles are usually shaped every other row. In squares and hexagons, this may be successful only in patterns with very wide stitches, such as garter stitch. It is often safer to work out the rows and stitches involved in one section, and calculate the shapings accordingly. When sections are divided by double shapings, take it as one single shaping at each end of each section.

Medallions worked on sets of needles are always best calculated.

Triangles

• Cast on three stitches and increase one stitch at one side (**Fig 41a**) or at both sides (**Fig 41b**). Alternatively, start at the other end and decrease. When three stitches remain, work a double decrease and pull yarn. Shape at the very edge or a few stitches in, on alternate rows for a tallish triangle, or on every row for a flatter one.

Fig 41a

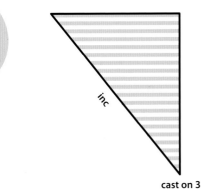

inc

cast on 3

Fig 41b

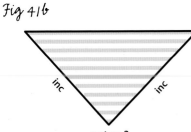

inc   inc

cast on 3

Fig 41c

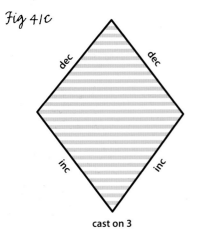

dec   dec

inc   inc

cast on 3

Diamonds

Two triangles, one on top of each other (**Fig 41c**).

• Increase, work a couple of straight rows and decrease.

Fig 42a

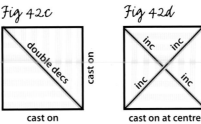

cast on

Fig 42b

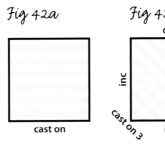

dec

inc   dec

cast on 3   inc

Fig 42c

double decs   cast on

cast on

Fig 42d

inc   inc

inc   inc

cast on at centre

Squares

Four possibilities (**Figs 42a–d**):

• (a) does not require any shapings.

• (b) is a diamond lying on its side. Calculate carefully so that the corners are square.

• (c) has double shapings along the diagonal. Start with two sides and end in three stitches, or vice versa.

• (d) is worked in rounds on a set of five needles; four needles hold the work, and the fifth is used to knit.

Other polygons

Hexagons and octagons can be worked in rows (**Fig 43a**) or in rounds. All the others theoretically could be worked in rows, but are usually worked only in rounds.

• However many sides there are, one line of double shapings goes from each outer angle to the centre (**Fig 43b**). If single shapings are worked, a swirl forms (**Fig 44**).

To keep good control of progress, each side needs to be on a separate needle – not very convenient if many sides are involved and the medallion is small.

Fig 43a

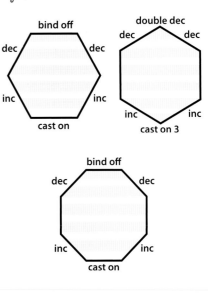

bind off

dec   dec

inc   inc

cast on

double dec

dec   dec

inc   inc

cast on 3

bind off

dec   dec

inc   inc

cast on

Fig 43b

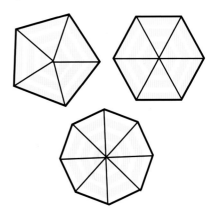

Fig 44

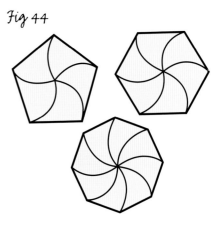

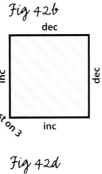

Circles

(See also **Medallions**, page 103.)
Circles can be worked as many-sided polygons, but other ways are possible, such as having 'shaping circles' rather than 'shaping lines' – many more shapings are worked in the outer circles than in the inner ones (**Fig 45**). Large medallions can be finished on a circular needle.

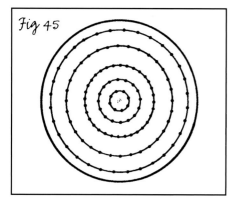

Fig 45

Embossed knitting

(See also **In a Twist**, pages 110–111 and **Getting a raise**, pages 112–113.)
Often a combination of increases and decreases with other techniques. The raising and receding effects of knit and purl stitches can be emphasized with increases and decreases. The knit blocks will stand out on one side of the fabric and recede on the other side.
Figs 46 and **47** show the two sides of such a pattern. The diamonds are first increased and then decreased at both ends, on alternate rows. Stitch total is maintained by staggering the diamonds. The three stitches between diamonds swing from side to side. Many patterns can be worked on this principle. The secret is to use shapings that leave no holes.

Fig 46

Fig 47

Eyelets

• A knit decrease next to an eyelet increase with three or more strands between holes.

Decreasing first gives a marginally rounder eyelet. A pair of single decreases each side of a double increase, and other combinations, are also possible.
Often arranged in horizontal, vertical or diagonal lines, when cords or ribbons can be threaded through to make drawstrings (**Fig 48**). Fancy and geometric designs are also popular (**Fig 49**).

Fig 48

Fig 49

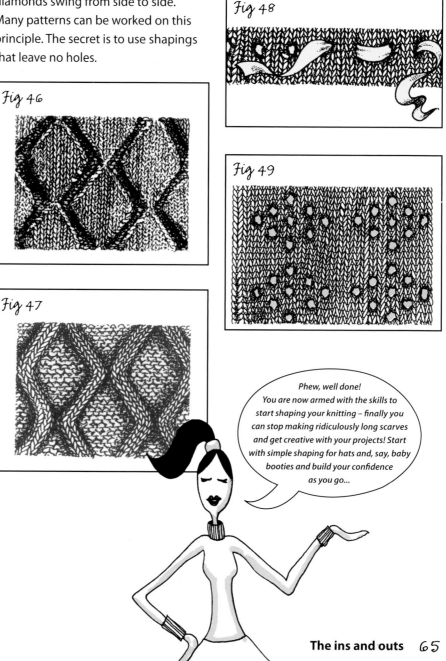

*Phew, well done!
You are now armed with the skills to start shaping your knitting – finally you can stop making ridiculously long scarves and get creative with your projects! Start with simple shaping for hats and, say, baby booties and build your confidence as you go...*

On the edge

Any simply fabulous piece of knitting should have firm edges – not tight, or they will break, and not sloppy, or they will crinkle and look terrible. To achieve this, you need to watch your yarn tension when changing rows. If you cannot obtain firm edges with slippery yarns, try the double chain selvedge technique explained on page 69. The right selvedge for the job makes life easier, and gives more rewarding results when it comes to finishing a project. Plan your selvedges ahead, because you will not be able to change them later. If you are following a commercial pattern, check what selvedges (if any) it recommends. You can alter or add to them if you are not satisfied.

Most flat patterns, including garter stitch, benefit from a slipped garter selvedge. Seed (moss) stitch and a few others, however, may look best without a selvedge if they have been worked to a fairly tight gauge. Try knitting some samples. If the pattern has deep rows and the slipped garter selvedge pulls too much, use a garter selvedge instead. If planning a crochet edging, use chain selvedge.

Use these same selvedges on curly fabrics if you want to maintain the curl. Otherwise, work a border in a flat pattern (see **Knitted-in borders**, below and **Picked-up borders**, page 73).

Classy clickers... *do not 'always slip the first stitch' or 'always knit the first and last stitch', just because they are in the habit of doing so. This can be a sound practice, but only if used in the right place.*

Style secrets
If you want a crisp-looking and stylish garment, plan your seams first (see page 130) before casting on. Choose the appropriate seam or join – these will recommend a selvedge and advise if any extra stitches need to be cast on.

In seams to be turned back, if the selvedge is taken in by the seam, bind off the selvedge stitch(es) then cast on again at the point where the seam will change from one side of the work to the other.

Shaped edges

The selvedge of a strongly shaped edge must be worked loosely or it will pull. The selvedge is now on the diagonal rather than on the vertical, and its usual row depth is not enough. Knitted-in borders will require additional short rows (see **Row adjustments**, page 101). In shaped free edges, always work any increases or decreases inside the selvedge or border.

In edges for seams or for picking up stitches, be flexible. Shaping inside the selvedge (perhaps even two or three stitches from it) gives a clearer straight line for sewing or picking up. It might even add interest to a plain design. But, at times, it is best to shape on the selvedge to avoid interrupting the pattern with increases or decreases, or to add much-needed length to a strongly shaped edge.

Style secrets
On edges for picking up stitches you will probably need a chain selvedge, but check **Picking it up** (pages 70–73) first. Free edges should be especially tidy, so avoid joining in yarn.

Style secrets
For a hint of decoration, use double slipped garter or picot selvedge.

Knitted-in borders

A border in a flat pattern, apart from being decorative, keeps the edge of a curly fabric flat. This is far from saying that it makes the entire fabric flat. Take the typical cardigan in stockinette stitch with a rib border. It stays flat because the body of the wearer is inside and corrects the curling-in tendency. But make it up so that the purl side shows and, unless it is carefully buttoned up, the curling-out tendency is so strong that the whole border folds back.

Classy clickers... work a certain number of stitches by the edge of the fabric in a different pattern than the rest. They know that a knitted-in border:
• *may* need row adjustments;
• *can* be worked as a continuation of a horizontal border;
• *if* worked consciously tighter than the rest, may save you from working a separate border on finer needles;
• *may* require a selvedge;
• *if* in rib, will look better with knit rather than purl stitch(es) next to the selvedge.

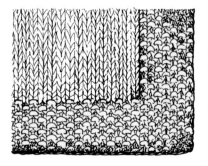

In borders knitted separately, the seam edge is likely to need a different selvedge from the free edge (see **The seamy side**, pages 129–135). If the border is to fit a curve, use a tightening selvedge for the inner curve (say, slipped garter or even double chain) and a non-tightening selvedge for the outer curve (say, no-selvedge, or garter if the pattern rows are shallow).
A different type of border consists of using the natural curliness of some fabrics to make a roll. **Fig 1** shows a reverse st st roll at the edge of a st st fabric. The roll cord in **Fig 2** shows another possibility. Secure with a slip stitch seam, or leave free.

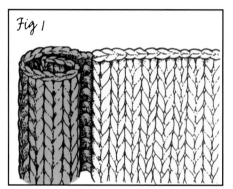

Fig 1

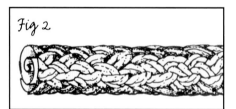

Fig 2

No-selvedge selvedge

Use this for ladder stitch seams and whenever it is essential not to disrupt pattern structure. In free edges, it is usually best avoided, although there are exceptions. Try knitting some samples. **Fig 3** shows a stockinette stitch fabric with no special selvedges.

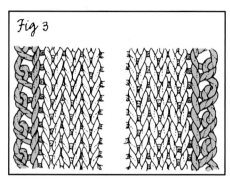

Fig 3

• Simply work the whole row in pattern, from end to end, taking care not to loosen the yarn tension when turning rows. In complex patterns where it is best to work with complete pattern repeats, and where taking the last stitch into a seam would spoil the arrangement of repeats, make a stockinette stitch selvedge:
Right-side rows: k 1st and last sts.
Wrong-side rows: p 1st and last sts.
If this makes the edges of a particular pattern pull or wave, loosen or tighten yarn tension on the selvedge stitches.

Chain selvedge

Good for some seams such as backstitch, and excellent for picking up stitches and crochet edgings. (**Fig 4**). (See also **Chain-garter** and **Double-chain selvedges**, below.) Some people like it on free edges, but I feel that it often looks unfinished.

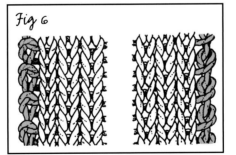

Fig 4

There are several ways of obtaining the same result:
- Right-side rows: sl 1st st kwise, k last stitch.
- Wrong-side rows: sl 1st st pwise, p last st.

Or:
- Last stitch: sl kwise on all rows.
- First stitch: k-b on right-side rows, p on wrong-side rows.

Or:
- Right-side rows: sl kwise 1st and last sts.
- Wrong-side rows: p 1st and last sts.

Slipping knitwise rather than purlwise, and vice versa, gives a twisted chain. For a variation in garter stitch:
- All rows: sl 1st st pwise, wyif; yb and k to end.

Garter selvedge

The first of a family of three selvedges that prevent curling of the edge stitch(es) and form a neat row of 'pips' – hence their name 'beaded selvedges' in French and Italian. Each pip equals two rows. Good for patterns with medium stitches, such as stockinette stitch (**Fig 5**).
- All rows: k 1st and last sts.

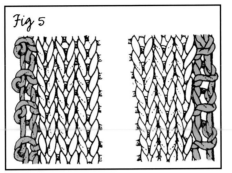

Fig 5

Slipped garter selvedge (Fig 6)

A firmer edge than garter selvedge. Good for patterns with wide stitches or when extra tightness is required.
- All rows: sl kwise 1st st, k last st.

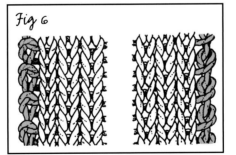

Fig 6

Double slipped garter selvedge (Fig 7)

A slightly more decorative version than slipped garter, often used in free edges. All rows:
- Sl 1st st kwise, through back of loop.
- K 2nd st.
- K last 2 sts.

A variation slips the first stitch also knitwise but in the usual way.

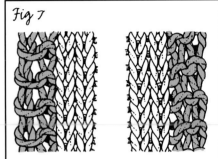

Fig 7

Chain-garter selvedge (Fig 8)

Same uses as chain selvedge, but the garter stitches add firmness and a hint of decoration.
- Right-side rows: sl 1st st kwise, wyab; p 2nd st; p last but one st; sl last st kwise, wyab.
- Wrong-side rows: p 1st 2 and last 2 sts.

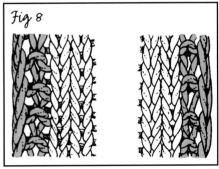

Fig 8

Double-chain selvedge
(Fig 9)

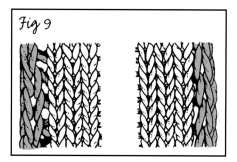

Fig 9

(See also **Chain selvedge**, above.)
To control sloppy edges when working
with slippery yarns, when all else fails.
Or, when a tightening effect, plus a
chain, is required.

• Row 2: work to last st, pick up
horizontal strand between last 2 sts
and place on right needle; sl last st
kwise.

• All following right-side rows: k-b tog
1st st and lifted loop; end as for Row 2.

• All following wrong-side rows: p tog
1st st and lifted loop; end as for Row 2.

Picot selvedge

Slightly decorative (**Fig 10**). This is good
for free edges in openwork patterns
and for some seams. Pin the loops away
from the fabric when blocking.

• Right-side rows: selvedge over, k 1st
2 sts together; ssk last 2 sts.

• Wrong-side rows: selvedge over, p
1st 2 and last 2 sts.

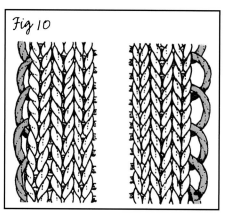

Fig 10

*Well, peering over the edge
wasn't so bad, was it? You can now
create accessories and garments that
have that professional, designer finish. They
will also keep their shape, making your
knitted creations look fabulous for
so much longer.*

Picking it up

Picking up stitches is something you do to create a finished edge such as the collar or neckband of a sweater. 'Pick up stitches' is a universally accepted term, yet it is misleading because it encourages the bad practice of catching the edge loops of a knitted fabric with a needle. 'Pick up and knit' and 'knit up' describe much better the action of taking a ball of yarn and making a row of entirely new loops. Enclosing the edge is a high priority, both to avoid holes and to hide yarn joins and any other causes of unevenness. This attention to detail creates a stylish finish to a garment.

For perfect pick-ups:

• Plan ahead so that any edge or selvedge to be knitted up is of the most appropriate type (see below).

• Aim for sharpness. Keep straight lines straight, curves smooth and angles pointed.

• Use a knitting needle or crochet hook one or two sizes finer than used so far, even if you revert to the original size on the first row.

• Secure the new yarn by tying it to the work before knitting up the first stitch, or by knitting up the second stitch with the short end as well as the long end of yarn; on the first row, work only the long end – the short one will unravel when you drop the stitch.

• Do not split the yarn when inserting the needle or hook.

• Do not leave holes; if inserting the needle or hook into a certain stitch makes a hole, insert it into a different stitch, or make it go first through an adjoining strand.

• If about to knit in a contrast colour, consider knitting up with the original colour and changing to the new one on the first row.

• If knitting up a stretched edge, thread a contrast, slippery yarn along the edge and pull to correct length. Remove the contrast yarn after a few rows.

Catching the edge loops is bad practice because it:

• distorts the original fabric;
• leaves holes;
• badly reduces elasticity and may lead to the join pulling, and even breaking;
• does not hide the edge.

perfect pick up stitcher

Distributing stitches

To calculate the number of stitches to be picked up is like calculating any other number of stitches: measure the edge, find out the tension of the fabric to be added, and multiply the number of stitches in 1in (1cm) by the total length.

Or, you can make things even easier. Divide the edge into 1, 2 or 4in (2.5, 5 or 10cm) lengths, using fabric markers (**Fig 1**) and knit up between markers however many stitches the new pattern has in that distance.

In diagonal edges you will need to knit up more often than if you were working on the same number of stitches horizontally, or the same number of rows vertically. A diagonal line will always be longer.

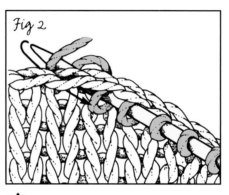

Fig 1

Classy clickers... *know that if you want the new piece of work to gather the original fabric, or vice versa, you start by knitting up in the usual way. In the first row, decrease or increase as the case may be. If working with sets of double-pointed needles, decide beforehand which are the best points for changing needles. Knit up accordingly, even if some needles end up with more stitches than others.*

From right to left

The most common direction for knitting up. The right side is facing. In flat knitting, the first row will be a wrong-side row – consider the knitted-up stitches a foundation row, rather like a cast-on.

Knit up as explained, whatever stitch pattern follows. If all, or some, of the knitted-up stitches are twisted, work them through the back of the loop on the first row.

The last of the three methods explained here is the fastest, once you get the hang of it.

Knitting-needle method (Fig 2)

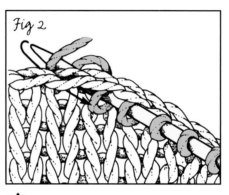

Fig 2

✿ *Knit it now...*

a Insert right needle into fabric.
b Wind yarn around needle as if to k.
c Draw through a loop.

First crochet method

Possibly a good method for left-handed knitters (**Fig 3**).

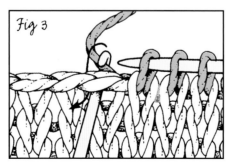

Fig 3

✿ *Knit it now...*

a Insert hook into fabric.
b Draw through a loop.
c Place loop onto knitting needle.

Second crochet method (Fig 4)

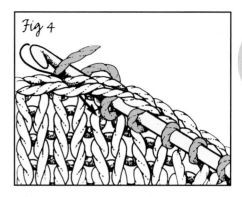

Fig 4

✿ *Knit it now...*

a Keep inserting hook into fabric and drawing loops, until hook is full.
b Sl the sts from back of hook, onto a knitting needle.

Sometimes hooks have large central areas that do not allow stitches to slip through, but the usual flat, thin area is rarely any problem in medium to thick hooks.

From left to right

When picking up from left to right, the yarn is ready to start a right-side row. Occasionally, this is an advantage.

• Left-handed knitters can use the knitting-needle and second crochet methods in reverse. Right-handed knitters might prefer the first crochet method in reverse (**Fig 5**).

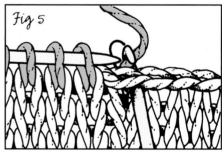

Fig 5

Horizontal edges

For greatest elasticity, use a provisional cast-on or provisional bind-off. Unravel and catch the free loops with a knitting needle (**Fig 6**). Make sure that the needle points towards the end you want to start knitting. If you need more or fewer stitches than there are, increase or decrease regularly on the first row. When picking up from a provisional cast-on, you will very likely find there is one loop fewer than there were stitches.

Classy clickers... *make sure that all the stitches you knit up from are on a straight line.*

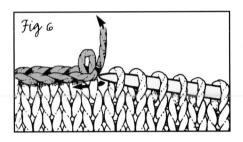

Fig 6

For a slightly decorative effect, use chain cast-on, or loop cast-on and pick up without unravelling. These are two of the exceptional instances where, if the cast-on was loose enough, you could catch the loops directly with a needle, without yarn.

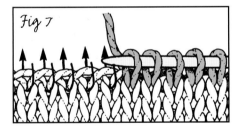

Fig 7

When a non-decorative edge cannot be unpicked (see **Curves**, page 73, for a possible situation), knit up into the row below the edge (**Fig 7**). For extra stitches, knit up between original stitches as well as into them.

Vertical edges

Best done from a chain, chain-garter or double-chain selvedge (see pages 68–69).

Each chain spans two rows. Knit up from under each complete chain (**Fig 8**). For extra stitches, knit up also, as required, from the tight point where two chains overlap. On the wrong side the chain should look quite untouched (**Fig 9**). With any other edge, knit up at least two strands in from the end of the fabric.

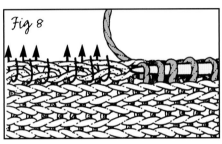

Fig 8

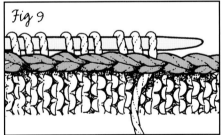

Fig 9

Classy clickers... *for a sharp angle, knit up a stitch from the very corner.*

Diagonal edges

(See also **Shaped edges**, page 66) Try to work from a chain, chain-garter or double-chain selvedge. If the selvedge is not interrupted with shapings, proceed as for vertical edges.

If the selvedge is interrupted by shapings, knit up at least two strands in from the edge on the interruptions. Take care to keep a straight line.

When the shapings are groups of cast-on or bound-off stitches, work as for horizontal edges. In between groups, knit up at least two strands in from the edge. For a smooth line, do not hesitate to knit up further from the edge if there is a step that breaks continuity (**Fig 10**).

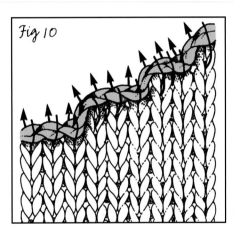

Fig 10

Style secrets
For a more eye-catching and bolder effect on your picked-up edges, try using a decorative cast-on or bind-off and knit up from wherever is most convenient, without affecting the original edge.

GET CLICKING

Curves

When the edge is a combination of horizontal, vertical and diagonal, follow the rules explained for each one. It might then seem a good thing to leave in waiting, rather than to bind off, the horizontal areas. Many patterns actually recommend that. But there are good reasons against this seemingly brilliant idea:

• the waiting stitches are larger than the ones being knitted up on a finer needle;

• knitting up inside the edge gives a slight 'lift' to the new stitches because a double layer is formed – the horizontal stitches remain flat and look less crisp;

• there might be a difference in level between the edge and the stitches in waiting.

Style secrets
If you are picking up stitches from a curved edge worked in seed (moss) stitch or garter stitch, be aware that you need decreases to make a good shape. In garter stitch these are almost unnoticeable.

Centre of work

Knit up in any direction you want, using one of the crochet-hook techniques explained above. Keep the yarn under the work, in your left hand, and the hook on top (**Fig 11**). Run a coloured thread through the fabric to keep a straight line.

On purl and some other fabrics it is possible to knit up without going through the fabric – for instance, for a pocket lining. Draw the new loops through the stitch heads (**Fig 12**). This is an exception to the rule of knitting up through at least two strands. The large arrow shows the direction in which work will continue, when the needle or hook is inserted as shown by the small arrows.

Fig 11

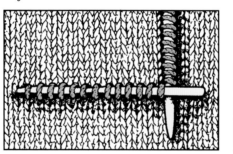

Fig 12

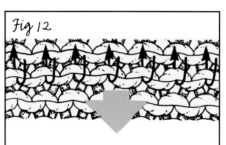

Picked-up borders

(See also **Knitted-in borders**, page 67.) A border is generally worked in a flat fabric, but sometimes a curly fabric such as stockinette stitch is used. It can be left to curl into a roll or folded in two and sewn into place.

Ribbed borders are often folded to hide the chain of basic bind-off, but this gives an unattractive thick edge. Tubular bind-off solves the problem much better.

Curves, such as necklines, are often given a ribbed border for elasticity. The knitted-up end is kept fairly stretched, and the bound-off end is left to gather in (**Fig 13**). Closed curves are much better worked in rounds. If you are worried about sets of double-pointed needles and cannot find a circular needle short enough, work flat by leaving one seam undone (see **Planning for seams**, page 130).

Fig 13

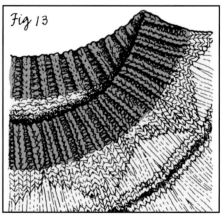

• Pick up sts from the edge, work for required depth of border, and bind off.

Classy clickers... make their borders on the tight side so they control the fabric edge. Be careful they do not pull, however.

Buttoned up

If you are set on becoming an accomplished garment knitter, you will need to know how to make slits and buttonholes. Slits are straight-line cuts in the knitted fabric. They can be horizontal, vertical or diagonal. They can also be closed or open, knitted-in or cut. Buttonholes are small closed slits with the practical purpose of fastening a button. They also can be knitted-in or cut, and travel in any direction. Additionally, they can be spot-like and loop-like. Buttonholes are often placed in borders (whether these are knitted-in, picked-up or separate).

For simply fabulous results:

• Choose a method that will not require oversewing or reinforcing. If you need a rescue measure, stitch around the buttonhole with buttonhole stitch.

• Leave at least three stitches between the edge and the start of a buttonhole or closed slit.

• In ribs, start and end horizontal slits or buttonholes in purl and keep vertical ones also in purl. In other patterns, work wherever the texture makes a 'low' rather than a 'high'.

• Knit-in for speed and neatness. Cut to avoid planning ahead.

• If working with slippery yarns, a strand or two of matching sewing thread will add stability. Use only on the slit or buttonhole area. Join in one row in advance.

• A button will not stay right in the centre of a horizontal buttonhole – movement will pull it to the outer end. If buttons are to be on a certain line, place buttonholes off-centre.

• Avoid tiny buttonholes for even tinier buttons in thick yarn. They look out of scale.

• Remember that knitting is elastic. A button may easily go through a smaller hole than you think. Try making some samples.

• Place men's buttonholes on the left side, and women's on the right side, if you want to follow convention.

• Choose buttons first if you can. To make a buttonhole that fits is easy – just try making a couple of small samples. To find a button to fit a hole might be impossible.

Spacing buttonholes

Don't place first and last buttonholes too close to the edge. Don't worry about the lower edge pulling open below the buttonhole. If you cast on all the necessary stitches at the correct gauge, the edge will stay where it should.

Having placed the two end buttonholes, space the rest evenly between. You need one more space than there are buttonholes left to place. And you need to know the exact number of rows or stitches between end buttonholes – a tape measurement would be far from accurate.

Style secrets
Two or three buttonholes close together at the bottom of a jacket front help to control rib waistbands.

Spot buttonholes

Traditionally used in baby clothes and whenever a very small button is required. Start work on right side, unless samples suggest otherwise. In heavy yarns, the size of button that can go through such a buttonhole is almost always too small to look good, unless many are used in close arrangement.

Ordinary eyelet

The simplest of all. Work an isolated eyelet (see **Fig 48**, page 65). Either make a front-to-back over and k2 tog, or ssk and make an over.

Reinforced eyelet

Stronger and neater (**Fig 1**).

Fig 1

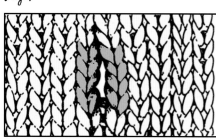

✿ *Knit it now...*

Row 1:

a Work to buttonhole position.

b Front-to-back over. Continue work.

Row 2:

c Sl over.

d Front-to-back over. Continue work.

Row 3:

e Sl kwise st before overs.

f K overs tog. Do not drop from left needle.

g Pass sl st over st just made, as in basic bind-off.

h K3 tog – overs and next st.

Horizontal buttonholes

Most common (see **Cut slits**, page 78). Start on right side unless samples suggest otherwise. Beginners should try standard or increase button-holes. Standard has weak sides, especially the left. Reinforced or one-row buttonhole have no weak sides. The second is strongest, but has less give and may require more stitches.

Standard buttonhole

Simplest procedure (**Fig 2**):

Fig 2

✿ *Knit it now...*

a Bind off required number of sts in one row.

b Cast on same number of sts in next row. Use basic bind-off and work two stitches past the buttonhole position before passing the first stitch on top of the next. Pass the last bound-off stitch over the stitch that forms the buttonhole left edge. Pull edge-stitch tight; it tends to loosen up.

For firm fabrics use buttonhole cast-on or double-twist loop cast-on.

Reinforced buttonhole

A stronger version of standard buttonhole. The instructions may look lengthy but they are not difficult (**Fig 3**).

Fig 3

✿ *Knit it now...*

Row 1:

a Work to buttonhole position.

b Right lifted increase: k first the back head of the st below next st, then k the st.

c *k1, pass previous st over*. Repeat as in basic bind-off for all the buttonhole sts but1.

d Right lifted increase as before, then pass previous st over the 2 sts of the increase. Continue work.

Row 2:

e Work to 2 sts before buttonhole.

f P2 tog.

g Cast on total buttonhole sts plus 2 (see cast-on methods under **Standard buttonhole**, above).

h P2 tog. Continue work.

Row 3:

i Work to st before buttonhole.

j Ssk side st and last cast-on st.

k Work to 1st cast-on st.

l K2 tog – 1st cast-on st and side st.

One-row buttonhole

Very strong and neat (**Fig 4**). May need more stitches than other methods as it has less elasticity. Very unobtrusive in garter stitch and in reverse stockinette stitch when worked from the knit side.

Fig 4

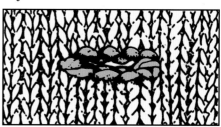

✿ *Knit it now...*

a Work to buttonhole position.

b Slip 1 pwise wyif.

c Yb, and leave it there; it will not be used for **d** and **e**.

d *Slip 1 pwise, pass previous st over as in basic bind-off*. Repeat for all buttonhole sts.

e Sl last cast-off st back to left needle. Turn work.

f Yb.

g Cable cast-on all buttonhole sts.

h Cable cast-on another st, but yf before placing it on left needle. Turn work.

i Slip 1 kwise and pass extra cast-on st over it.

Bound-off buttonhole

Matching top and bottom edges. **Fig 5** shows the results in backstitch bind-off.

If working in fancy pattern, knit or purl one stitch at either side on the buttonhole row, plus all the stitches between these two on the row before and the row after. Knit-and-purl combinations do not count as fancy patterns.

Fig 5

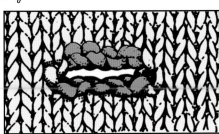

❀ *Knit it now...*

a K buttonhole sts in contrast yarn, preferably slippery. Leave a long loop of main yarn at back, for later finishing – at least 12–16in (30–40cm). Cut contrast yarn. Finish work. Block.

b Remove contrast yarn and place free loops on spare needles or holders.

c Cut main-yarn loop and crochet, backstitch or stem-stitch bind-off all around edge, working into the loops and edge sts.

d Darn and trim ends.

(See **Cut slits**, page 78 for variation.)

Tubular buttonhole

Ideal for single rib (**Fig 6**), with knitters who can use the tubular bind-off.

Fig 6

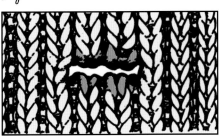

❀ *Knit it now...*

a Work buttonhole sts in single rib with a short length of contrast yarn, preferably slippery. Leave a long loop of main yarn for later sewing – at least 12–16in (30–40cm). Cut contrast yarn. Finish work.

b Remove contrast yarn and place lower sts on a needle and upper loops on a holder.

c Cut the yarn loop in half and tubular bind-off lower sts. Anchor yarn, to the side, darn and trim.

d Again with a sewing needle, thread 2nd yarn end through upper loops and anchor to side with a vertical st.

e Repeat **d** 2 or 3 times more, alternating direction. Darn and trim.

Classy clickers... *For immaculate results, use tubular buttonhole in single rib and related fabrics, and bound-off buttonhole in other patterns. For circular knitting, use increase or one-row buttonholes.*

Once you've got to grips with making buttonholes, you can think about what sort of buttons to buy to add a touch more style to your garment. There are some beautiful styles around now, in every colour and finish you could want, from handmade glass to mother of pearl. The Internet is an excellent source for vintage buttons – the perfect finishing touch for a retro-inspired knit.

Horizontal slits

A closed horizontal slit is simply a large version of a horizontal buttonhole. An open horizontal slit is placed at the edge of the fabric. Binding off, therefore, starts at the beginning of the row. Broadly speaking, any buttonhole technique can be used. Tubular buttonhole needs adapting if the top edge is to be elastic. Instead of working with a contrast yarn, try this:

 Knit it now...

a Leave lower sts on a holder.

b End row and work next row to slit position. Leave work in waiting.

c Tubular cast-on the sts required with new yarn and new needles, leaving yarn tail long enough to tubular bind-off lower sts and anchor sides. Stop before tubular st st rows. Cut yarn.

d Return to main work and join in cast-on sts. On next couple of rows, work tubular st st across new sts if desired.

e To finish, anchor 1st side, bind off lower sts, anchor 2nd side. Darn and trim.

> *Classy clickers...* know that if a fabric is not flat, the slit will curl, either in or out. To avoid this, you need to work a flat border around the four sides of closed slits (*Fig 7*), or around the three sides of open slits. In open slits, the border could be continued along the free edge. Needle markers will be useful between the border and the main pattern.

Fig 7

Overlapping slits

The top edge starts behind lower edge, making a second layer. Borders are restricted to the overlap. Closed slits are the basis for horizontal slit pockets.

✿ *Knit it now...*

a Having reached start of overlap, continue working complete rows, but use border pattern across slit area. Increase or decrease on 1st row and/or introduce row adjustments if necessary. Consider working tighter across border sts, especially in ribs. Needle markers might be useful.

b At top of overlap, bind off slit sts or leave on holder for tubular or other special bind-off. End row. Leave work in waiting.

c With new yarn and needles, cast on slit sts plus 2. Leave long end for sewing one side.

d Work in border pattern for same number of rows as before. Cut yarn – leave end long enough to sew other side, and to bind off lower edge if necessary.

e Return to main work, joining 2nd border on 1st row. Work sts at either side of slit together with edge sts of 2nd border, to add strength.

f To finish, sew sides of overlap with a slip stitch and bind off lower edge if required. Darn, and trim yarn.

Fig 8 shows an unseamed, open, overlapping slit.

Fig 8

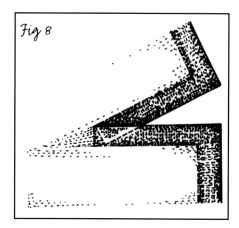

Vertical buttonholes

Use when the fastening will have a vertical pull, or for horizontal buttonholes when working vertical rows (see also **Cut slits**, page 78). The two sides are worked separately. Either work at the same time with two balls of yarn, or work first one side and then the other, cutting the yarn as required. Stitches left in waiting can be kept on holders or on the working needles. Leave yarn tails long enough for darning. Although it is possible to work either without a special selvedge, or with a garter or slipped garter selvedge, and although it is usual to keep the number of stitches unaltered, for neatest results work as follows (**Fig 9**):

Fig 9

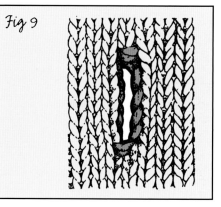

✿ *Knit it now...*

a Work right side with a chain selvedge (first method).

b Before starting left side, make a right lifted increase on 1st st.

c Work left side also with a chain selvedge (second method) – the selvedge is the increased st.

d On 1st row across at top of buttonhole, work together the 2 selvedge sts. End work.

e To finish, make a couple of horizontal sts at top and bottom ends with a sewing needle, to add strength. Darn up and down the back of the selvedge chains. Trim yarn.

Both sides of the buttonhole must end with either a right-side or a wrong-side row.

Vertical slits

A closed vertical slit is a large version of a vertical buttonhole. An open slit is placed at the cast-on or bound-off end of the fabric, so that it has three sides instead of four.

To prevent curly fabrics rolling, work a knitted-in border. In closed slits the border starts before, and ends after, the actual slit. The result will be similar to **Fig 7** on its side. A decorative selvedge could also be used just along the slit. Try samples. In open slits, the border can be continued along the cast-on or bound-off edge.

If the two sides are not worked at the same time, keep the stitches in waiting on holders.

Overlapping slits

Either the right or the left side gets wider and makes a second layer behind the other side. Borders, or decorative selvedges, are restricted to the overlap. Closed slits are the basis for vertical slit pockets. An open slit at the start of work is often used for sweater side vents or buttoned cuffs. At the end of work it can be used for buttoned necklines.

✿ Knit it now...

a Work upper layer, with border if there is one. (Use a needle marker.)

b Before starting under layer, cast on sts for overlap, leaving yarn tail long enough to sew side of overlap. Or, for neatness and strength, pick up overlap sts as in **Fig 12** on page 73 if pattern is such that sts will not show on right side.

c Work under layer.

d At top of slit, bind off all overlap sts but 1 on the last under-layer row; on 1st row across, work together the edge upper-layer st with the remaining overlap st. Or, for best results, DO NOT bind off; on the 1st row across, work together 1 st from each overlap layer, as in cast-on edge hems.

e To finish, sew under layer with a slip stitch if necessary. Darn and trim yarn. An overlapping open slit at a cast-on or a bound-off edge would look like **Fig 8** on page 77 on its side.

Cut slits

Use when you do not want to decide the slit or buttonhole position beforehand, or when it is too late to knit them in. Always try on samples first. Block the work before cutting. For horizontal or vertical slits or buttonholes:

✿ Knit it now...

a Mark precise position with contrast thread.

b Work one line of close stitching at each side of mark (see **Cut and sew**, page 125).

c Cut fabric by mark.

d Reinforce.

Fig 10

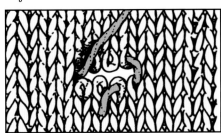

Bridges

(See also **Cut and sew**, page 125) Used in circular knitting to prepare the work for vertical slits, especially open ones. Invaluable for working jacquard and whenever seeing right side of work all the time is an advantage; make a bridge for each opening (such as a jacket front, armhole, sleeve top, neckline). **Fig 11**:

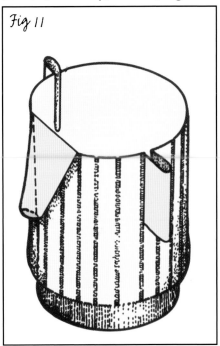

Fig 11

✿ Knit it now...

a Cast on a few sts (8 to 14 depending on yarn) at start of slit, to form bridge base. Use one of the end of rows methods.

b K the bridge sts for length of slit. If working with two colours, k1 in each colour.

c At top of slit, bind off bridge.

d To finish, work one or two rows of close stitching at either side of centre line. Cut through centre and stitch back – consider binding for neatness.

Loop buttonholes

Generally used on the edge of the fabric.

• For the thinnest loop, crochet a chain (**Fig 12**). Attach to wrong side with the ends of yarn coming out of first and last chain (**Fig 13**). A row of loops could be made out of one single chain.

• If you prefer sewing, anchor matching yarn to the selvedge, leaving a shortish end. Anchor again a few stitches away, and then again on first stitch, each time forming a loop. Buttonhole stitch over the two loops and the yarn end (**Fig 14**).

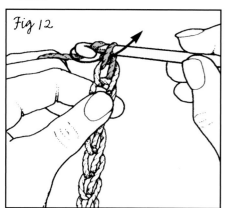

Fig 12

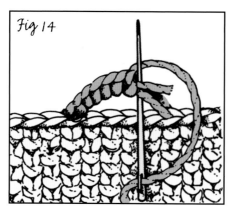

Fig 14

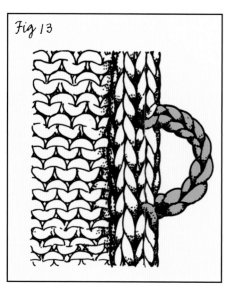

Fig 13

• For contrast, make the loop with a piece of leather thong. Closely overcast the two ends, jointly or separately, with matching cotton, on the wrong side. Other materials and other structures (see **Cords**, page 136) could be used.

Perfect pockets

Pockets can be another way of adding a simply fabulous touch to a beautifully made garment. Pockets can be practical or purely decorative. In clothes, they fall neatly into three categories: patch pockets attached to the right side; slit pockets attached to the wrong side; and loose pockets hanging from a slit.

For simply fabulous pockets:

• Pick up stitches and graft, in preference to casting on or binding off and slip-stitch seaming, to increase elasticity, strength and neatness.

• Before starting a border or edging that will need sewing on the right side, decide how it is going to be sewn and what selvedges, if any, will look best.

Style secrets
It can be difficult to make pocket flaps look really good, so avoid them unless you are an experienced designer or are following very good instructions. Block the work carefully.

• Keep straight lines straight, angles sharp and curves smooth.

• If you're not sure about size and/or exact pocket position, use patch pockets or cut pockets (see **Horizontal slits**, page 77, and **Loose pockets**, below). These can be decided when the work is finished.

• In general, work linings in the same yarn as the rest of the item. Use also the same pattern, unless highly textured, and try to align with a change of pattern on the main fabric.

• Unless using different patterns, check lining depth by counting rows rather than measuring.

• With very thick yarns, work linings in a finer, matching yarn. Adjust stitches and rows as required.

• If working linings in different patterns and/or yarns, the area closest to the opening must be like the rest of the work. Allow at least 1¼in (3cm), more for large pockets.

• Cloth is difficult to add successfully, but consider it for patch pockets and for linings of loose pockets.

Take some care with your knitted pockets – they will not be as robust or sturdy as the pockets on commercially manufactured garments. Don't overfill them or you will probably stretch and distort them, and be careful not to put anything in them that might poke through or damage the knitted fabric. Lining a pocket with fabric will give it some extra resilience.

Patch pockets

Two types: applied and picked up. Square picked-up pockets look very much like slit pockets (see below), which are actually easier to make.

Applied pockets

(See **Choosing seams**, page 130.)

• Work an independent shape such as a medallion and sew it onto the right side, leaving an opening.

Pockets in flat patterns are easiest to apply. Thin fabrics are tricky because the seam is difficult to hide. The edge may have to be turned in. These are bulky methods, based on dressmaking, and not always successful in knitting.

For easy sewing and a much-improved pocket, work an edging all around the edge.

Style secrets

Use picked-up pockets when you want a funky colour change, a drastic pattern change, or a fun shape.

✿ *Knit it now...*

a Pick up sts from centre of work, following outline of pocket, except for opening. One st per st and/or row is required.

b Start work from one row of picked up sts.

c At start and end of each row, work 1 of the picked-up sts still on needles together with the edge st. Increase or decrease if necessary.

d If pocket ends with a straight row, finish as suggested for overlapping horizontal slits. If it needs shaping with short rows, finish as for diagonal slits.

Or, pick up only sts for the first row, then knit on the edges.

Slit pockets

Worked exactly like overlapping slits (horizontal, vertical) but with a lining instead of the hidden overlap layer.

Horizontal pockets

The most common pocket of all (**Fig 1**). Work as for overlapping horizontal slits but with a long upper overlap layer that will become the lining. Instead of **c** and **d** in first method:

Fig 1

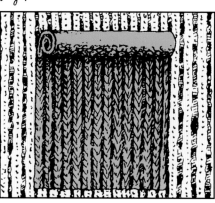

• work an independent lining or, preferably,

• work a lining from stitches picked up as in **Fig 12** on page 73, or

• work a lining from stitches picked up both at the bottom and at the sides.

Loose pockets

Like horizontal slit pockets, only a slit and an edging or border shows on the right side. But on the wrong side, instead of a one-layer lining attached to the fabric, they have a two-layer lining dangling from the slit and so are bulkier. Having reached the top of the pocket:

Fig 2

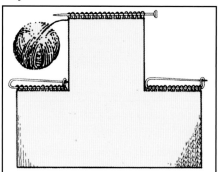

✿ *Knit it now...*

a Leave any sts at either side on holders.

b Continue on pocket sts for twice the required depth (**Fig 2**), to form pocket lining.

c Fold lining in two and join in sts on holders. Finish work.

d Pick up sts from pocket edge if necessary. Work border or edging.

Vertical pockets

Work in isolation, with the opening to the left (**Fig 3**) or to the right, or make a large pocket with two openings, one on each side.

Work as for overlapping vertical slits but, in **b**, cast on (or preferably pick up) extra stitches to make a lining rather than an overlap. You could also pick up stitches for the side of the lining, and work together one of them with the edge stitch of each row.

Fig 3

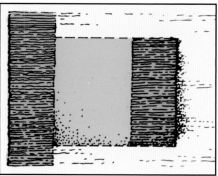

Hems and casings

If you want to make a truly stylish-looking garment, you should pay just as much attention to the hems and casings as to the main body of the garment. A crisp-looking hem creates a very professional finish. Hems and casings can be vertical or horizontal, knitted in or picked up.

Horizontal hems

The most popular type. When the fabric is to remain flat, it should be the same width as the main layer of fabric. At most, it may have one stitch less at each end, to make sure that the edges do not stick out. But when the fabric is to form a closed or open tube (as in skirts and jackets) the hem becomes a ring, inside the tube, and must be smaller than the tube.

A popular way of making the ring smaller is to work the hem in finer needles – one to three sizes finer. This also tightens the gauge and makes a stiffer hem. If the extra stiffness is not desired, try the less common method of having 10 per cent fewer stitches in the hem. Increase or decrease (depending on whether the hem is made at the start or end of work) one row away from the fold-line.

> **Classy clickers...**
> • **Choose** hems that do not require sewing.
> • **If** they do need a sewn hem, they make sure that the fold-line is straight and pin or tack before sewing. The stitches must not show on the right side.
> • **Do** not measure with a tape; count rows (or stitches) instead.
> • **Use** only tubular hem for ribbings.

If you want to mark the fold-line, work one of the following:
  • a contrast row – such as a purl row on a knit fabric (**Fig 1**) or vice versa;
  • a row on a thinner needle;
  • a row where every other stitch is slipped.

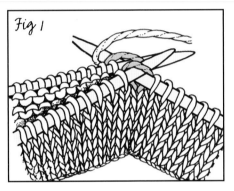

Fig 1

Cast-on edge hems

(See also **Picked-up hems** and **Tubular hems**, below) The first method gives the strongest and neatest results.

FIRST METHOD:

❋ *Knit it now...*

a Provisional cast-on sts required for hem.
b With hem yarn and pattern, work for desired depth – with fewer sts until the last row but one, or on finer needles, if appropriate.
c Mark fold-line, if appropriate. Change to main yarn and needles, if required. If not marking fold-line, place a fabric marker.
d Continue in main pattern, to obtain exactly the same depth of work from fold-line.
e Unravel provisional cast-on and place

free loops on a spare needle, pointing in same direction as last needle worked.
f Fold and work together I st from each needle (**Fig 1**). If hem has fewer sts than main layer, work some evenly spaced, main-layer sts by themselves. If hem has more sts, work 2 tog with a main-layer st at regular intervals.
g Continue main layer.

SECOND METHOD:

❋ *Knit it now...*

Work **a** to **d** as before but leave a long strand of hem yarn when joining it in for later sewing. Then:
e Place a fabric marker on last row. Finish work.
f Unravel provisional cast-on and place free loops on a spare needle.
g Free-loop slip stitch sts on needle to the corresponding sts on row with marker (**Fig 2**). If hem does not lie quite flat, work on next row. If hem has fewer sts than main layer, skip row sts as required. If hem has more sts, sew 2 tog to a row st as required. For an even neater hem, see **Grafting to rows**, page 128.

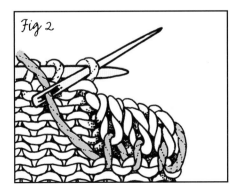

Fig 2

Bound-off edge hems

Like the second version of cast-on edge hems, but at the other end of work.

✹ *Knit it now...*

a Work main layer up to fold-line.

b Mark fold-line if appropriate, then change to hem yarn and needles if required. If not marking fold-line, place a fabric marker.

c Continue in hem pattern. If requiring a hem with fewer sts, decrease after one row.

d When desired depth of hem is reached, do not bind off. Fold work, and free-loop slip stitch last row to main layer, as just explained for cast-on edge hems. Alternatively, see **Grafting to rows**, page 128.

Picked-up horizontal hems

For a crisper and/or more decorative fold-line. Use on either cast-on or bound-off edges.

✹ *Knit it now...*

a Cast on or bind off with a decorative method. Or, work a provisional cast-on, finish work, unpick cast-on yarn, and decorative bind off the free loops.

b Pick up sts from the wrong side of the cast-on or bind-off, possibly as in **Fig 12** on page 73.

c Work for required hem depth.

d Free-loop slip stitch last row to main layer (see **g** in 2nd version of **Cast-on edge hems**), or see **Grafting to rows**, page 128.

Tubular horizontal hems

Ideal for single rib (**Fig 3**). Useful for other fabrics when only very small hems are required. If no stitches are added, it is likely to gather the work.

Work a tubular cast-on or a tubular bind-off, but with a few more rows in tubular stockinette stitch than the usual two or four. Total number of tubular rows must be an even number, and they must be worked with open sides.

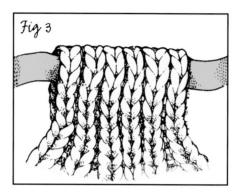

Fig 3

Vertical hems

Vertical hems tend to be used flat. But if the fabric is to form a tube (as in skirts knitted across), the difference in length is solved with row adjustments.

To mark the fold-line, either:
- work a slip chain: slip 1 pwise wyab on right-side row; p on wrong-side row; or,
- work 1 single garter stitch.

Or, for a crisper fold-line, work a picked-up hem (see below).

Ordinary vertical hem

✹ *Knit it now...*

a Cast on sts required for main area of work, plus additional hem sts.

b Work to end, marking fold-line and adjusting rows, if required.

c To finish, fold and sew selvedge to main layer of fabric with a slip stitch.

Picked-up vertical hems

Work as for horizontal picked-up hems, except:

✹ *Knit it now...*

a Work a decorative free-end selvedge or, work a chain selvedge, pick up sts from it, and work a decorative bind-off.

Mid-way casings

These happen somewhere in the centre of work. They can be worked in tubular knitting, adjusting the stitches before and after the casing.

They can also be worked as two layers:

✹ *Knit it now...*

a Increase on every st, or as required, to continue the main layer and obtain a 2nd layer to form the casing.

b On next row, work main-layer sts only; sl the others pwise onto a holder.

c Continue on main layer for depth of casing. Leave sts in waiting.

d Work sts on holder for same depth.

e Join the 2 layers by working together 1 st from each layer (**Fig 1**).

f Continue work.

For afterthought casings:

✹ *Knit it now...*

a Pick up sts from the wrong side (**Fig 12**, page 73).

b Work casing for desired depth.

c Free-loop slip stitch (**Fig 2**) or see **Grafting to rows**, page 128.

A colourful life

If you've fallen in love with knitting, chances are that you are already inspired by colour. If this is something you want to pursue, a next step is to try knitting with several yarns of different colours. You can create something relatively simple, such as a sassily striped jumper or scarf. Or you can try making fabric with intricate motifs, pictures and patterns. There are two main methods to achieve this: intarsia and jacquard. Both are explained in this section. You can create your own designs if you are feeling ambitious; otherwise, you'll need to follow a chart. Most instructions for colour patterns are perfect examples of a picture being worth a thousand words – crystal clear from a chart, but laborious to decipher when written row by row.

GET CREATIVE

Tangle-free colour knitting!

Working with fifty, ten, or even two different balls of yarn is, of course, more awkward than working with one single ball. Here are some ideas to make life as easy as possible.

ALWAYS:
• Twist yarns only to prevent holes, say for intarsia (see page 90). As explained in jacquard (see page 91), instructions may ask you to twist unnecessarily.
• Turn work so that tangles untwist rather than twist further.

Knitting with two colours
• Keep one to your right and one to your left, or both on the same side but well apart and in different bags.

Knitting with several colours
• Thread each colour through a hole, either of a large button or a stiff piece of card.
• Clip balls not in use to the cast-on edge with stitch holders.
• Keep each ball in its own container – a box or jar. Move the containers around if the colour order changes.
• Keep the balls in a long container, not wider than the largest ball, and place the working ball(s) always at the right end.
• Divide a shoe box into compartments, by pushing strips of card through slits made at the sides, or by placing several small boxes inside. Make a hole in the lid above each compartment. Place the yarn in the compartments and thread it through the holes. Tie the box and turn it every time you turn the work.
• Keep only the working yarns attached to the work. Cut and join in new colours as required. Weave in the ends as you work.
• Use bobbins, unwinding only enough yarn for immediate needs.

Knitting with many colours
• Use bobbins, as above.
• Use short lengths of yarn, never ever more than 2yd (2m) long; half that length if you want them really manageable. Leave them dangling. To untangle one particular colour, simply pull. Weave in all the ends as you work.

Choosing colours

Experimenting with colour is one of the most inspirational aspects of knitting. If you want to spark off some creative ideas, try this:

• Open your eyes and **look around**. Whenever you see something (room, mountain, picture, garment, floor rug, bird, flower, stone wall, river…) that appeals to you, try to identify the different colours. You may discover unexpected combinations, and be surprised to see how bright a colour needs to be when only specks of it appear.

• Try knitting a **colour scheme** that pleases you, in as many shades as the original, or picking up just a few of them. Choose colours very carefully – a colour darker or lighter than the original might break the balance and ruin the effect.

• Knit **several samples** with the same pattern, but changing the colours around. Some combinations will make the pattern more obvious; others will blur it. Have the samples around for a few days, and keep looking at them. If they are dull, add small amounts of a bright colour for accent. If they are too harsh, try again in more muted shades or introduce a neutral colour. If you still like a sample after a few days, start knitting.

• If you are **working stripes**, wrap the yarns around cards or around your fingers in different combinations before doing any samples.

• **Be open** to new colour combinations. Colours interact with each other. By itself, you may not like one colour, but knitted with others you may love the final effect – or vice versa.

• Consider using **more than one dye lot** of the same colour to increase subtlety.

• If colour knitting inspires you, **stock up** on balls of yarn in as many shades and hues as you can find. Keep them together by colour: reds, blues, greens, pinks, purples.

Multicolour yarns

Perfect for a lazy day. Take, for instance, an ombré or a twist yarn, and from cast-on to bind-off you will never have more than one strand. Or, work together several fine strands in slightly different or highly contrasting shades. You will still have several balls to contend with, but because they are worked at the same time, tangles become far less likely to occur.

Yarns with great colour, and perhaps texture interest, are usually best worked in simple patterns. However, the obvious choice of stockinette stitch can make them flat and dull. Sometimes, merely using the reverse side, perhaps worked sideways, is enough to improve the look.

An additional problem with ombré yarns regularly spaced at short intervals is the zebra, or colour-blob, effect they produce. To keep the effect regular, do not break the colour sequence when joining in new yarn, and start at the same point in the sequence when working identical pieces.

Shapings, or dividing the work for, say, a neckline, will always have an effect. If you want to mask the 'zebra', use two balls of yarn and change from one to the other every two rows.

Style secrets
To achieve striking effects with multicolour yarns, try using patterns that break the straight row arrangement, such as slip stitch (see pages 52–53).

Stripes

Horizontal stripes are the easiest way of working with two or more colours. Simply join in a new colour at the start of a row.

Vertical stripes are worked in jacquard if they are narrow and in intarsia (see page 90) if they are wide. They can also be worked horizontally and used sideways.

With very wide stripes, it is best to cut the yarn at the end of each stripe. Otherwise, the yarn can be carried up the work to avoid darning or weaving in. Wrap the working yarn around the other yarn(s) every 1in (2–3cm). Make sure the yarns do not pull. Stripes in stockinette stitch make a clean line on the knit side and a broken line on the purl side (**Fig 1** – see also **The knitted stitch**, page 13). In garter stitch, one side is clear-cut and the other not. In other words, on the purl side of the change-in-colour row the colours overlap. If you want a clean stripe in your ribbings, make the first row of the new colour a knit row (purl row if worked on the wrong side). Expect some loss of elasticity.

Fig 1

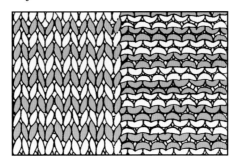

Odd-row stripes

In flat knitting, it is easier to work stripes with an even number of rows. Odd-numbered or single-row stripes, however, need only a little planning or a little cunning.

Carry some colours up the right edge and some up the left edge. Arrange the stripes so that the colour you want next is already at the appropriate edge (**Fig 2**). You will need at least three balls of yarn.

Or, work with double-pointed or circular needles – if not all the time, at least for the last row of the odd-row stripe. At the end of this row go back to the beginning of it, without turning the work, and join in the new colour. This method may involve more darning or weaving than the first one.

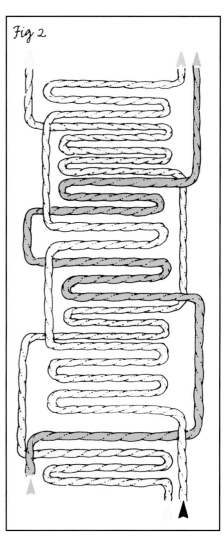

Fig 2

Helix stripes

This is an ingenious way of avoiding steps at the start of the rounds, and having to carry yarns at back of work, when knitting one-row stripes in circular knitting.

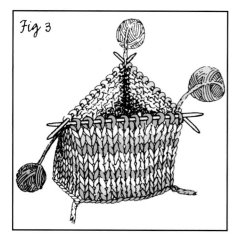

Fig 3

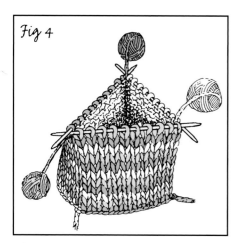

Fig 4

✿ Knit it now...

a Divide the work into as many, roughly equal, groups of stitches as colours you want to use. Either put each group on its own double-pointed needle, or use needle markers if working with a circular needle.

b Work 1st group in 1st colour, 2nd group in 2nd colour, etc. **Fig 3** shows an example with 3 colours.

c Work next round similarly, but using the colours as they come – 1st group with last colour from previous round, 2nd group with 1st colour (**Fig 4**).

Repeat **c**.

If you are working in this way right from the start, cast on each group in a different colour.

Interlocking stripes

Use slip-stitch techniques to make the old colour blend into the new one whilst never working the two at the same time. In **Fig 5**:

Fig 5

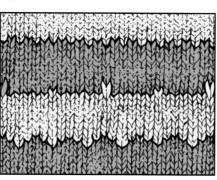

• the top stripe starts with a *k1, slip 1* row.
• the centre stripe slips every 6th st on 1st row and every 12th st on 2nd row.
• the lower stripe slips 3 sts out of 4 on 1st row, and the centre st of the group of 3 on 2nd row.

Many other combinations can be used.

Pattern stripes

A far cry from conventional stripes. Many patterns have rows that are not straight; a colour change often produces interesting results.

Zigzags are possibly the best-known example. Other good examples would be daisy stitch worked in two-row stripes (**Fig 6**) and reverse st st bobbles worked in the first of two rows of garter stitch on a st st background (**Fig 7**).

Fig 6

Fig 7

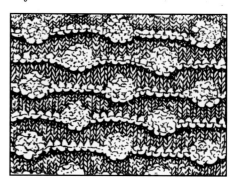

Intarsia

This technique is used for working totally independent blocks of colour, as in large geometrical arrangements and 'picture knitting' (**Fig 8**). This technique is also called geometric, tartan, collage or patchwork knitting.

Each colour block has its own ball of yarn. Depending on how large the blocks are, use a complete ball, a bobbin, or an unwound length of yarn. When changing from one colour to the next, twist one yarn around the other to join the two blocks (**Fig 9**). Expect the twist to show on the purl side (**Fig 10**).

On vertical lines, twist the yarns on every row. On diagonal lines, twist only on the rows, if any, on which the yarn changes at the same point that it did on the previous row.

After changing colours, check that the last stitch of the previous block is the correct size and shape.

In circular knitting, the yarn is at the wrong end of the block on the next round and needs to be cut and joined in – this is an awkward job, leaving many tails to be darned or woven in.

Classy clickers... *always work from a chart for intarsia and jacquard – row-by-row instructions are not enough.*

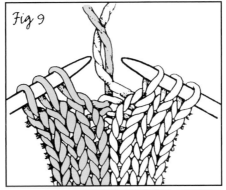

Fig 9

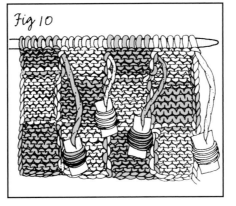

Fig 10

Style secrets

Stockinette stitch is the most popular pattern for intarsia. Other patterns can be used, but you may have to experiment to stop the twisting of the colours from showing on the right side, or to use this to your advantage.

You can use intarsia to add a lively personal touch to hand-knitted accessories. Think of a symbol or motif that you particularly like or that means something to you – a heart, a star, a calligraphic symbol – a favourite cartoon character, even. You could feature this on a bag, on the pocket of a sweater, or round the brim of a winter hat.

Fig 8

Jacquard

Also called Fair Isle, stranded, two-colour, and double knitting, jacquard employs two-colour or multicolour motifs rather than blocks of solid colour (**Fig 11**). Two or more yarns are carried from end to end of each row, although only one is worked – usually in stockinette stitch – at any one time.

Fair Isle is basically a type of jacquard, with its own rules and characteristic patterns. It is confusing and wrong to say that if a pattern uses only two colours in a row it is Fair Isle, and if it uses three or more it is jacquard. Many non-Fair Isle patterns use two colours only.

Circular knitting is often the most sensible way of working jacquard. If you knit all the time (as opposed to purling), you see the pattern forming before your eyes and mistakes are easily avoided or spotted. Much traditional knitting is done this way.

Floats can be stranded or woven in. Stranding (see page 92) is easiest, but keep to the rules below. Weaving in (see page 93) can show on the right side; this adds subtlety to some projects, and ruins others.

Isolated motifs (**Fig 12**) can be worked in either technique but using individual bobbins, or short lengths, of the contrast colour(s) for each motif. This avoids carrying yarn unnecessarily across wide areas of background. Very small and isolated motifs, or non-horizontal fine lines, might be best embroidered in Swiss darning (see below).

Fig 11

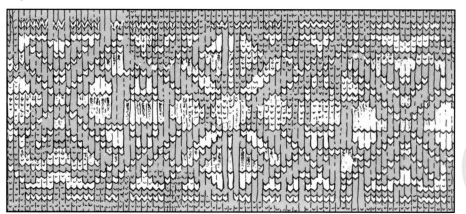

Jacquard knitting tips

• Jacquard fabric tends to be thick and warm as the floats (the extra strands carried at the back) form an additional layer. More yarn is therefore often required.

• Very thick yarns may result in an uncomfortable and heavy fabric.

• Pulled floats are the most common cause of a tight gauge; try making the floats longer before changing to thicker needles.

• On the right side the pattern is clear; on the wrong side only the floats of the non-working colour(s) show.

• Floats, whether stranded or woven in, must be loose enough for the intervening stitches to stretch, yet not so loose that they sag. They are easier to control when not too long. Long-stranded floats are easily caught in fingers or buttons.

• More than two colours in a row add thickness, warmth, yarn weight and technical difficulty.

• Jacquard may give you a different stitch size from self-coloured work in the same stitch pattern. Be aware that it may also give you a less elastic fabric.

Swiss darning

Swiss darning imitates the knit stitch – hence its other names: embroidered jacquard and duplicate stitch. Traditional Swiss darning is used for motifs similar to those in jacquard. It works better than jacquard when there are long gaps between stitches of the same colour in one row, and for vertical lines set widely apart. The two techniques can be combined, but the embroidered stitches will look slightly larger and raised. Work in Vs, as shown in **Fig 13**, from right to left. When working blocks of stitches, work to the end of the first row, then turn the work upside down so that

the second row also goes from right to left, after an initial half-stitch. It's like stitching a zigzag backstitch.

Fig 13

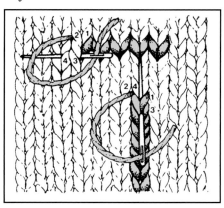

Fig 12

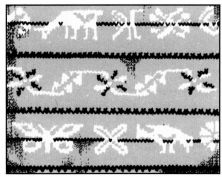

Holding the yarns

There are several ways of holding the yarn for jacquard work:

FIRST METHOD

Keep the working colour in one hand, and drop it to pick up the next colour. This is a slow method, especially when the instructions say twist the yarns around each other at each colour change. This, essential in intarsia, is totally unnecessary in jacquard, except sometimes to prevent a hole in the first colour change of the row or round.

SECOND METHOD

Often recommended: keep one colour in each hand (**Fig 14**). As we have only two hands, working with three or more colours causes problems. The technique then needs to be combined with the first or the third method. In either case, it may persuade you to have only two colours in any one row.

One problem with this method is that you may need to learn a second, unfamiliar way of knitting. This takes time. To start with, carry the colour with fewer stitches in the less-practised hand. Another problem is loss of rhythm. A group of stitches requires the right needle to move and the left needle to be still, whilst the next group requires the opposite.

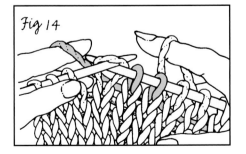
Fig 14

THIRD METHOD

A good method: keep one colour over the index finger in the usual hand, and the other colour over the middle finger of the same hand (**Fig 15**). Try a third colour over the ring finger. This method needs getting used to, but the change is not as drastic as with the second method, and there is no loss of rhythm. (See also **Needle know-how**, pages 18–21, and **Stranding** and **Weaving in**, below.)

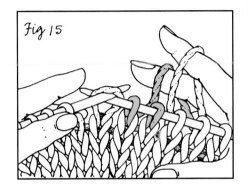
Fig 15

Style secrets
You can devise your own unique jacquard patterns by adapting tapestry or embroidery charts.

Stranding

The floats are left loose and untwisted, with one colour always on top of the other (**Fig 16**).

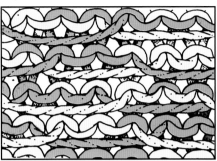
Fig 16

If holding the two yarns in one hand, keep the index finger above needles whilst working with the middle finger, and the middle finger below needles when working with the index finger. If holding one yarn in each hand, keep the right colour to the right of needle tips whilst working with the left colour, and the left colour below needles whilst working with the right colour.

DO NOT pull the floats. Spread the last group of stitches to their full width before bringing in the new colour. Otherwise, the floats will tighten up the gauge and you will not obtain the expected width. Keep measuring the overall width to make sure that the work is not pulling.

AVOID long floats. If they are longer than about 1in (2–3cm), floats are difficult to work even. They also snag more easily when in use. Consider introducing odd contrast-colour stitches, or small complementary motifs, to break up long stretches of colour. If long floats are essential to maintain a balanced pattern, weave them in.

Weaving in

The floats are caught by the working yarn, either on alternate stitches (**Fig 17**), or about every 1in (2–3cm). DO NOT pull the floats. Keep measuring overall width to make sure that they are not tightening the gauge.

Fig 17

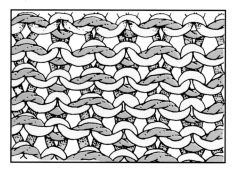

ONE YARN IN EACH HAND
To weave in left yarn (kept above needles when not weaving it in):

Fig 18

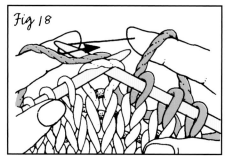

Fig 19

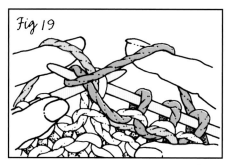

❀ *Knit it now...*

a Either on k (**Fig 18**) or p (**Fig 19**), bring the float up.
b Insert right needle into st and under float.
c K or p st as usual, under float.

To weave in right yarn (kept to the right of needle tips when not weaving it in, and more awkward than left yarn):

Fig 20

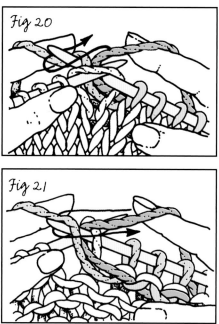

Fig 21

❀ *Knit it now...*

a Insert right needle into st.
b Wind float around needle. On k, wind float as if to k (**Fig 20**). On p, wind float first under and then over needle (**Fig 21**).
c Wind working yarn around needle as usual.
d Return float to its previous position.
e Draw st through.

BOTH YARNS IN RIGHT HAND
To weave in index-finger yarn (kept above needles when not weaving it in):

Fig 22

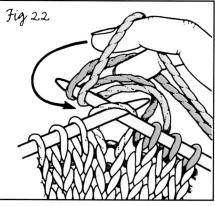

❀ *Knit it now...*

a On k (**Fig 22**) or p, insert right needle into st.
b Wind float and working yarn around needle as usual.
c Return float to its previous position.
d Draw st through.
Work next stitch keeping float above needles.

 ***Classy clickers...*** *always leave yarn tails long enough for darning if they are not weaving them in. Longer lengths for sewing different areas with matching colour are not necessary if the ladder stitch seam is to be used.*

To weave in middle-finger yarn (kept below needles when not weaving it in, and more awkward than index-finger yarn):

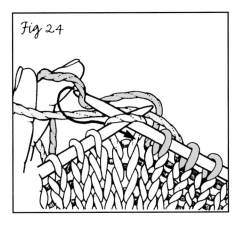

Fig 23

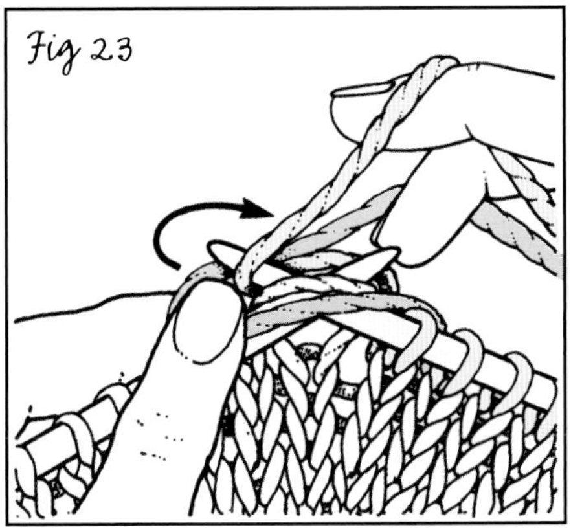

✿ Knit it now...

a On k (**Fig 23**) or p, insert right needle into st.
b Take float over both needles and hold with left thumb and/or index finger.
c Wind working yarn around needle as usual.
d Return float to its previous position.
e Draw st through.
Work next stitch keeping float below needles.

BOTH YARNS IN LEFT HAND
To weave in index-finger yarn (kept above needles when not weaving it in):

Fig 24

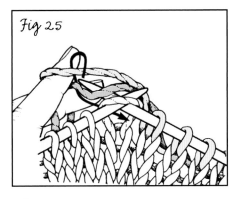

✿ Knit it now...

a On k (**Fig 24**) or p, insert right needle into st.
b Take right needle over float and work st as usual, drawing it from over the float.

To weave in middle-finger yarn (kept below needles when not weaving it in, and slightly more awkward than index-finger yarn):

Fig 25

✿ Knit it now...

a On k (**Fig 25**) or p, insert right needle into st.
b Pass right needle under float and work st as usual, drawing it from under the float.

Jacquard variations

Although stockinette stitch is by far the most popular base fabric for jacquard, other patterns can also be used.

Knit-and-purl jacquard

Purling some of the stitches adds texture and breaks the horizontal line between colours (**Fig 26**). The occasional slip stitch adds even more subtlety and intricacy.

Fig 26

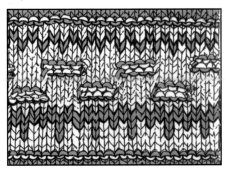

Garter-stitch jacquard

Two rows instead of one are worked for each stitch, always in garter stitch. The result is thicker and sharper because there are no Vs as in stockinette stitch, and squarer because of the nature of garter stitch (**Fig 27**). To avoid floats showing on the right side, on alternate rows each yarn has to be taken to the wrong side when not in use, and brought back when required for working.

Fig 27

Double-sided jacquard

A fascinating way of knitting, which gives a very thick and firm fabric. Clever use of the double-pointed needle version of tubular knitting can produce reversible fabrics with two-colour patterns on both sides. The patterns may be identical, totally different, mirror images or colour-reversed as in **Figs 28** and **29**.

Fig 28

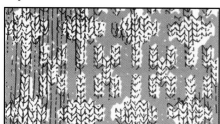

Fig 29

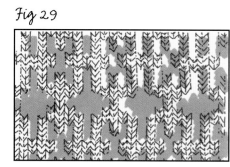

Mosaic knitting

A type of geometrical multicolour slip stitch worked from charts in garter stitch, stockinette stitch, or a combination of knit and purl stitches.

Each line of the chart is worked in two rows. The second row repeats, in the same colour, the sequence of worked and slipped stitches. The two rows of the following line are worked with the second colour. The third line is worked with the first colour, and so on.

Each line of the chart must start with the working colour for that line. **Fig 30** shows a characteristic pattern, out of the thousands possible.

Fig 30

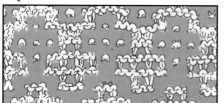

Multicolour slip stitch

This technique can produce a huge variety of textures. The number of slipped stitches in any one row makes the patterns slow to grow, but on the plus side there is no need for more than one yarn at a time. **Figs 31** and **32** show some examples.

Fig 31

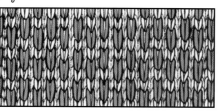

Fig 32

Slip-stitch patterns are excellent for oddyarn knitting. Another advantage is that the wrong side can sometimes be used in its own right, especially in patterns worked with double-pointed needles where rows can start at either end. The result is a reversible fabric. (See also **Slipping away**, pages 52–53.)

Beautiful beads

Beads, sequins, and other gorgeous embellishments can be incorporated into a knitted fabric, often with stunning results. If the fabric shows between the beads, it is called beaded knitting. If the beads are so close together that the fabric is pushed behind the beads, it is close-bead knitting. The beads, in most cases, show only on the right side. The gauge should be tight enough to keep the beads on the side they are meant to be.

Bead threading

Thread the beads onto the yarn before starting. If they are to form a pattern, work from a chart and thread the beads in strict order, starting with the one to be used last. In flat knitting, check carefully where the bead rows end. Some may end at the right edge and some at the left edge.

In general, the bead hole will be too small for a sewing needle large enough to carry the yarn. To thread the beads, refer to **Fig 1**.

> **Classy clickers...** use beads with holes just large enough for the yarn to go through.

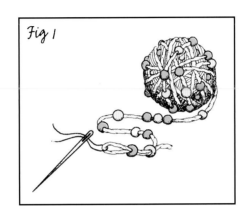

Fig 1

✿ Knit it now...

a Thread the two ends of a short piece of sewing cotton into a dressmaker's sewing needle.

b Pass end of yarn through cotton loop.

c Thread beads, push down the yarn, and rewind ball.

When many beads are used, a marker between beads of different rows is a help. The marker must be removable (use knotted yarn, a paper clip or a coil ring) and the beads should not be able to slip through it.

For large numbers of beads, thread a few rows at a time. This means there are more tails to be darned or woven in, but the work is more manageable.

> **Classy clickers...** *know that it's best not to have beads at the selvedges. Leave one or two stitches on each side.*

Beaded knitting

Beads are knitted into the fabric, and the fabric remains visible. The shape of the bead, the way it is threaded, the position and direction of the hole, and the technique of insertion, will determine how the bead hangs. For projects with large numbers of beads, try samples with different beads, different inserting techniques and even different knitting patterns. The possibilities are endless:

• Working in garter stitch, place one bead after each stitch on all wrong-side rows (**Fig 2**). This gives the closest possible arrangement in beaded knitting.

• Place beads at random, or in isolated motifs, over any unobtrusive pattern. Stockinette stitch is often used, although other patterns are better – like seed (moss) stitch in **Fig 3**.

• Arrange beads in regular patterns such as lines, squares, diamonds or chevrons.

• Use the beads to highlight an edge (**Fig 4**).

• Use the beads to highlight a knitting pattern such as fur stitch or eyelets.

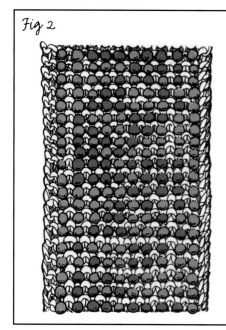

Fig 2

Fig 3

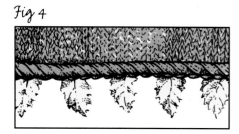

Fig 4

Beads on purl stitches

Refer to **Fig 5**. Because the yarn makes a loop between every two purl stitches, it is easy to insert a bead by simply bringing it up next to the fabric after working a stitch. This applies to reverse stockinette stitch, garter stitch and any pattern with at least two consecutive purl stitches on the right side. The beads can be inserted either when purling from the right side or when knitting from the wrong side. The bead stays perfectly horizontal but, because of its position between stitches:

• a single bead cannot be centred on an odd number of stitches (top left-hand corner of illustration);
• the number of stitches required to insert a line of beads is always 'number of beads plus one';
• unless very small, a bead will push the fabric to the sides; many beads could distort the fabric.

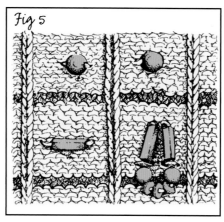

Fig 5

To have a central bead on an uneven number of stitches, plus an undisturbed fabric, slip purlwise one stitch after bringing the bead next to the fabric (top right-hand corner of the illustration). If the bead is very wide, slip several stitches (bottom left-hand corner). Bead loops need a little trick to prevent a hole forming (bottom right-hand corner):

✿ *Knit it now...*

a P-b1, but do not drop.
b Bring the beads next to the st.
c P tog 1st st and st next to it.

Beads on knit stitches

Inserting beads on knit stitches comes less naturally. If it does not interfere with the design, consider purling the stitch before and the stitch after the bead. Any of the first three purl situations above could then be used.

Close-bead knitting

The beads are so placed as to hardly let the fabric show. Every stitch of every row has a bead, and every stitch is twisted to ensure that the bead goes right across the stitch and hides it. The base fabric is twisted stockinette stitch.

Compare **Fig 6** with the beaded knitting on a garter stitch base of **Fig 2**. Both have the same pattern, but it shows better in the former because the beads are closer together. The overall size of **Fig 6** is smaller, despite having one stitch more than **Fig 2**. Finally, the fabric of **Fig 2** was flat, whilst that of **Fig 6** required drastic blocking. Apart from the natural fabric curl, it also slanted badly due to the twisting. In circular knitting, the slant will create a spiral effect, which, used properly, might enhance a project. Another advantage of circular knitting is that it avoids the awkward purl rows.

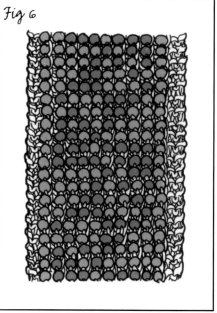

Fig 6

Match carefully stitch and bead sizes. Small beads will not hide the fabric and will tend to go through it onto the wrong side. Very large beads will be awkward to work and may give uneven gauge.

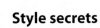

Style secrets

The slanting that is a feature of twisted stockinette can be used to advantage. Choose patterns that will not be spoiled by it. Try mixing twisted with plaited stockinette stitch, which slants in the opposite direction. If straight side edges are required, you may need to increase at one end and decrease at the other.

Both on knit (**Fig 7**) or purl (**Fig 8**):

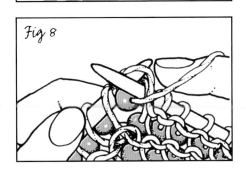

Fig 7

Fig 8

✿ Knit it now...

a Insert needle into back of loop. When purling, the right needle should be placed above bead of previous row.
b Bring bead up, but not so close as in beaded knitting.
c Wind yarn in the usual way; the bead should now be behind the right needle, from where it will more easily go through the st.
d Draw yarn and bead through st.

Blind objects

Objects that cannot be hung have to be enclosed, usually in a tubular pocket. Use ordinary tubular stockinette stitch when you want to stuff the pocket but do not want to show what is inside it. Otherwise, wrap the yarn two or three times around the needle to make elongated stitches (**Fig 9**). On right side or wrong side:

Fig 9

✿ Knit it now...

a Work a single increase on every st of the pocket area.
b Work in tubular stockinette stitch for a few rows over the pocket area, and in the usual way over the rest of the fabric.
c Sl the front tubular layer onto the right needle, and the back tubular layer onto a cable needle, to open the pocket.
d Drop the object inside the pocket.
e Return the sts to left needle, without twisting them or changing their order.
f Work 2 tog across top of pocket.

Be inspired by beautiful beads

Bead markers

Make counting rows easy with bead markers (**Fig 10**). They also help remind you of changes in pattern or shapings to be worked at regular intervals. This is invaluable for knitters with poor eyesight, but very useful even if your eyesight is perfect.

Use lightweight beads in more than one colour or shape. In circular knitting, position at the start of the rounds. If using a circular needle you will not need the usual needle marker. In flat knitting, position between first and second stitches at one of the edges or at any convenient place.

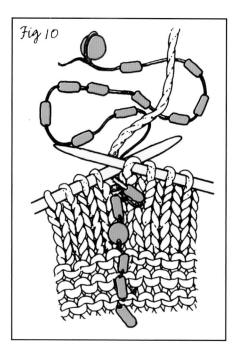

Fig 10

✿ Knit it now...

a Take a piece of yarn, preferably slippery, about twice the expected length to be knitted. Tie one end to the cast-on tail.

b On the slippery yarn, thread a bead for every 2 rows you are to work. Use a contrast bead when you have to change pattern or work a shaping. If not sure about the total number of rows required, thread more beads than you think you will need.

c Thread an extra bead or small button and tie at the free end. Leave beads dangling at back of work.

d Work one row or round. When you reach the beads, take them to front of work under the needles – the slippery yarn should not be caught when making the next stitch.

e Work another row or round. Now, take the beads to back of work but leave one bead at the front.
Repeat **d** and **e**. If you had too many beads before a change of pattern, leave the extra on the wrong side.
When the work is finished and you are sure that you will not need the beads any longer, cut the tied end of the slippery yarn and pull the other end. The beads will drop – to stop them going all over the place, hold the knitting over a box or bowl.

Beads and sequins can add glamour, texture and interest to your knitting. Create fabulous evening accessories with sparkling sequins, or, for a funky look, use chunky, colourful beads on everyday items.

Short rows

Short rows (or turning) is a useful shaping technique that can be used to create darts, corners and curves. Short rows can be used for features such as shaped collars, curved hems and for sock heels. This technique can also be used to create some innovative decorative effects.

GET CREATIVE

In short row knitting, the rows, or rounds, do not need to be worked from end to end. You can stop anywhere, turn and work backwards. If only a few stitches are involved, consider working from left to right on return rows.

Avoiding holes

Merely turning the work leaves a hole. Depending on the pattern, the hole will be an asset or an eyesore. There are three ways of avoiding holes, which are explained here. Over is the loosest; catch is very neat; and tie is easier and also neat. The instructions given are for stockinette stitch. Other fabrics may require adaptations.

Tie

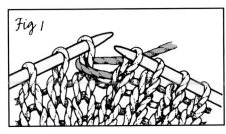

Fig 1

✿ Knit it now...

a Before turning, take yarn to other side of work.
b Sl next st pwise.
c Return yarn to original side of work.
d Sl st back to left needle (**Fig 1**).
e Turn; work back; sl 1st st pwise if desired.

If the tie interferes with your pattern, on the first long row work it together with the stitch it wraps. Insert needle first into the loop made by the tie, from underneath, then into the stitch.

Over

Fig 2

✿ Knit it now...

a Turn work.
b Make an over.
c Work the short row – sl first st pwise if desired.
d On 1st long row, work over and next st together (**Fig 2**). If this is a p row, reverse order of over and st: drop over, sl st, pick up over, return st to left needle and p2 tog.

Catch

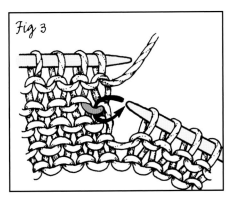

Fig 3

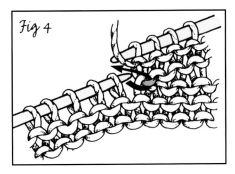

Fig 4

✿ Knit it now...

a Turn work.
b Sl 1st st pwise and work short row.
c First long row: on k: pick up strand shown in **Fig 3** and work it together with next st.

On p: pick up strand shown in **Fig 4** and work it together with next st after reversing their order (see **d** in **Over**, above).

Horizontal darts

These are a series of increasingly shorter, or longer, rows. They smoothly lengthen one side of the fabric.

Long to short rows (**Fig 5**) can be combined with short to long rows (**Fig 6**), to form a double dart (**Fig 7**). Each line in the diagrams is a row. If working two symmetrical darts, one will be turned on right-side rows and the other on wrong-side rows (**Fig 8**). Use needle markers to highlight the turns. To calculate, consider the depth of the dart in rows and the width in stitches. Half the number of rows gives the number of turns. Dividing the stitch total by the number of turns tells you by how many stitches each row will be shorter, or longer, than the previous row. If the result has a decimal point, make a few of the turns one stitch shorter, or longer, than the others.

Style secrets
Many shallow darts give a smoother edge than fewer deep darts.

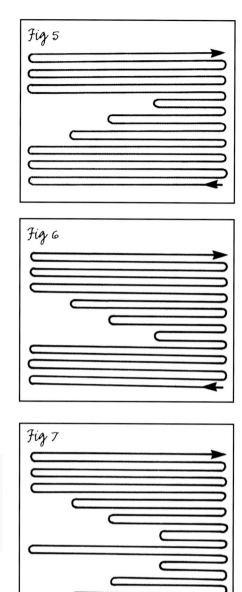

Fig 5

Fig 6

Fig 7

Fig 8

Mitred corners

(See also **Mitred corners**, page 61.)

Mitred corners can easily be achieved with a double horizontal dart (**Fig 9**).

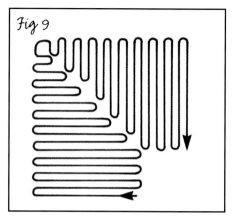

Fig 9

• For a right angle, leave 1 st unworked each time (and work 1 st extra later on) if the sts are nearly square; 2 sts if they are very wide; alternate 1 and 2 sts if they are medium. For obtuse/acute angles, leave fewer/more sts. Do not use any of the methods explained to avoid holes, but sl pwise the 1st st after turning. A neat row of holes will mark the mitre; for no holes, when lengthening the rows, work together sl st and head of st below next st.

Row adjustments

When working vertical or diagonal blocks in different patterns, unless they all have the same row depth, some areas will pull. Avoid this by working extra pairs of rows on the shallower patterns as required.

• Either keep checking and adding short rows until a sequence is established, or calculate the sequence beforehand from samples: if Pattern One has 30 rows in 4in (10cm), and Pattern Two has 34 rows, add 2 rows to Pattern Two every 15 rows.

Usually, there is no need to avoid holes. They disappear after a few rows. Use fabric markers to keep track of the extra rows.

Vertical gathers

• To gather an insertion, work frequent pairs of short rows (**Fig 10**). Frequency depends on patterns used and amount of gathering required. An extra pair of rows every other main row will double the length of the insertion.

Very wide insertions will drape. The effect can be emphasized by lengthening the centre with symmetrical darts (**Fig 11**).

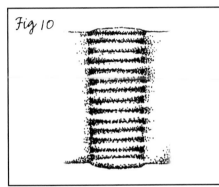

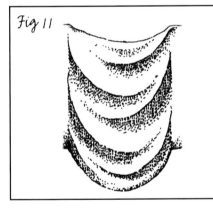

Ruffles

Like vertical gathers but worked at one end of work, or forming a separate edging (**Fig 12**).

The illustration shows how the pattern (a reverse st st welt) can help accentuate the ruffling effect. The straight edge is in garter stitch.

Curves

(See also **Curves**, page 63.)

Placing one dart after another will shape the work into a curve (**Fig 13**). This is a technique often used in decorative knitting and in garment making – collars, yokes, skirts etc.

• Calculate the number of rows needed at either side of the curve, and the number of stitches across. If, for example, the outside needs 30 rows more than the inside, you can have 3 darts 10 rows deep, or 5 darts 6 rows deep. The rows needed for the inside edge are evenly distributed between darts and worked from end to end.

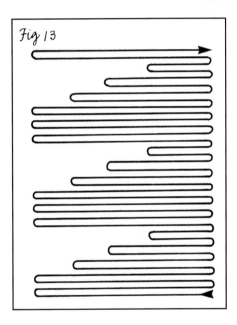

One of the many useful things that you can use short-row shaping for is to create extra rows at the front of a garment to accommodate a fuller bust. If you've been blessed with a curvy figure, show it off by knitting something that fits you just right!

Medallions

Individual geometric shapes. Only circular medallions can be achieved with short rows. For all other shapes, see **The ins and outs**, pages 54–65.

Medallions are created using the same idea as curves, but the inside edge has no rows between darts. The outside edge is as long as the circle. Medallions usually have between 6 and 16 darts, defining a similar number of sections (**Fig 14**).

The main drawback is that they need a seam. In solid patterns this can often be solved by grafting the last row to a provisional cast-on. Remember that grafting will create a new row, so make the last section one row short.

In lace work, even a grafted join is unwelcome and invariably ruins the work. If you must use short rows to work circular medallions, try to incorporate two plain rows to match the grafting at the end of each section, on the principle that 'if you cannot beat them, join them'. Alternatively, make a feature of the join – use a decorative cast-on or bind-off and hide the seam under it.

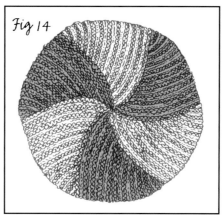

Fig 14

Style secrets
A straight piece between two end medallions gives an enclosed cylinder – great for bolsters and decorative work. Removing one of the medallions gives a cylinder with an open end, which is good for baskets and hats.

Style secrets
Shape a medallion over half the stitches, and a second medallion over the remaining stitches, and you have a casing for a sphere.

Special throws

Throwing the yarn means that you change its position, often wrapping it around the needle in the process. The most common throws are those used to knit and to purl. In this section, we describe the special throws that can be used to make a variety of creative effects, including the throws that are often used in lace knitting, and the very funky-looking loop stitch.

Yarn under

The throw is done under the needle, and the stitch count is not affected.

Yarn forward (yf or yfwd)

• Bring yarn from back to front of work, under needles.
To be done automatically between a knit stitch and a purl stitch (**Fig 1**). Also used in fancy patterns. In this case, the instructions are specific, but between knit and purl stitches the instructions assume the knitter knows that it must be done.

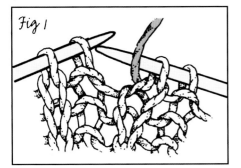

Fig 1

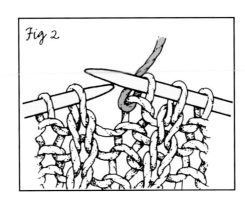

Fig 2

Yarn back (yb)

• Take yarn from front to back of work, under needles.
To be done automatically between a purl stitch and a knit stitch (**Fig 2**). Also used in fancy patterns (see **Yarn forward**, above).

With yarn in front (wyif)

Often found in patterns with slip stitches when the yarn needs to change sides, or just to ensure that it is left on the correct side.
Sl3 wyif is another way of saying yf, sl3, yb. If the yarn was already at the front of the work, leave it there.

With yarn at back (wyab)

(See **With yarn in front**, above.)
Sl3 wyab is another way of saying yb, sl3, yf.
If the yarn was already at the back of the work, leave it there.

Yarn over (yo)

Also called over and yarn round needle (yrn). Used mainly in increases (eyelet, closed eyelet, double eyelet and over).

If worked as it comes on the next row or round (sometimes through front of loop, sometimes through back of loop, but always in the easiest way, without twisting), it will leave a hole. Unless instructions say otherwise, patterns with overs must be worked in this manner.

Ways of avoiding the hole include twisting, as in closed eyelet increase, and decreasing by working the over with the stitch next to it as in brioche knitting (see page 114). Notice that, depending on the stitches before and after, some overs are much longer than others.

Front-to-back overs

The most commonly used.
• Take yarn up front of needle, over the top, and down the back.
From knit stitch to knit stitch: start by bringing yarn forward (**Fig 3**). Sometimes abbreviated in instructions to yf, k.
From purl stitch to purl stitch: end by bringing yarn forward (**Fig 4**).
From knit stitch to purl stitch (the longest): start and end by bringing yarn forward (**Fig 5**).
From purl stitch to knit stitch (the shortest): no extra yarn winding required (**Fig 6**).

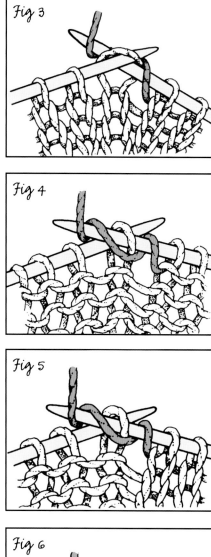

Fig 3

Fig 4

Fig 5

Fig 6

Back-to-front overs

Used to obtain perfect symmetry in paired increases, or identical results in increases worked on either side of work. Also used to avoid working some stitches of the following row through the other side of the loop in specific situations. In twisted stockinette stitch, a back-to-front eyelet increase will be worked through the back just like all the other stitches. In garter stitch, a back-to-front closed eyelet increase (sometimes called garter increase) will be worked through the front, also like the rest of the stitches.

• Take yarn up back of needle, over the top, and down the front.

From knit stitch to knit stitch: end by taking the yarn back (**Fig 7**).

From purl stitch to purl stitch: start by taking the yarn back (**Fig 8**). Be careful not to tighten up the over or the stitch, something easily done because the over ends at the top of the needle. It may be necessary to loosen up the yarn after purling the stitch.

From knit stitch to purl stitch (the shortest): take the yarn up the back to the top of the needle, where it will be ready to purl (**Fig 9**). Loosen up the yarn after purling, or the stitches before and after the over will get distorted.

From purl stitch to knit stitch (the longest): start and end by taking the yarn back (**Fig 10**).

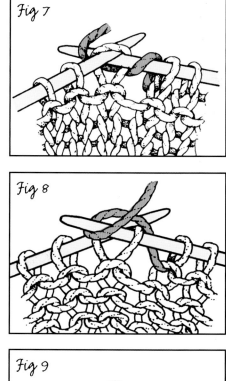

Fig 7

Fig 8

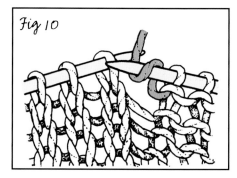

Fig 9

Fig 10

Double over (yo twice)

End any of the overs described above by wrapping the yarn a full extra turn around the needle. **Fig 11** shows a front-to-back double over, from knit stitch to knit stitch.

Used in double eyelet increase and in pattern construction, where it can either be used to make two new stitches or to obtain a larger hole. In the first case it is worked twice (once twisted, once untwisted). In the second case it is worked only once, and the second wrap is dropped.

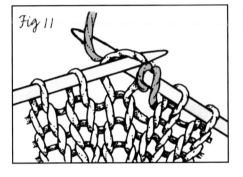

Fig 11

Selvedge overs

Used to increase at the start of a row, either for decorative or for purely practical reasons.

Before a knit stitch, work a front-to-back over around the free needle (**Fig 12**).

Before a purl stitch, work a back-to-front over around the free needle (**Fig 13**). Be careful not to work too tight. Hold with finger or thumb if necessary.

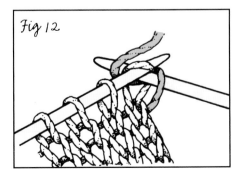

Fig 12

Fig 13

Elongated (dropped) stitch

Knit or purl in usual way, but wrap yarn two or more times around needle (**Fig 14**). On following row, work only the first wrap and drop the others (**Fig 15**).

Or, work single overs between ordinary stitches, then drop the overs on next row.

Or, work elongated rows with a much thicker needle (oddpin knitting). If this needle is much thicker than the ordinary one, it may be awkward to insert into the smaller stitches. Extra long rows, however, can be worked onto a ruler (**Fig 16**), which becomes the holding needle in the following row.

Fig 14

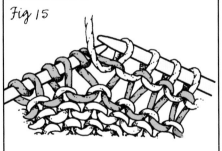

Fig 15

Style secrets

- Use elongated stitch all over for very soft and very loose areas, so stretchy that they will need controlling with adjoining areas of tight knitting. Or use it:
- on alternate rows for a more controlled effect;
- in occasional rows, to create loose stripes;
- in groups, to create a wavy effect.

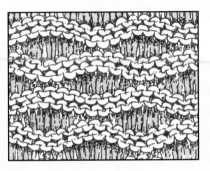

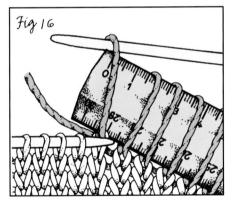

Fig 16

Fur stitch (loop knitting)

You can make loops by wrapping the yarn round needle and finger or card. A number of stitch patterns can be used as a background and made to interplay with the loops. The loops themselves are always made on knit stitches, which are generally worked twisted on the next row. Most often, the base fabric is stockinette stitch, or garter stitch for a flat finish.

The loops are usually worked every two (or a multiple of two) rows, and they show on one side only (**Fig 17**). Working the loops on every row (or on every third, fifth…) would make them show on both sides.

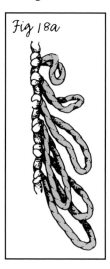

Fig 17

For a really dense pile, work a loop on every stitch. For less density, work them on every other stitch (or on every fourth, sixth…), and stagger the next loop row.

Fine yarns might be more successful. To increase density, use several strands together on each loop row and/or make several wraps around needle and finger or card. (Multiple wraps are treated as one single loop and drawn together through the base stitch, if appropriate.)

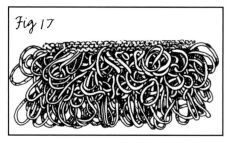

Fig 18a   Fig 18b

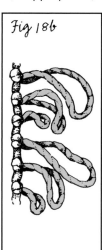

- Work fur stitch loops in blocks of colour.
- Grade the loop length. Either wrap yarn around more or fewer fingers, or change width of card. Mix loops of different length to create layers: short over long (**Fig 18a**) and long over short (**Fig 18b**).

Loops at front of work

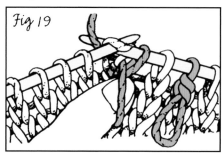

Fig 19

❀ *Knit it now…*

a K1 but do not drop from left needle.
b Yf.
c Wind yarn around left thumb, or around a piece of card.
d Yb.
e K original st again (**Fig 19**) and let it drop.
f Yo from front to back.
g Pass last 2 sts on right needle over the over, as if binding off.
h Withdraw thumb from loop.

Loops at back of work

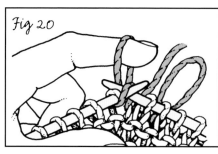

Fig 20

❀ *Knit it now…*

a K1, wrapping yarn around piece of card, or around one or more left fingers, as well as needle. Do not drop st from left needle.
b Place new st on left needle (**Fig 20**).
c K-b together the new st and the original st.
d Withdraw finger(s) from loop.

Loops on a ruler

❀ *Knit it now…*

On a wrong-side row:

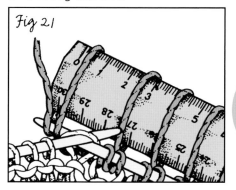

Fig 21

a K1, wrapping yarn first around needle, then around ruler held behind the right needle, then again around needle (**Fig 21**).
b Draw the 2 wraps around right needle, and drop st from left needle.
On next row, k-b together the 2 wraps from each loop. Withdraw ruler at the end of the row.

Style secrets
Cut the loops for a shaggy finish. Starting at the top, draw a knitting needle through the first row of loops, pull and cut close to the needle. Brush up and cut next row. At the end, brush down, spray with water, comb, pin the edges down and allow to dry.

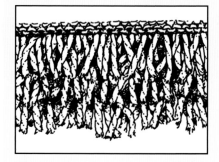

In a twist

Cross stitches and cables offer you another way of embellishing your knitted pieces with some potentially stunning textures and features. The effect can be as extensive or as subtle as you like; one line of cables running down the central panel of a bag or the sleeves of a sweater, for example, could add just the touch of extra interest that you want without being overwhelming.

GET CREATIVE

In crossed work, one stitch (or group of stitches) is worked after the stitch or group that follows. If only two stitches are involved, the result is cross stitch. If two groups of stitches are involved, the result is a cable and an auxiliary cable needle is required. For a right cross, the first stitch or group stays at the back. For a lft cross it stays at the front. Crossing always increases gauge, thereby making a denser fabric.

Cross stitch

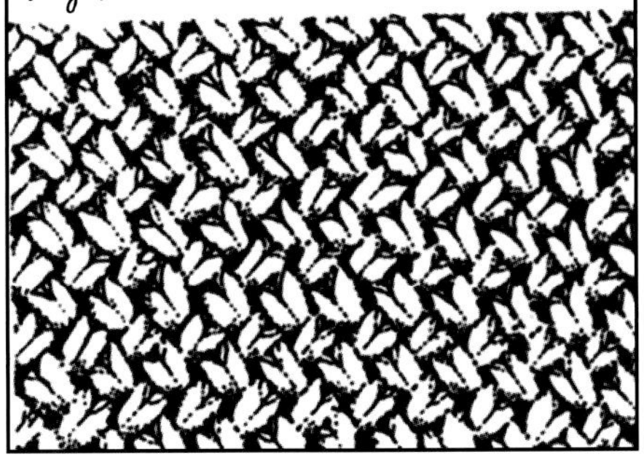

Also called twist stitch, one-over-one stitch, cross-over stitch, travelling stitch and wraparound. Used in many stitch patterns, either as miniature cables, as backgrounds (**Fig 1**), or in eye-catching, carefully designed arrangements (**Fig 2**). In fabrics made with many cross stitches, consider working with fairly thick needles and expect some loss of elasticity. The standard version of the technique includes one or two awkward movements. Several variations exist.

Standard cross stitch
RIGHT CROSS
On knit:

A less orthodox variation knits the second stitch also from the front but without drawing front of loop across first stitch. **Fig 4** shows a mock cable obtained by applying this technique to three stitches: k, 1st, 3rd st; then 2nd st; then 1st st.

On purl:

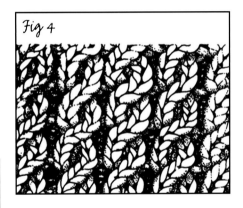

Fig 4

❀ *Knit it now...*

a P 2nd st.
b P 1st st.
c Drop the 2 sts from left needle.
Easier than the orthodox knit version.

Fig 1

Fig 2

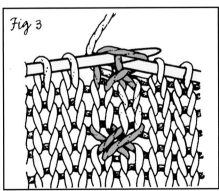

Fig 3

❀ *Knit it now...*

a Insert right needle into 2nd st from the front, drawing its front loop across 1st st (**Fig 3**).
b K 2nd st.
c K 1st st.
d Drop the 2 sts from left needle.

LEFT CROSS
On knit:

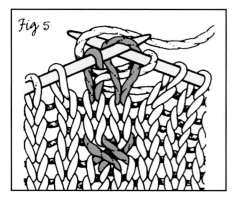

Fig 5

✿ Knit it now...
a Working round back of 1st st, insert right needle into front loop of 2nd st and k.

b K 1st st (**Fig 5**).

c Drop both sts from left needle.

A variation, not so orthodox but easier and practically identical in appearance, works the second stitch through the back loop.

On purl:

✿ Knit it now...
a Sl2 kwise (1 at a time).

b Insert left needle from right to left into the 2 sts and sl them back together. They are now in reverse order.

c P the 2 sts as they are.

Twice-worked cross stitch
This version is somewhat more raised and compact.

RIGHT CROSS
On knit:

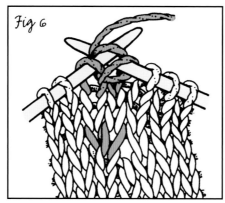

Fig 6

✿ Knit it now...
a K2 tog, but do not drop.

b K 1st st again (**Fig 6**).

c Drop the 2 sts from left needle.

On purl:

✿ Knit it now...
a P 2nd st.

b P 1st and 2nd sts together.

c Drop the 2 sts from left needle.

LEFT CROSS
On knit:

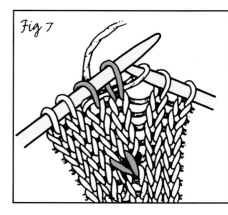

Fig 7

✿ Knit it now...
a K-b 2nd st (**Fig 7**).

b K 1st and 2nd sts together, inserting needle into front of 1st st and into back of 2nd.

c Drop the 2 sts from left needle.

A variation, which leaves a twisted top stitch, knits-back both stitches together.

On purl:

✿ Knit it now...
a Sl2 kwise (1 at a time).

b Insert left needle from right to left into the 2 sts and sl them back together. They are now in reverse order.

c P the 2 sts together. Do not drop.

d P 1st st again.

e Drop the 2 sts from left needle.

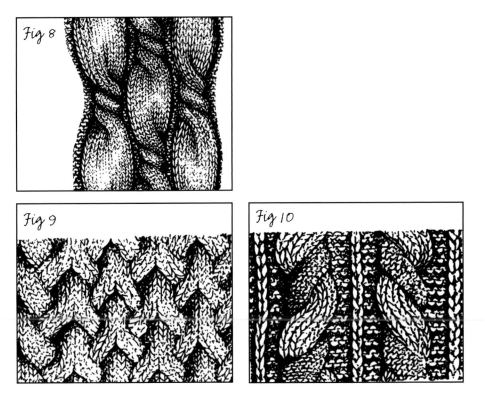

Fig 8

Fig 9

Fig 10

Cables

Cables are most often worked as knit stitches over a purl background (**Fig 8**). They are also possible on a knit background (**Fig 9**), and even in other patterns (**Fig 10** shows a purl and single rib cable on a garter stitch background).

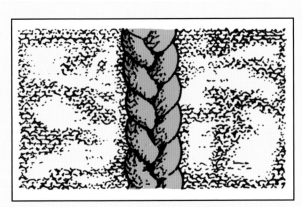

Use one colour for the cable and another one for the background.

Use one colour for the right side and another for the left side.

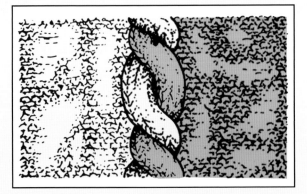

Make 'braids' travel across the background (by cabling the braid with one adjoining stitch, possibly on every alternate row), then interlace the braids.

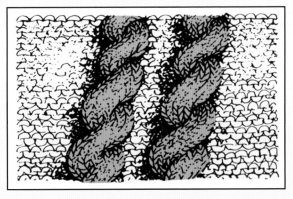

Make cables travel diagonally by using the principle of increasing and decreasing outlined in **Embossed knitting** (see page 65), or by off-setting the pattern sequence one stitch to right or left on the row after each crossing.

Style secrets

Cables have a very marked effect on the width of the fabric, and sometimes a slight effect on its length. The loss in width can be as much as one-third as compared with stockinette.

There are only two techniques involved. What makes one cable different from another is the width in stitches, the number of rows between crossings, the sequence of right and left crossings, and the number of background stitches in between.

In general, cables have an even number of stitches, divided in two equal groups when crossing, and are crossed from the right side of the work. Asymmetrical cables, and cables crossed from either side of the work, are possible.

Right cross for cables

Also called back cross.
On right-side or wrong-side rows:

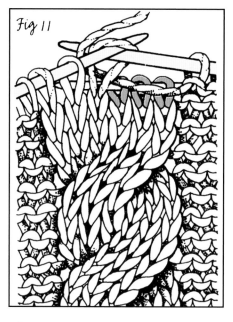

Fig 11

✿ Knit it now...

a Work to cable position.

b Sl half the cable sts (or appropriate number) onto cable needle.

c Place cable needle at back of work.

d Work the cable sts still on left needle (**Fig 11**).

e Work the sts on cable needle in their original order.

Left cross for cables

Also called front cross.
Work as for right cross but keep cable needle at front of work (**Fig 12**).

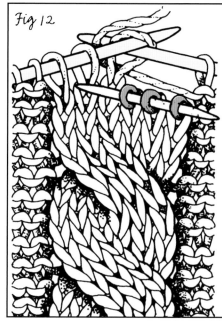

Fig 12

Classy clickers...

• **Use** a cable needle thinner than the needle(s) used for knitting.

• **To** avoid gaps, pull yarn firmly when knitting the first stitch from left needle.

• **To** avoid a left-edge stitch larger than the rest in knit cables on purl background, see page 21.

• **Use** fabric markers to keep track of the rows between crossings.

You might associate cables with chunky, clunky, shapeless masculine sweaters. Think again, though. Cables can add an attractive twist to snuggly throws, funky ponchos and chunky scarves. They're also fun and satisfying to make.

Getting a raise

Knitting raised motifs is an eye-catching way to add texture and visual interest to a piece. Subtlety is often the key here, unless you want to deliberately create a wacky-looking item.

All the techniques in this section create motifs that stand above the fabric surface. Try to emphasize this effect when blocking (see pages 122–124). The motifs can be worked individually, in rows, in vertical or diagonal or curved lines, in clusters, in geometrical shapes, evenly or randomly spaced, or all over the fabric – with a further choice of the same or a different colour(s) from the background. Some motifs, such as bobbles, can be worked independently and then sewn onto the fabric. This is useful for afterthoughts, but best results are obtained by knitting the motifs in. If not random, plan them on ratio graph paper.

Almost any pattern can be used as background. However, when many motifs are involved the result will be considerably thicker and heavier. Allow for extra yarn. Gauge may be affected too, so work some samples before committing yourself.

Style secrets
Avoid raised patterns where they will get flattened, as at the back of skirts.

Classy clickers... *use needle and fabric markers to show the position of motifs.*

Tufts or popcorns

This is the smallest of all raised motifs, consisting of a multiple increase followed, immediately or almost immediately, by a multiple decrease. Work this over one stitch on the right side. Always work the next stitch firmly and pull the tuft neatly onto the right side.

To follow is a selection of tufts out of the many that could be devised. The exact size of increase is not given – the larger the increase, the larger the tuft.

Flat tuft (Fig 1)

Fig 1

✿ *Knit it now...*

a Work a multiple over increase.
b On next row, p together all the sts of increase. Use a crochet hook if action is awkward.

Crested tuft (Fig 2)

Fig 2

✿ *Knit it now...*

a Work a multiple knit-and-purl increase.
b Pass all extra sts over last st made, starting with the one furthest from it.

Cock's comb tuft (Fig 3)

Fig 3

✿ *Knit it now...*

This stands out quite vertically.
a Knitted cast-on a few sts.
b K all sts made and drop original st from left needle.
c Pass all extra sts over last st made, starting with the one next to it.

Thimble tuft (Fig 4)

Fig 4

✿ *Knit it now...*

a K1, but do not drop from left needle.
b Place new st on left needle, k it and drop it. Repeat **a** and **b** as desired, always working from same original st.
c Drop original st.
d Pass all extra sts over last st, starting with the one next to it.

Bobbles

A tuft with added rows, worked so that they are independent from the base fabric. Bobbles can be worked in stockinette stitch or in reverse stockinette stitch (**Fig 5**). Their size depends on the size of the original increase and on the number of back-and-forth rows. Work next stitch firmly. Consider working the return rows from left to right rather than turning (remember to adapt wrong-side rows – p for k and k for p).

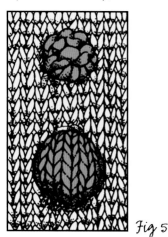

Fig 5

❀ *Knit it now…*

a Work a double or a multiple increase.

b Turn. Slip 1 pwise, p to end of bobble, for a k bobble; slip 1 kwise, k to end of bobble, for a p bobble.

c Turn. Slip 1 kwise, k to end of bobble, for a k bobble; slip 1 pwise, p to end of bobble, for a p bobble.

Repeat **b** and **c** as desired. With only 3 sts, end with a **b** row, then:

d Straight decrease.

With 4 or more stitches, end with a **c** row, then:

d Decrease as necessary along next row to leave only 3 sts.

e Straight decrease.

Hoods

Unlike the previous motifs, hoods stem from a platform of cast-on stitches placed between two stitches of the base fabric. A shape is worked over the following few rows on this platform, cunningly decreasing until no stitches remain.

Hoods should be worked on a fabric, such as stockinette stitch, which curls in the same way as the hood. Choice of decreases is equally important, because of their decorative role.

Bells (foxgloves)

The most popular shape of hood, it starts from a triangle (**Fig 6**).

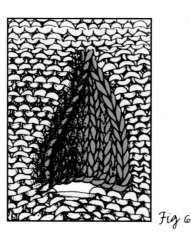

Fig 6

❀ *Knit it now…*

a Row 1 (right side): cast on, say, 8 sts, with one of the methods recommended for ends of rows.

b Work 3 rows in st st, or chosen pattern, right across work.

c Continue in pattern – ssk at start and k2 tog at end of every bell on right-side row.

d When only 1 st remains, work together with 1 of the adjoining sts.

Flaps

Totally independent motifs, attached to base fabric on their last row (**Fig 7a–c**). Work any shape you like (see medallions), on a flat fabric, unless you want a curly effect.

Knit in by placing the needle with the flap next to the main left needle, then working one stitch from each one of these together (**Fig 8**).

Fig 7a

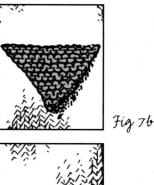

Fig 7b

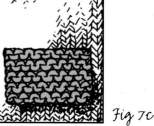

Fig 7c

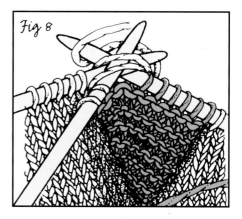

Fig 8

All sorts

This is a selection of individual techniques – these are useful for specific situations or just downright quirky!

Double stitch

Double because it is drawn through two stitches – the one in the row being taken off the left needle and the one immediately below it. Working through the stitch two rows below makes a treble stitch. Double stitches cannot be worked closer than on alternate stitches, otherwise the previous row would unravel. Mainly used in all-over patterns, especially brioche (see below).
The resulting fabric tends to be very wide, but also short.

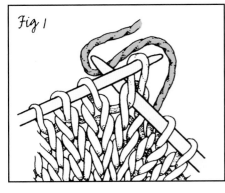

Fig 1

✿ *Knit it now…*

a K into centre of st below next st (**Fig 1**).

b Drop st above off left needle.

Brioche knitting

FIRST METHOD
Fabrics in which up to every other stitch of every row is a double stitch. They are thick, soft and often deceptive. To the untrained eye, the popular fisherman's rib (**Fig 2**), for example, may look like single rib worked on thick needles. The selvedge must be slipped at the start of every row, or the edges will ripple. Make sure that selvedges do not interfere with pattern. All patterns need a preparatory row, usually a purl row on the wrong side. It takes quite a few rows to see the pattern forming.

SECOND METHOD
Another way of working these patterns uses increases and decreases instead of double stitches:

a Row 1: an over is made next to a sl st.

b Row 2: yo and sl st are worked together.

It is more tedious, but there is a subtle difference. In the first version, the long strand (of the unravelled stitch above) lies UNDER the head of the final stitch. In this second version, the long strand (of the over) lies ABOVE the head of the final stitch. The preparatory row becomes, in this version, a series of overs, slip stitches and ordinary stitches.

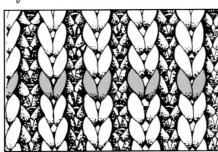

Fig 2

Dip stitch

A loop drawn from a stitch a few rows below to make a long, ornamental stitch over the fabric. Used in stitch patterns such as daisies (**Fig 3**). Depending on the pattern, the long loop is maybe passed over the next stitch or taken together with a neighbouring stitch on the next row.

Sometimes the loop will need untwisting, by dropping it and then inserting the needle from the other side, so that it lies flat.

Fig 3

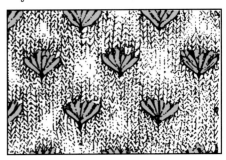

✿ *Knit it now…*

a Insert right needle into a st a few rows below. This can be directly under, to the right, or to the left of the st last made.

b 'K' and draw a long loop (**Fig 4**).

Fig 4

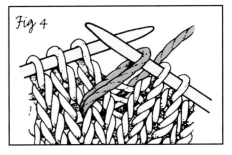

Classy clickers... *make sure that the loop in dip stitch is long enough. Remember that a similar loop appears at the other side of work, and that neither must pull.*

Three-into-three stitch

• Work three stitches together so that three new stitches result.

Fig 5 shows a cornflower motif worked on the right side in this way. The three stitches are first purled, then knitted, then purled again (always together), and finally dropped off left needle.

Fig 6 shows daisy or star stitch, an all-over fabric worked very similarly, but this time from the wrong side. The three stitches are purled, knitted and purled as before (or p, yo, p for a less dense fabric). One knit stitch divides each group, and the sequence is staggered on the following wrong-side row. The right-side rows are knitted.

Fig 5

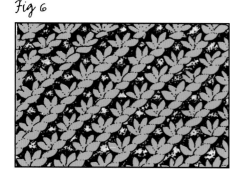

Fig 6

Classy clickers... *know that you may need thicker needles for three-into-one stitch.*

Pull-up stitch

Go for deeply textured effects with this technique.

• Catch the head of a stitch a few rows down and work it with the first stitch on left needle (**Figs 7** and **8**). If a whole row is pulled up, you will get cording or horizontal soft pleats (top of **Fig 8**), depending on how far down that row was. It might be convenient to pick up all the heads of the row below with a fine needle, hold this needle next to the left needle, and work together one stitch from each.

Fig 7

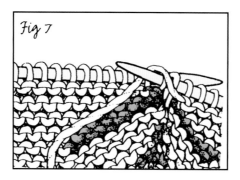

Fig 8

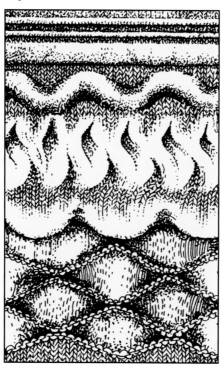

Style secrets

For horizontal waves, pull up a few stitches at regular intervals. Repeat, staggering the arrangement, a few rows further up. For diagonal effects, pull up consecutive stitches, one at a time, over several rows.

Stockinette, pulled up from the wrong side, is most often used. Picking from the right side is also possible. The effect is then reversed (bottom of **Fig 8**), and often some purl stitches, or a couple of rows of garter stitch, are introduced to make pulling up easier.

Oddyarn knitting

Mixing yarns of different thickness and/ or texture (and perhaps even colour) may be a disaster or a revelation, but is certainly worth experimenting with. There are thousands of possibilities, such as raised motifs or pairs of garter stitch rows in thick bouclé on a thinner, high-twist background.

Take care with gauge. Large chunky areas on a solid, medium-weight fabric are likely to require adjustments in the number of stitches as well as a change in needle size.

Style secrets

Knit two yarns in bands so that the fine yarn is so loose that it becomes quite lacy, whilst the thick yarn ensures that shape is retained with, say, slip stitches connecting the thick bands.

get it together

By now you should have a good understanding of the essential skills that you need to create simply fabulous knitting. So what now? You've got piles of gorgeous knitted fabric, but nothing to wear. So the next step is putting everything together. Learning how to make perfect seams might appear a bit of a chore, but just think – you're only a short way from creating the divine designs you've been dreaming of ever since you picked up the needles.

Let's make up...

Making up is the art of giving life to the assortment of knitted pieces you have created. When you start, these pieces may look shapeless and crumpled. It just takes a little making-up skill to turn these into smooth, stylish and wearable pieces that are a proper reflection of your craftsmanship. Great results can be obtained so long as you use the right techniques.

GET IT TOGETHER

Three approaches

Knitwear can be viewed in three ways:
  • a fabric to be dealt with exactly as cloth;
  • a continuous fabric that grows in many directions and avoids seams at all costs;
  • a fabric that will be joined by some seams but which is not like cloth.
The first is the tailoring approach. It makes great use of pressing, binding, lining and other dressmaking techniques. The second is the circular knitting approach. Favourite techniques are leaving stitches on holders, picking up stitches, provisional cast-on and bind-off, and grafting. The third approach uses seams in moderation, taking advantage of their structural possibilities, and planning seams ahead so that they either 'disappear' or become part of the design. Work is mainly flat and may well use some of the techniques favoured by the second approach. Shaping plays an important role. Pressing, lining and binding are totally out. Cold-water spray blocking is in.

Classy clickers...
  • **Buy** yarns they are sure of
  • **Choose** a good project
  • **Work** gauge samples
  • **Double** check the size they need
  • **Constantly** check and measure the work
  • **Don't** expect to finish making up in half an hour!

Making-up order

The following list is a very general guide, to be adapted as required.
a Fitting. Tack pieces in position with contrast yarn, or join with safety pins. Try on, wrong-side out. Allow for the fabric not having been blocked.

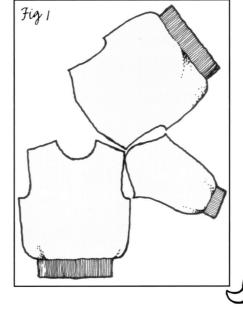

Fig 1

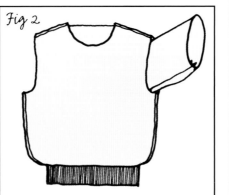

Fig 2

b Darning of all yarn tails not needed for sewing.
c Blocking, including improving fabric.
d Cutting.
e Cutting of lining.
f Grafting or seaming of joins. Tubes are easier to join when they are open. In knitwear, it is easier to join the shoulder seam, then fit the sleeve, then join the side and sleeve seams (**Fig 1**), than to fit the sleeve after the side and sleeve seams have been joined (**Fig 2**).
g Blocking or pressing of joins.
h Edgings and borders, if any.
i Fixing of fastenings and elastic.
k Lining if necessary.

Classy clickers... know that
  • **Fabrics** that are to be stretched will only fit properly after blocking. But the yarn will then be 'set', and will need reconditioning if something has to be unravelled.
  • **Yarn** tails of fabrics to be stretched are best darned after blocking, to avoid pulling.
  • **Some** seams may be easier to block before joining other seams.
  • **Zips** may be easier to insert before seaming, when the two sides can be laid flat.

Darn it!

Darning is one step towards creating smart-looking items. Except for long tails that can be used for sewing, all yarn ends should be darned, in such a way that the fabric loses no elasticity. Pull the fabric gently before changing direction or trimming, to ensure that the darning 'gives'. If unsure, leave trimming for after blocking. Fabrics to be stretched should have their tails darned after blocking.

For simply fabulous darning results:

• Check that you are not leaving a hole or a flaw on the right side; two ends, at mid-row or at the edge, usually need crossing.

• Leave yarn tails not shorter than 6in (15cm).

• Darn up and down for anchorage. With slippery yarns consider darning the yarn a third time.

• Unpick any knots or double stitches made when joining in yarn.

• Avoid darning along edges that will be stretched and released whilst in use (such as necklines or waistbands). If darning is unavoidable, work at right angles to the edge.

• Avoid darning in free edges.

• Avoid unnecessary darning. In colour knitting, consider carrying the colours up the side of the work, or use woven yarn joins.

Classy clickers... *know that darning must not show on the right side. Keep checking. Sometimes it helps to follow knobs or ridges, or darn each tail over its own colour.*

Types of darning

Basic darning can be horizontal, vertical or diagonal. There are tricks for neatening loose loops, and long jacquard floats. Finally, there is knotting.

Free edges

Neaten loops if required. Use either horizontal or vertical darning, whichever shows least. In general, garter stitch requires horizontal, and ribbing vertical darning. Try working vertical darning one or two stitches in from the edge.

Seam edges

Neaten loops if required. Use vertical darning right on the edge if the selvedge is taken in by the seam. Use diagonal if not, and knotting when the number of ends is overwhelming.

Middle of row

Use diagonal darning, unless texture or colour suggest otherwise. Neaten any floats if required.

Neatening loops

Long loops, such as the ones that sometimes form at the end of basic bind-off, should be controlled either whilst darning or whilst seaming. Choice depends on whether or not there is a tail to be darned next to the loop. In both cases (**Fig 1**):

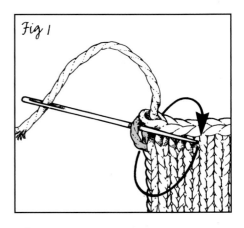

Fig 1

✿ *Knit it now...*

a Insert a sewing needle through the loop.

b Give the needle a complete turn, so as to twist the loop.

c Catch a strand at back of work – whichever will make the loop look tidiest.

d Darn or sew in the usual way. Missing loops or half-loops can be corrected by imitating knitting with the sewing needle. The general idea is to add, or hide, as required to make the fabric look perfect.

Horizontal darning

Figure 2. With wrong side facing:

✽ *Knit it now...*

a Follow a row of 5 or 6 sts, taking advantage of fabric texture. Either insert needle always from the top (or from the bottom), as in illustration, or alternate once from the top and once from the bottom. Choice depends on pattern.

b Repeat in opposite direction, either over same row or over next one.

If there is a second end, repeat away from the first one over the same row(s). At free or seam ends, repeat on a parallel row (**Fig 3**). Remember that, if there are two ends, they will probably need crossing to avoid holes.

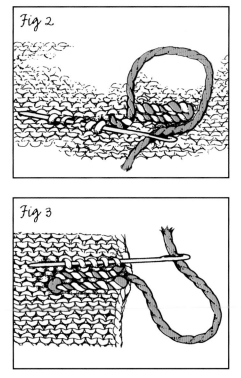

Fig 2

Fig 3

Vertical darning

Figure 4. With wrong side facing:

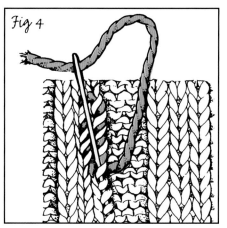

Fig 4

✽ *Knit it now...*

a Follow a st line for 5 or 6 rows. Either insert needle always from the same side (as in illustration), or alternate once from the right and once from the left, depending on pattern.

b Repeat in the opposite direction, either over the same st line or the next one.

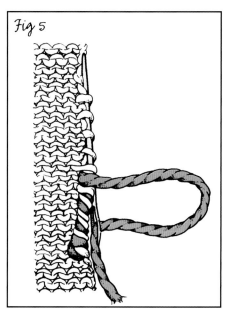

Fig 5

If there is a second end, repeat away from the first one over the same stitch line, as in illustration. Or work parallel to the first end, over an adjoining stitch line. In free edges, try to work one or two stitches in from the edge. In seam edges, work right at the edge (**Fig 5**). If there are two ends, remember they may need crossing to avoid holes.

In desperate need of darning?

Diagonal darning

Figure 6. This is more elastic than the other two. With wrong side facing:

Fig 6

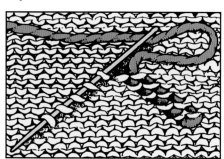

❀ *Knit it now...*

a Follow a line of 5 or 6 sts, each 1 row and 1 st further away from the 1st. Take advantage of fabric texture, and follow the line that leaves a better surface on the right side – usually going down and left (right) if you are darning the right (left) tail.

b Repeat in the opposite direction, either over the same sts or the ones next to them.

If there is a second end, repeat following a different diagonal, possibly forming a V with the first one.

> *Classy clickers... know that instead of a sewing needle, you can darn with a crochet hook, or a latch hook as used in machine knitting or rug-making.*

Knotting

Use this only at edges, such as seams, that will remain hidden from view. **Fig 7**.

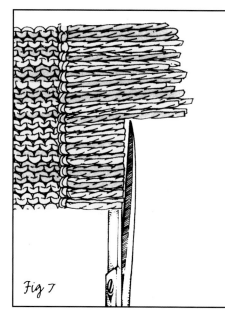

Fig 7

❀ *Knit it now...*

a Tie ends in pairs, using square knots. Ordinary, 'granny' knots, tend to come undone.

b Trim to leave a neat fringe, not too short.

Coarse yarns, and yarns that 'plump up' when washed should not cause trouble. Fine yarns, and especially slippery yarns, may be best secured with a running stitch or backstitch in matching thread. If you are worried about the fringe, cover it with binding.

Neatening floats

If you have a mass of lengthy floats, you can do one of two things: add a lining or secure the floats. Lining is best used for wall-hangings and other decorative projects, and for tailored knitwear. Never line knitwear if you want to preserve the elastic moulding qualities of the fabric.

To secure the floats (**Fig 8**):

  • Work a vertical running stitch, catching the back of the st on every 2nd row. If worried about the stitching showing on the right side, insert needle through yarn instead of lifting the whole stitch-head. Repeat at about 1in (2.5cm) intervals.

An alternative is to work lines of slip-stitch crochet at similar intervals.

If the original yarn is thick, use finer yarn matching the main colour.

Fig 8

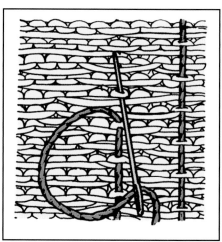

Round the block

Blocking is another step to ensuring the best-looking finish for your knitwear. Blocking gives a permanent 'set' to knitting. There are two steps to blocking: dampening and shaping. Using cold-water spray works for all fabrics, even flat ones that are sometimes left unblocked – it improves the nature of the fabric.

Dampening with cold-water spray

This is a foolproof method. It minimizes shrinkage risk because wetting is done after shaping. There is total control of dampness and of texture. No pressure is applied, and so raised textures can be raised even further. Uneven stitches can often be successfully corrected. With very limp fabrics, try spraying a little starch after a first spray with water.

Classy clickers... know that if you want to reuse yarn that has been blocked, you should first straighten it by reconditioning.

KEEP KNITTING HORIZONTAL whilst drying.

a Shape each knitted piece right side up.

b Spray with an ordinary, fine-mist plant sprayer. Some fibres need more water than others. Wool may only require a light spray. Manmade fibres or silk may require much more, but no fibre is likely to need as much wetting as if you were to wash it. Use gauge samples to check degree of dampness.

c Allow to dry, away from direct sun or heat, but in a warm atmosphere if possible.

Blocking can be your best friend because it evens out any irregularity in the knitted fabric, whether that's been caused by mistakes in knitting or it's just the nature of the yarn. Blocking can help you ensure that the garment you've spent so much time working on will actually fit you properly and make you look as fabulous as you hoped.

Classy clickers... washing for blocking should only be necessary when the yarn changes character after washing. Check the gauge on a washed sample before any work is done.

Shaping

• Work on a surface that will take pins, such as a bed, carpet, or large foam cushion. Beds are good because you can sit on them – and it's more comfortable than kneeling on the floor. Use ironing boards only for small items.

• Cover pinning surface with clean cloth. A checked cloth helps in keeping straight lines, but avoid small checks because they are confusing.

• Use long glass-headed pins and half-push them only.

• Improve fabric texture as much as you can.

• Respect the fabric's natural tendencies. Although you may want to eliminate excessive curling, do not expect a curly fabric to become perfectly flat!

Classy clickers... know that cotton, lace, limp yarns and heavy decorative work may benefit from starching.

Pinning

With tape measure in hand, spread the knitting until it reaches the intended main length and width. With natural fibres you may be able to adjust minor discrepancies by slightly shrinking or stretching the knitting, but do not rely on it. For best results, the knitting must be totally devoid of wrinkles and lightly tensioned, without being stretched. Pin all strategic points (**Fig 1**). Then pin between these points at close intervals – how close depends on how flat the fabric is. The edges must be quite smooth (**Fig 2**). If each pin draws out a point, you are either stretching too much or not using enough pins. Make sure you have plenty.

Fig 1

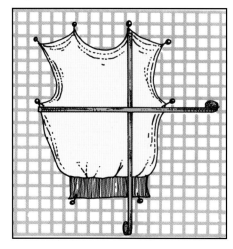

Fig 2

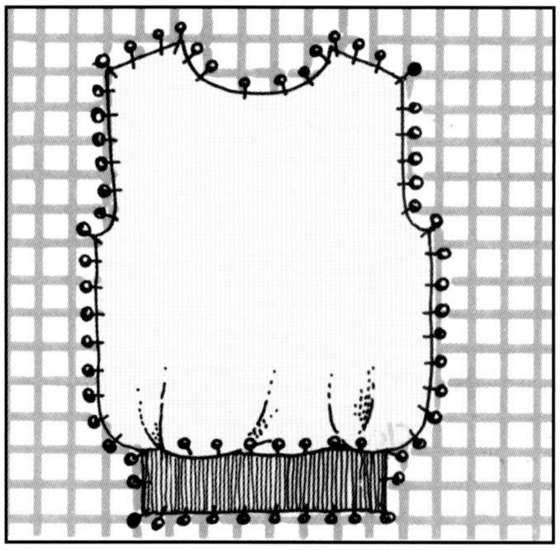

Ribbings should be dampened without the slightest tensioning, unless the design specifically requires them to remain open. If the adjoining fabric is so gathered that it cannot be blocked without stretching the ribbing:

✿ Knit it now...

a Stretch the ribbing and cover with a dry towel, plastic sheet or foil.
b Spray or steam the rest. Allow to dry.
c Release the ribbing.
d Cover what has already been blocked and spray the ribbing. Allow to dry.

If dealing with gathering borders, or other areas, that have no give and cannot be stretched, block around a cushion (**Fig 3**).

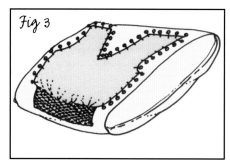

Fig 3

The pieces of a sweater to be joined into a circular yoke, and any other similar cases, are also best blocked before joining. Totally circular and seamless projects should be sprayed thoroughly, then dried (see page 33).

Stretching with pins

Non-resilient yarns should be stretched, to avoid them going out of shape later on. Stretch evenly in all directions. Slippery yarns, and fabrics expected to sag, should be stretched sideways but kept short. Once hanging, they will adopt the intended shape.

Lace and some other openwork patterns are usually stretched. Squares and rectangles can be stretched on a checked cloth.

For circular shapes:

✿ Knit it now...

a Attach a pen to the end of a tape measure, or of a piece of string, and draw a circle to exactly fit the medallion to be blocked. You can draw the shape on the back of tracing or greaseproof paper, or see-through thick plastic, and place this on top of the pinning surface.
b Mark the points of the medallion at regular intervals.
c Draw a second circle if the edge is scalloped.
d Pin centre and main points of medallion.
e Pin remaining loops (**Fig 4**).

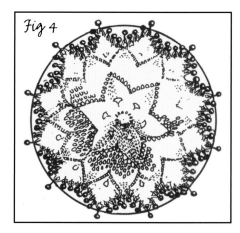

Fig 4

Some people prefer stretching wet, rather than dry, items. And, of course, if something is being restretched as part of its aftercare, it will have been washed; it then makes sense to stretch it wet. After a few hours of drying, check whether retensioning is necessary; some fibres become longer when they dry. If you are uncertain about whether to stretch before or after wetting, try both methods on samples.

Knitting that has been stretched wet can be dried upright. Knitting sprayed after stretching must be dried flat, so that the moisture permeates the fabric.

Improving fabric

The three golden rules of blocking to improve fabric are: block flaws out, block texture in, and be crisp.

- Stretch edges that are pulling.
- Make sure that rows and vertical lines of stitches are absolutely straight.
- Make tight stitches larger by drawing yarn from a couple of stitches at either side. Use a cable, or sewing, needle.
- Make larger stitches smaller by easing up the side stitches.
- Straighten up the loops in rows that have become lopsided after being too long on the needles. Use a cable, or sewing, needle.
- Draw out points and secure with a pin at the tip. Draw in corners and keep in place with a pin on the outside (**Fig 5**). Points and corners should be made as sharp as possible without distorting.

Fig 5

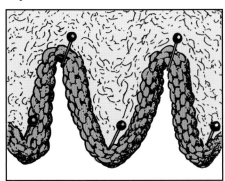

- Draw the sides of slits and buttonholes together and keep in position with as many pins as required.
- Draw back and pin any strand that cuts across what should be a neat line of a hole. As with corners, the pin should push the strand or fabric back, but should not go through it.
- Push pins down to their heads to flatten raised stitches that should be flat.

After sewing

Seams do not always need blocking, but when they do the difference really shows. As far as possible, block seams unfolded, otherwise a crease can form. If an unavoidable crease bothers you, block seam again, unpinned, around a convenient mould. It is often possible to block one or more seams unfolded, if one last seam has not yet been sewn. This last seam is later blocked folded.

- To block unfolded seams, push many pins at either side of the seam line, down to their heads. The pins should be on top of the fabric taken in by the seam, on the wrong side, and they may need to be nearly touching (**Fig 6**). In folded seams, there is room for only one row of pins (**Fig 7**), on the right side. Wet the seam very well, spraying cold water from very close. Allow to dry.

Classy clickers... *know that matching pieces can be blocked in pairs, if they have a smooth texture. Shape the first one and spray wrong side up. Place the second one on top, right side up, re-pin and spray.*

Fig 6

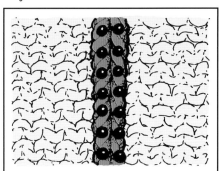

Fig 7

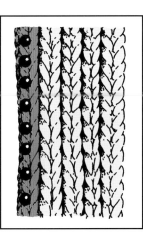

Cut it out

Cutting your knitting may sound like a dangerous idea, but it can play a big role in the tailoring approach to knitting. It is also used for restyling, adapting to size, changing damaged areas and providing openings in circular knitting. It is safer to cut knitting after blocking. Once the yarn has 'set', it does not ladder so easily. Horizontal cuts are made by pulling a thread. Cuts in all other directions are made by the cut and sew method. Practise first with samples, worked in the appropriate stitch pattern and preferably the same yarn.

Pulling a thread

This is based on the idea that rows are interlocked yarn waves (see **The knitted stitch**, page 13). Cutting a row at the two ends, and then pulling the thread, frees the crest of the wave below and the trough of the wave above. Notice that the unlocked crest shows a row of real stitches, and can be unravelled. The unlocked trough, on the other hand, cannot be unravelled, although it can ladder. In stockinette stitch, the waves are very clear. In other patterns they may be far less distinct. Usually, the trough has one loop less than the crest.

Having cut the fabric, thread a fine needle through the free loops. You can then do a number of things:

• Unravel part of the lower section, and graft what is left to the top section (see pages 126–128).

• Add rows to the lower section, and graft to the top section.

• Discard one of the sections and bind off or add rows to the other one. You can do this to the troughs of the top section, as well as to the crests of the lower section, but only stockinette stitch will look unbroken – except for a half-stitch kink at the edges. Changing stitch pattern gets over this problem.

To cut (**Fig 1**):

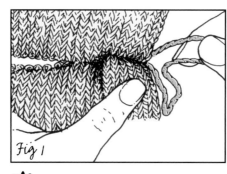

Fig 1

✿ Knit it now...

a Snip a st some 2in (5cm) away from left edge.

b Pull right-edge st of same row, first with a needle, then with your fingers. The fabric will gather.

c Once the gathers reach the cut st, smooth them towards the left and continue pulling the thread until the cut end reaches the right edge.

d Unpick the sts remaining at the left edge. Some yarns and patterns are easier to pull than others. If the yarn breaks, smooth the gathers towards the right, find the new yarn end and continue pulling in stages. If the pattern is very awkward, unpick the row stitch by stitch.

Classy clickers... *who are working with a slippery yarn thread a contrast thread through the rows above and below the one to be cut.*

Cut and sew

Or, rather, 'sew, cut and sew'. Some cuts can be planned ahead.

a Baste (tack) the cutting line in contrast thread.

b Work 2 lines of close stitching (see below) on the inside of the cutting line, almost touching each other, in matching thread.

c Repeat **b** about ¼in (0.5cm) further in, if working with slippery yarns.

d Cut along tacking (**Fig 2**).

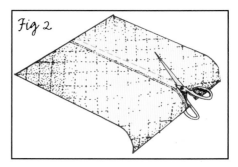

Fig 2

The best close stitching is done by machine. Try on samples first; you may need a fairly loose setting. If the fabric is very thick and gets caught, try placing tissue paper on top of it; this can easily be removed afterwards. Be careful not to stretch the fabric. To close-stitch by hand, use a very small and tight backstitch and dressmaker's thread. Don't be surprised if the edge ripples after cutting.

The hard graft

Grafting (also know as or weaving, or Kitchener stitch) is a very neat-looking and professional way of joining two pieces of knitting with an imitation row. The join is done with a sewing needle, but looks knitted. Although real grafting is done between two sets of free loops, rows of free loops can be grafted to solid rows or edges. Fake grafting uses the same technique but with solid rows and edges, rather than free loops, on both sides.

Knit stitches are the easiest to graft. Stockinette stitch is the easiest fabric, and the only one that will not betray two sections knitted in opposite directions, except for a half-stitch kink at the edges. All other fabrics will only graft successfully if the two sections are worked in the same direction.

Classy clickers…
- **Work** *flat on a table, or over a cushion placed on your lap. DO NOT keep the two needles together in your left hand with the knitting back to back.*
- **Check** *that the tips of both needles are pointing to the right. Transfer to spare needles if necessary.*
- **If** *you can, use yarn coming out of one of the two rows to be grafted. You will need about four times the width of the rows.*
- **Keep** *tension even or keep it loose and later ease all the excess yarn towards the left edge with a cable, or sewing, needle. The grafted row must not look different from the rest.*
- **If** *one needle has more stitches than the other, work together two stitches of the longer row at regular intervals.*

Grafting is easier to understand when the stitches are off the needles, as in the illustrations. In real life, drop them off the needles one at a time, as you need them. To practise, try this:

 Knit it now…

a Work 2 st st samples in very thick yarn. Do not bind off.
b Pin them as for blocking. Remove needles and keep each free loop in place with a pin.
c Spray well with starch, and allow to dry.
d Graft with a yarn of similar thickness but of contrast colour.

Style secrets
Grafting at a change-of-pattern line can disguise changes in fabric direction, making a different gauge in the grafting row less noticeable. This may allow you to join two complex patterns with simple knit grafting.

Knit grafting (Fig 1)

Fig 1

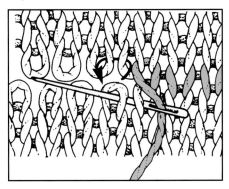

Knit it now…

a Insert needle UP 1st lower loop.
b Insert needle DOWN 1st upper loop, then UP 2nd upper loop.
c Insert needle DOWN 1st lower loop, then UP 2nd lower loop.

Repeat **b** and **c**, always going DOWN on the loop you have already gone up. If the two sections were worked in opposite directions, you will have to go 'UP the 1st upper loop only' the first time you work **b**.

Purl grafting

If the whole row is purl, turn the work and knit graft from the other side.

In purl grafting, the needle works in an up-and-down movement (**Fig 2**):

Fig 2

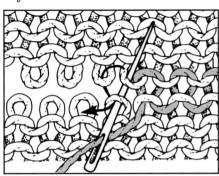

✹ *Knit it now...*

a Insert needle DOWN 1st lower loop, then UP 1st upper loop.

b Insert needle DOWN 2nd upper loop, then UP 1st upper loop.

Repeat **a** and **b**. You will be going first DOWN a new loop, then UP a loop you have already been through.

Garter-stitch grafting

To keep the pattern unbroken, the lower section must show the purl side of the stitch, and the upper section the knit side (see **The knitted stitch**, page 13).

The grafting movement is a combination of knit grafting on the lower loops, and purl grafting on the upper loops (**Fig 3**):

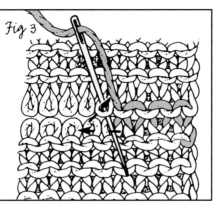

✹ *Knit it now...*

a Insert needle UP 1st lower loop.

b Insert needle UP 1st upper loop.

c Insert needle DOWN 2nd upper loop.

d Insert needle DOWN 1st lower loop, then UP 2nd lower loop.

Repeat **b** to **d**.

Ribbing grafting

This is another combination of knit and purl grafting.

Single rib

Assuming that the first stitch is a knit (**Fig 4**):

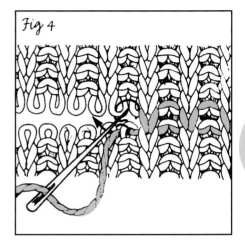

✹ *Knit it now...*

a Insert needle UP 1st lower loop.

b Insert needle DOWN 1st upper loop, then UP 2nd upper loop.

c Insert needle DOWN 1st and 2nd lower loops.

d Insert needle UP 2nd upper loop, then DOWN 3rd upper loop.

e Insert needle UP 2nd and 3rd lower loops.

Repeat **b** to **e**.

Grafting may seem a bit complicated, but it's a technique well worth learning. It means that you can create 'seamless' seams that lie flat and look invisible, for example, on the shoulders of a garment. You get a really stylish-looking, smooth finish.

Single rib worked in opposite directions (such as the two sides of a jacket frontband meeting at back of neck) can be joined by knit grafting (**Fig 5**). The result is not elastic, but quite adequate.

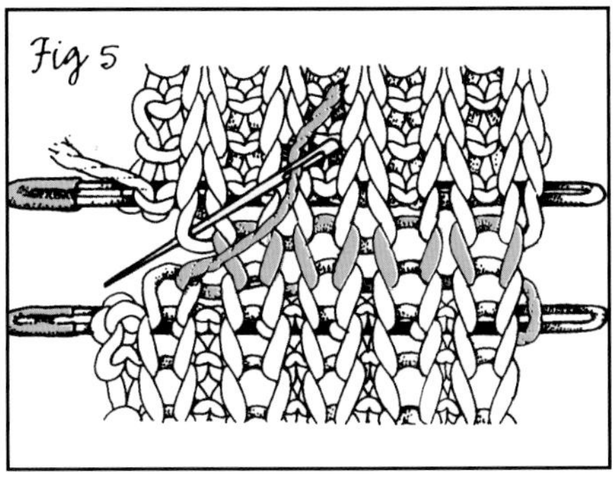

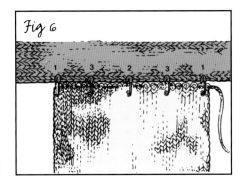
Fig 5

❋ *Knit it now...*

a Sl the k sts of one side onto a needle, and the p sts onto a holder.
b Repeat with the other side.
c Knit graft the sts on the needles.
d Turn work, transfer the remaining sts onto the needles and knit graft.

Other ribs

Work as for single rib, changing to knit or purl grafting as suggested by the knit and purl sequence.

Grafting to stitch lines

This is often done to an edge (such as the last row of a sleeve being grafted to an armhole), but could be done to any other line of stitches.

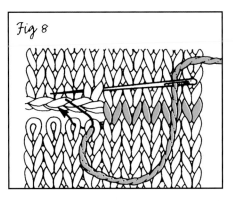
Fig 6

❋ *Knit it now...*

a Pin the edges with safety pins, without overlapping the fabric if grafting to an edge. Gather one of the sides if you want to. Count stitches and rows to find the centre line and insert another pin. Add more pins to divide into quarters, then eighths, and so on until there is a pin every 2in (5cm) or so (**Fig 6**).
b Knit graft (or graft as suggested by the free loops), taking as much or as little of the top fabric as required to keep the join flat (**Fig 7**). Make sure you follow a straight stitch line. If gathering one side, take more from that side than from the other.

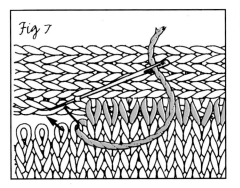
Fig 7

Grafting to rows

Pinning, as in grafting to stitch lines, is only necessary when either the numbers of stitches or the widths of the two sections are different. To graft a knit row to a knit background, proceed as for knit grafting, but catch a top stitch instead of a top loop (**Fig 8**).

To graft a knit row to a purl background (which could easily be the case in hems), proceed as for garter-stitch grafting, again catching a top stitch instead of a loop (**Fig 9**).

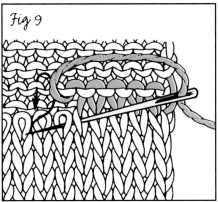
Fig 8

Fig 9

The seamy side

Knitters often hate seams, mainly because they love to knit, not sew. Many knitters have a bundle of unfinished objects that languish in piles, waiting to be sewn up, while the knitter moves on to their next must-start-it-now project. But take a deep breath, try to be patient, and learn how to make professional-standard seams that really do justice to your hard work and craftsmanship.

There are some real eyesores of seams around that are described as 'neat', 'professional' and 'almost invisible'. A striking example is the joining of garter selvedges (used to prevent stretched edges) with an edge-to-edge seam (chosen to keep the fabric flat). The result is a highly visible, often uneven line that can ruin the overall effect. It makes much more sense to prevent stretched edges by holding the needles efficiently, and to restrict edge-to-edge seams to those situations where they can be integrated within the design, such as a throw made up of dozens of separate pieces, with edges carefully thought out to accommodate the seams. The sides of a sweater are usually best joined with seams that tuck in the edges of the knitting.

Style secrets
Soften seams by blocking them after sewing. If carefully chosen, they might turn out to be undetectable – and this is much more desirable than complete flatness.

Simply fabulous seams

a Plan seams to fit with the pattern. They are not afterthoughts.
b Choose seams carefully and allow for the appropriate selvedge when you cast on.
c Use the right sewing yarn, in the correct way.
d Block seams that bulge or make the fabric curl the wrong way (see pages 122–124).

Straight lines should be straight. Stitches and rows are often of help. If necessary, mark them beforehand with a running contrast thread.

Matching sides should be joined accurately. Count stitches or rows rather than relying on a tape measure. Use fabric markers.

A number of seams do not need tacking or pinning. If pinning, use either safety or long glass-headed pins. Follow the sequence explained in **Grafting to stitch lines** (**Fig 6** on page 128).

Anything to be turned back (such as cuffs or hat brims) must have the turnover section, plus another ½in (1.5cm), seamed from the opposite side to the rest of the seam. If there is a selvedge, ideally bind off at the appropriate place, then cast on again on the next row.

*Classy clickers... know that it is easier to sew flat pieces than tubes (see **Figs 1** and **2** on page 130).*

Shapings worked two or three stitches in from the edge do not interfere with sewing, but are not always desirable. If sewing across an increase or decrease, simply remember to take the seam gradually over it and not to leave any holes.

Loose cast-on or bound-off loops by a seam edge can be neatened when sewing. Secure them onto the seam, or twist them as shown in **Fig 1**, page 119.

Style secrets
Sewing seams on light-coloured items needs more care than dark ones. They make cheating difficult!

Style secrets
Joins show less behind a raised line, such as that provided by knit stitches in ribbings, than in front of a raised line.

Planning for seams

A seam, or join, has to fit in with the overall design. It can play a decorative role, a functional one, or both. In each case it has to relate to the adjoining stitch pattern(s). In merely functional seams, the fabric should look unbroken. Add selvedge stitches, and plan the pattern repeats to match once the selvedges have been taken in by the seam.

Ribbings, because they are so often used, are a good illustration.

• A single rib join should have one side ending in knit and the other in purl (**Fig 1**). A sweater back, for example, requires an odd number of stitches, starting and ending with a knit stitch. The front must start and end with a purl stitch. Cuffs, being round, need an even number of stitches.

• A double rib join should have three knit stitches at one side and three purl stitches at the other (**Fig 2**). This makes sweater fronts and backs multiples of four stitches, and cuffs multiples of four stitches plus two.

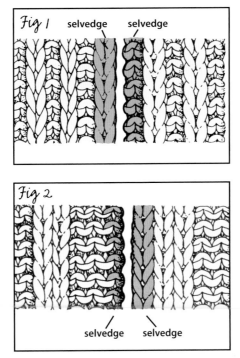

Fig 1   selvedge   selvedge

Fig 2

selvedge   selvedge

Notice that the double-rib seam lies at the meeting point of knit and purl, taking advantage of fabric texture to 'hide'. In broader patterns, consider making the front larger than the back, and adjusting the stitch difference at the armholes.

Choosing seams

Remember, this must be done at planning stage, so that the appropriate selvedges can be allowed for. If all you need is something as inconspicuous as possible, go for ladder stitch. For more elaborate seams, it is best to experiment in advance. Either incorporate different selvedges into the gauge samples, or work narrow strips (half a dozen stitches may be enough) for the sole purpose of trying seams. Look also at the list below.

If you like the idea of a fully knitted project, use **Knitting on** (page 135), and see also **Seam bind-off** (page 47) and **The hard graft** (pages 126–128). Seams can be joined with crochet if you prefer that to sewing – look up in a crochet book.

Some seams can only be used along rows, some only along selvedges; but most seams can be used in either situation, or even to join a row to a selvedge.

ORDINARY EDGES
ladder stitch
backstitch

**BORDERS,
knitted separately**
Attaching a row:
free-loop backstitch from right side
free-loop slip stitch
(grafting to stitch lines or to rows)
Attaching a selvedge:
ladder-stitch variation
edge to edge
knitting on

CUT AND SEW
slip stitch to
tidy up

EDGINGS
If they cover the fabric's edge, slip stitch from wrong side; otherwise, see
Borders, left

OVERLAPS
slip stitch from
wrong side

DECORATIVE SEAMS
slip stitch if sewing under a decorative selvedge
flat-felled seam
overcasting from right side
fishbone stitch
knitted stitch
alternate free loop (rows only)
knitting on

HEMS
free-loop backstitch
slip stitch if the edge is cast-on or bound-off
free-loop slip stitch
(grafting to rows)

PATCH POCKETS
slip stitch
ladder stitch
pick up stitches around edge and free-loop backstitch (or graft to lines of stitches or to rows)

**REVERSIBLE
PROJECTS**
flat-felled seam
*The other flat seams may
also be adequate, depending
on the fabric texture*

**POCKET
LININGS**
slip stitch

LOOP EDGES
Loop edge over solid fabric:
free-loop backstitch
free-loop slip stitch
(grafting to stitch lines or to rows)
Two loop edges:
edge to edge
overcasting
fishbone stitch
alternate free loop

**REINFORCED
SEAMS**
backstitch
knitting on

FLAT SEAMS
flat-felled seam
edge to edge
overcasting
fishbone stitch
knitted stitch
alternate free loop

GET IT TOGETHER

Sewing yarn

It's best to sew with the yarn used for knitting. Its thickness matches that of the fabric and gives just the right strength. If you cannot use matching yarn because its lack of twist makes it break, or its texture is too knobbly, find a plain one in matching colour, or a shade darker. Make sure that it can be cleaned in the same way as the main yarn, and that it will not shrink. As far as possible, use the same fibre you used for knitting.

Use vertical darning to anchor new yarn to the selvedge, if this is to be taken in by the seam. Repeat on the taken-in selvedge when yarn is running out (**Fig 3**).

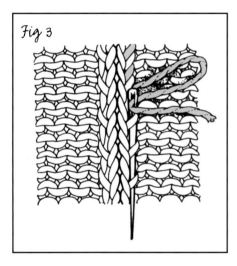

Fig 3

Classy clickers... *try to keep selvedges as neat as possible; anchor the yarn wherever it will show least.*

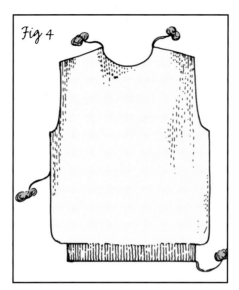

Fig 4

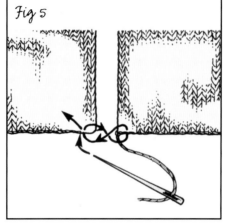

Fig 5

If using the same yarn, try to leave long tails in strategic places as you knit, and tie them in little bundles (**Fig 4**). Using long tails will encourage you to start seaming from the lower, or the top, edge (rather than, say, from the underarm). This is excellent, because it makes it easier to leave a smooth edge, without 'steps'. To avoid the gap that often forms at the start of a seam, use a figure of eight (**Fig 5**). Repeat, if required, until the edge is totally smooth.

Ladder stitch

One selvedge stitch is taken in from each side except in garter stitch (see below). Some people take in only half a stitch to diminish bulk, but this often makes the seam more noticeable on the right side. Ideally, use a no-selvedge selvedge.

✿ *Knit it now...*

a Make a figure of eight.
b Place the two pieces in left hand, without overlapping, and with the two right sides facing you.
c Pick up strand between 1st and 2nd sts on top piece. Pull yarn.
d Repeat with lower piece.
Repeat **c** and **d** (**Fig 6**).

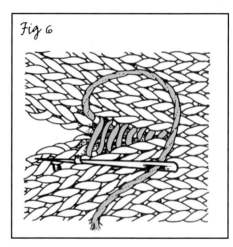

Fig 6

Style secrets
Ladder stitch is also called mattress stitch, invisible seam, weaving and vertical grafting. It creates a neat seam when joining pieces edge to edge.

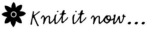

There is no need to baste the seam, but both sides must have the same number of rows unless you are gathering one of the sides, or they are in different patterns, or a side selvedge is being sewn to a cast-on or bound-off edge. In these cases, pick two strands instead of one from the appropriate side at regular intervals. Pinning may be advisable (see **Fig 6**, page 128).

The nature of the strand being picked up depends on the pattern. In reverse stockinette stitch and in garter stitch it is a 'bump'. Reverse stockinette stitch should alternate one lower strand with one upper strand (**Fig 7**). So should garter stitch, but this time closer to the edge to make the seam flat (**Fig 8**). With other patterns, proceed in the way that gives the least noticeable result.

Bound-off edges can be sewn in the same way, taking one stitch (half if the stitch is large) instead of one strand. If the yarn is not pulled tight, a row of knit stitches appears – this is fake grafting (**Fig 9**).

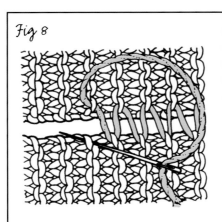

Fig 8

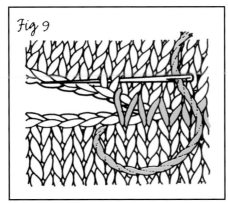

Fig 9

Variations

This variation is useful for carefully designed, well-integrated seams (perhaps for a border join); it makes a half-flat seam. One side (the border's) needs a garter or slipped garter selvedge; the other side needs a chain selvedge. Alternate one garter-selvedge 'bump' with the strands attaching one of the chains (**Fig 10**). This leaves a very near chain on the wrong side.

Another variation, leaving a double chain, uses a chain selvedge on both sides.

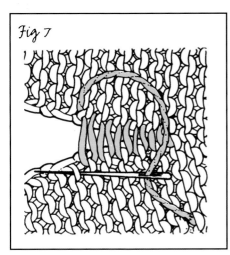

Fig 7

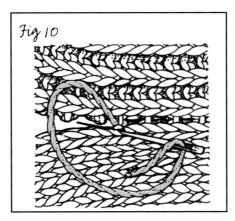

Fig 10

Backstitch

This is a strong seam that is worked from the wrong side. One selvedge stitch is taken in from each side. The selvedge that helps best to keep a straight line and to match the two sides (provided they have the same number of rows), is chain selvedge. This leaves a very neat pair of chains on the wrong side, but shows more on the right side when the fabric is pulled apart. Bound-off edges and no-selvedge selvedges can equally well be used.

✾ *Knit it now...*

a Make a figure of eight.
b Place the two pieces together in left hand, right sides against each other.
c Insert needle up between 1st and 2nd row. Pull yarn.
d Insert needle DOWN between 1st row and cast-on, then up between 2nd and 3rd row. Pull yarn.

Repeat **d**, always going DOWN where you first went up, and up one row further to the left (**Fig 11**).

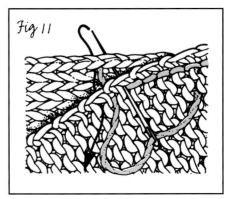

Fig 11

If using chain selvedges, insert the needle between the main fabric and the two strands of each chain.

Except with chain selvedges, baste before starting to sew. Blocking will probably be necessary.

Free-loop backstitch

This is used mainly for attaching separately knitted borders, or hems, from the right side. The border or hem is either started with a provisional cast-on, or finished with two additional rows, in contrast slippery yarn.

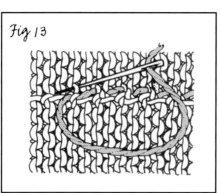

Fig 12

✿ Knit it now...

a Block the edge, so that the row to be sewn 'sets'.

b Pin or baste in position.

c Unravel slippery yarn, st by st and work a backstitch on the newly freed loops (**Fig 12**).

If you prefer, work the backstitch without unpicking the slippery yarn. In this case there is no need to block, but be careful not to catch the contrast yarn – you could have trouble when unravelling it later.

Consider omitting the extra rows and working the stitches straight off the needles.

Style secrets
Free-loop backstitch is a professional-looking way of joining ribbed neckbands.

Slip stitch

This is good for pocket linings, for neatening cut and sew edges, and for joining two pieces when one slides underneath the other – perhaps because the top one is making a flap, or has decorative selvedge or edging that covers the seam.

Work with the two wrong sides facing you.

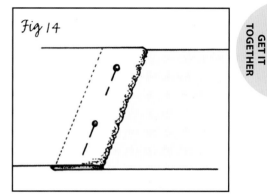

Fig 13

✿ Knit it now...

a Baste or pin the edge to be sewn onto the main fabric.

b Catch one or two strands from main fabric, then a couple of strands from the edge (**Fig 13**). Do not pull yarn too tight.

Flat-felled seam

This makes good use of slip stitch for reversible projects, or can be used to make a decorative thick line. The two sides should have selvedges appropriate to free edges, and all darning should be restricted to the seam overlap. If the project is reversible, avoid darning at mid-rows.

You will lose the width of the overlap, counted only once, from the overall fabric width.

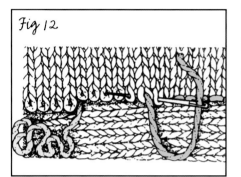

Fig 14

✿ Knit it now...

a Place one edge on top of the other. Pin or baste (**Fig 14**).

b Sew one of the edges with a slip stitch, taking care that the sts remain hidden. Instead of catching a couple of strands right at the edge, catch them from under the edge or edging. One strand may be enough.

c Repeat with the other edge, working from the other side.

Free-loop slip stitch

Mainly used for horizontal hems. Work a slip stitch, catching one strand from main fabric and one stitch from needle (**Fig 15**).

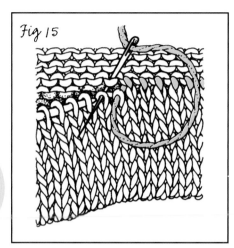

Fig 15

Edge to edge

This is the fateful 'flat seam' that has disfigured so much knitting. There are two versions, neither of which takes in any fabric. The first is like a ladder stitch worked at the very edge, from the wrong or the right side. The second places the two pieces together as for backstitch, then merely takes the yarn from one side to the other, without ever going back (**Fig 16**).

The only place for this seam is in carefully designed, fully integrated situations, for example:

• the ladder-stitch version joining two picot selvedges;
• the same version joining two contrast patterns (one perhaps a border), when both sides have garter or slipped garter selvedges. Try samples.

There should be no darning right at the edges.

Overcasting

This is another edge-to-edge seam that is particularly useful in fine lace knitting. It is generally worked from the wrong side, with the two right sides against each other, as for backstitch.

• The needle is always inserted up, from back of work, and moves one row at a time. Another version works from the right side with the two pieces side by side (**Fig 17**). The second version, using thick contrast yarn, can be used for decorative seams. The yarn must be thick enough to hide the edges, unless these have been worked neatly like free edges.

Fishbone stitch

Similar uses to the second version of overcasting.

• The needle is inserted up on both top and lower edges (**Fig 18**).

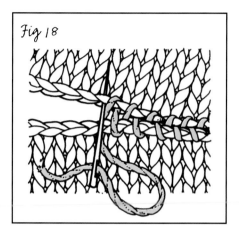

Fig 18

Knitted stitch

An imitation line of knit stitches, based on Swiss embroidery (**Fig 19**). Slightly raised. Could be worked in contrast for a decorative effect.

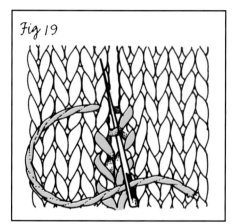

Fig 19

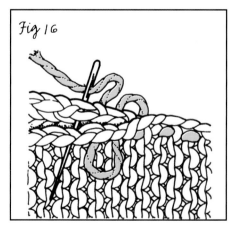

Fig 16

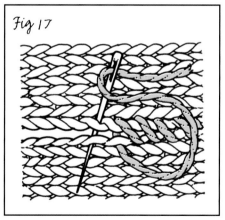

Fig 17

Alternate free loop

Decorative and simple, but only of use with two open rows.

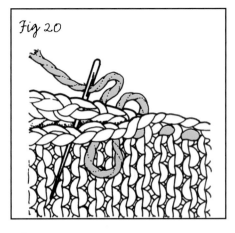

Fig 20

✿ Knit it now...

a Place one piece above the other, needles touching and both pointing towards the right. Preferably have one strand hanging from the right and the other from the left.

b Thread right strand through all the sts, alternating one from each needle, and removing the needles as you work.

c Repeat with the left strand in the opposite direction (**Fig 20**), or with the first strand starting on 2nd st.

Style secrets
Machine stitching is not recommended for the best-looking joins. It has to be done very carefully, basting very close to the edges and making sure that no loops are caught or distorted and that the edge does not ripple. A stretch stitch is best, but practise beforehand because it may take you a while to control.

Knitting on

This is a very strong and decorative join, with a great number of variations. One piece is knitted first, and the second joined to it on alternate rows (**Fig 21**).

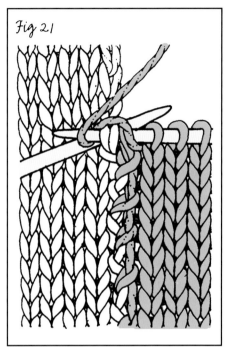

Fig 21

✿ Knit it now...

a Work 1st piece with a chain selvedge. Other selvedges could be used, but this is the neatest and most convenient.

b Work 1st row of 2nd piece to last st.

c Work together last st with the two strands of the chain selvedge. You can choose between k or p, taking first the st or first the chain.

d Work 2nd row in usual way. Repeat **b** to **d**.

You can also work the selvedge by itself, and knit or purl together the first 2 sts of the 2nd row (or, indeed, the 2 sts before the selvedge on the 1st row). And you can also knit on to the centre of work, in which case the selvedge is, obviously, immaterial.

Getting edgy

Edgings are the finishes given to a cast-on, bound-off, or selvedge edge. They can play a very powerful decorative role, or a very understated one. You could go for an elegant embroidered edge to trim a neckline, or simply add some fringing to add a fun touch to a colourful scarf. Edgings also have a functional purpose – to control the edge, so that it does not stretch or fray. Try to decide on the edgings before you start to knit, so that you can allow for any special selvedges.

Knitted edgings

Work roughly the length that you expect to need, but do not bind off or cut any strands. Pin the piece, starting at the cast-on end. Adjust the length once the edging has been joined, and its tightness checked.

Separate knitted borders

• Work a narrow band in any flat pattern, and sew to the edge of the main fabric. **Fig 10** on page 132 shows one possible seam.

If the band is to be buttoned up (a band going up one side of a jacket front and down the other, for instance), start with the buttonhole end; otherwise, the buttonhole arrangement could be spoiled when adjusting the length.

Classy clickers... *know that edgings must be worked, or joined, only slightly tight, or the edging will pull. Block the work, pinning the edging carefully so that it reaches the full length of the edge. After blocking, the piece should feel firm, but not pull.*

Classy clickers... *know that edgings that make a closed circuit around a project should disguise the start-and-end point. This may require careful spacing of repeats, grafting, or ladder-stitch seams. Avoid overlapping.*

Bias bands

These adapt well to curves and are also good for cut and sew.

• Strips of flat, bias knitting can be attached directly to the edge. Curly fabrics, such as stockinette stitch, should be folded over the edge and sewn separately on both sides (**Fig 1**). The wrong side is sewn with a slip stitch. The right side, which is normally joined first, can be sewn similarly if the selvedge is good enough to show. Otherwise, use a ladder stitch, turning the selvedge in. Block flat if the work looks too bulky.

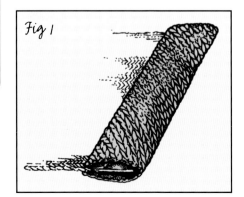

Fig 1

Cords

• Attach a knitted cord to the fabric edge with a hidden slip stitch.

Bound-off edgings

• Pick up stitches all around the edge (with a circular needle or several double-pointed needles, if necessary), and work a decorative bind-off.

Classy clickers... *turn their corners carefully. The outside of a curve is longer than the inside. The outside of an angle must be sharp and not pull, so the edging must be shaped to fit the corner.*

Fringe

Choosing a cast-on and choosing a bind-off give methods that make it easier to add fringes. **Fig 2**.

Fig 2

❃ *Knit it now...*

a Wrap yarn around a book or picture frame and cut at one end. This should give you a pile of strands somewhat longer than twice the fringe depth (knotting has a shortening effect).

b Take a few strands, and fold in two. How many depends on how thick you want the fringe and how close together the knots are.

c Insert a crochet hook up, and draw the strands through the fabric, by the fold line. The fabric should be right side up.

d Pass the ends of the strands through the loop, again with the hook, and fasten.

e When all the knots are done, tidy them carefully to make them look alike, and trim the ends straight.

Style secrets
The knots on a fringe should be evenly and thoughtfully spaced. Too wide apart will look straggly; too close will make the edge wave.

Embroidered edgings

Apart from the rather uninspiring basic blanket stitch (a buttonhole stitch with wide gaps), there are many ways of finishing an edge with embroidery. Two good edging stitches are Antwerp stitch (**Fig 3**) and Armenian stitch (**Fig 4**). A bead edging (**Fig 5**) is another possibility. Take great care with the spacing. Work, for instance, into every edge stitch of every second row, or into every stitch along the cast-on row.

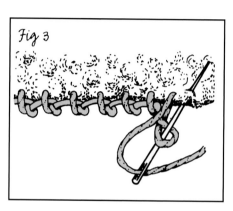

Fig 3

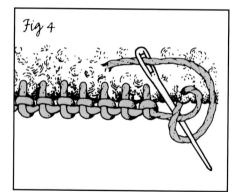

Fig 4

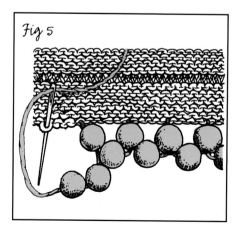

Fig 5

Style secrets
Knitting can be padded, wired, brushed, felted and even painted – have fun with it!

Style secrets
Embroider your edging in contrast yarn, unless you want to give just a hint of texture to a very delicate project.

Keeping it together

Often left as afterthoughts, fastenings can make or break a project. Think of them in the early stages – finding the perfect buttons for a garment could take you even longer than the actual knitting. Choose your buttons before knitting the buttonholes, so that these can be made to the exact size. Or make your own buttons using a button covering kit – cover with fabric to match your yarn.

Sewing buttons

Sew buttons with a shank using matching thread, or a shade darker. Make a thread-shank for buttons with holes (**Figs 1a–c**), otherwise they will pull the fabric or even come undone:

a Insert a cable needle or thin pen, between button and sewing yarn. The extra length must match the thickness of the buttonhole.

b Sew the button in the usual way.

c Remove the needle or pen, pull the button up and wind yarn around shank to strengthen it.

Style secrets
When buying buttons:
• A colour contrast may be better than a half-match.
• Try to emphasize the character of the yarn – shiny yarns should have shiny buttons.
• Buy buttons with shanks, or buttons with holes large enough for a needle, threaded with the same yarn used for knitting, to go through.
• Cheap plastic buttons make even pure silk look inferior. Hand-carved wooden buttons could make an inexpensive acrylic yarn look out of this world.

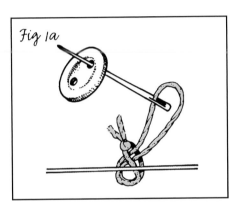

Fig 1a

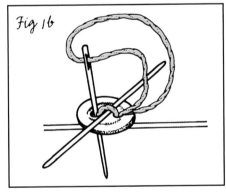

Fig 1b

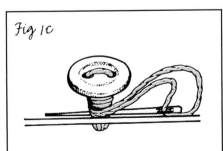

Fig 1c

Zips

Try to avoid zips. Their stiffness does not mix well with the elasticity of hand knitting. They remain at a constant length, whilst the knitting may stretch or shrink. A good colour match may be impossible. (If necessary, go for a darker colour.) The wrong side never looks very neat, unless the zip is concealed inside a double layer (**Fig 2**). This can be worked from picked-up stitches, or in tubular knitting – bind off the two layers separately.

Finding the exact length may also be a problem. Buy the zip whilst you are knitting, so that you can add or omit a few rows if necessary. Don't bind off until the zip has been fixed in position.

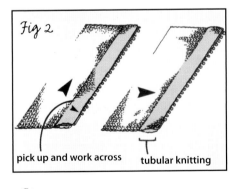

Fig 2

pick up and work across   tubular knitting

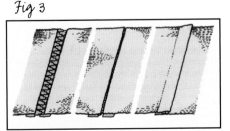

Fig 3

If you do want a zip, consider three types (**Fig 3**):

• Visible zips. The fabric just reaches the inside of the teeth. There should be a flat border or a free-edge selvedge at either side of the zip.

• Concealed zips. Same borders or selvedges, but the fabric is sewn so that the two edges meet once the zip is fastened; in other words, the fabric reaches the outside of the teeth.

• Concealed zips with flap. One side is sewn as for visible zips, but the other covers the zip and goes beyond it. If the flap runs in a central position, the zip needs to be sewn off-centre.

To fit a zip (**Fig 4**):

Fig 4

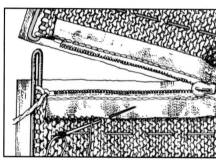

❀ *Knit it now...*

a Baste a strip of fine, stable cloth to each of the two edges, on the right side. The edges must be totally flat, and have identical lengths. The cloth will prevent stretching whilst sewing the zip, and consequent buckling.

b Baste the fastened, pre-shrunk zip to the wrong side, first one edge and then the other.

c Open the zip and backstitch next to the teeth with two strands of sewing thread. This must not show on the right side.

d Slip stitch the edge of the tape.

Drawstrings

Make a simple drawstring by running a cord or ribbon through a line of eyelets (see **Fig 48**, page 65). Space the eyelets evenly along a row – close together for shallow folds; far apart for deep folds.

There should be an even number of them, so that the cord starts and ends on the right side.

To avoid bulk, place the eyelets within a gathering strip of fabric. Decrease right across the fabric a couple of rows before the eyelets; increase in a similar, or different, sequence a couple of rows after the eyelets (**Fig 5**).

Fig 5

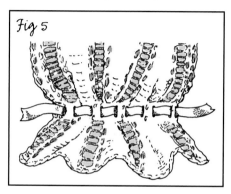

Another possibility is to make a hem or casing and thread a cord or ribbon through it. Try a tubular hem worked on the same number of stitches as the rest of the fabric.

Elastic on surface

A good, non-bulky way of attaching wide elastics, ideal for waistbands (**Fig 6**):

Fig 6

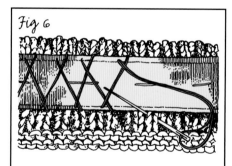

❀ *Knit it now...*

a Cut pre-shrunk elastic to required length plus about 1in (2.5cm). Check for comfort before cutting.

b For a closed elastic, overlap the extra length, overcast top and bottom edges, and slip stitch the ends (**Fig 7**). For an open elastic, fold under half the extra length at each end, and slip stitch in position.

Fig 7

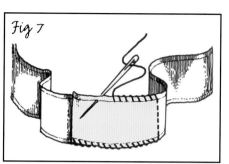

c Pin both fabric and elastic, first at midpoint, then at quarter points. Pin elastic to fabric at these points exactly, then pin at intermediate points, always slightly away from fabric edge.

d Baste.

e Herringbone stitch as shown with two strands of matching thread, catching the edges of the elastic. Avoid splitting the rubbery threads.

Keep the elastic stretched whilst basting and sewing. Catching the edges of the elastic with herringbone stitch gives an even distribution of gathers.

Elastic in casing

For heavy gathers, or when the wrong side needs to be as tidy as the right side. Draw the elastic through a hem or casing using a bodkin or safety pin.

• For an open elastic, fold under about 1cm (½in) at each end and anchor to fabric. Slip stitch the two fabric layers to close the casing. For a closed elastic, overlap the ends (as in **Fig 7**) after threading.

Knitting-in elastic

This is a very fine elastic made of the same elastane fibre used in swimming costumes and bras. It has incredible stretch and either comes in its natural state (see-through and rather shiny), or covered with a coloured thread. This is great for adding elasticity to ribbings.

• Work it together with the knitting yarn, just as if you were using two balls at the same time.

Fancy finishes

Some finishing touches have a very practical element. Sewn-in linings, for example, can be used to reinforce a knitted waistband or to add structure to a knitted bag, which otherwise would be likely to sag with the weight of whatever you put in it. Facings can be used to reinforce buttonbands or the brims of knitted hats. Other finishing touches are just for fun. Experiment with cord finishes to belts or hats, add tassels to fringe a comfortable knitted cushion, or add pompoms for a fun addition to a child's winter hat.

Lining

Lining is designed to neaten the wrong side and to help knitting keep its shape better. In the process, it makes it lose its elasticity, snugness and comfort. Certain skirts can take a loose lining, attached only at the waist, and there are probably other exceptions. But, in general, linings are best avoided for garments. If you work at the right gauge, without never-ending jacquard floats, and if you work heavy items such as coats in flat patterns (allowing for a certain amount of sagging), you will not need to line your hand-knitted garment. Linings can, however, be useful for giving structure and strength to knitted bags.

Binding

This may be used in cut and sew to hide untidy edges. It is also recommended to keep shoulder seams, back of necklines, and other lines of stress under control. In most cases, if the gauge is right there is absolutely no need for it, but there may be the odd exception.

• To tidy edges, slip stitch the two edges of a pre-shrunk binding tape, or bias, so that the edge is fully covered (**Fig 1**, page 136). To strengthen seams, use the same method, or backstitch the centre line of a narrow tape over the seam (or over the stress line).

Facings

Another addition best avoided, unless using cut and sew. Mainly used to reinforce buttonhole and button bands, so that they do not stretch. Use soft pre-shrunk, grosgrain ribbon – the one with ridges that comes in several widths and many colours (**Fig 1**):

✿ Knit it now...

a Tack the ribbon on the wrong side, working on a hard, flat surface. It must be the exact length of the edge, when flat.

b With matching thread, slip stitch first one side, then the other.

c Cut and stitch buttonholes, if any.

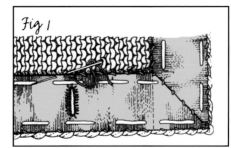

Fig 1

Cords

Cords can become powerful decorative elements – perhaps the only decorative element of a plain project – and great fun. Belts, edging cast-ons, fastenings, edgings (with or without loop buttonholes), appliqué, loops for hanging – these are just a few possible applications. Allow plenty of yarn – cords often take up tremendous amounts.

Cords often stretch if subjected to tension, so they should be stretched while blocking:

• Keeping the cord dead straight, pin the two ends and spray well; allow to dry.

Style secrets
Tubular cords can be stuffed with petersham, grosgrain ribbon or piping cord.

Knitted cords

Unless working purely decorative cords that will not undergo any stretch, work tightly.

Flat-pattern cords

Wide, flat cords. Patterns that look alike on both sides are the most successful. Try matching the cord to a flat-pattern border. Two methods:

• Cast on just a few stitches (could be as few as 3), and work on a flat pattern for required length. **Fig 2** shows a 5-stitch seed stitch cord.

• Cast on as many stitches as required to obtain length, work a few rows in a flat pattern and bind off. Length is not so easy to adjust as in the first method.

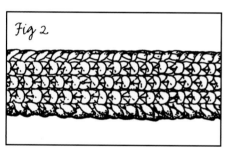

Fig 2

Roll cords

• Work as before but in a very curly pattern. Pull the ends to straighten, and run the fingers along to make a smooth roll. Slip stitch along the edge if desired. Stockinette stitch (see border illustrated in **Fig 1**, page 67) is an obvious pattern choice. **Fig 3** shows a more unusual cord in a basketweave pattern made up entirely of cross stitches. Because of the curl, at least about three times the required width has to be knitted.

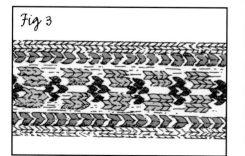

Fig 3

Cast-on bind-off cords

• Simply cast on the number of stitches required to obtain length, and bind off on the following row. There are innumerable variations – just think of combining all the casting on, and binding off, methods explained in this book.

Tubular cords

Wider, flat cords are made by working a long strip of tubular knitting. Alternatively, you could work the cord in double-sided jacquard. The slip cord is a piece of circular knitting worked on, say, 3 to 6 stitches, with double-pointed needles. It is also called idiot-cord or I-cord (**Fig 4**):

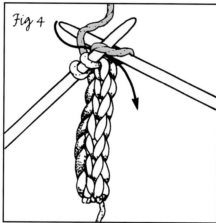

Fig 4

✿ *Knit it now...*

a Cast on and k 1 row.
b Without turning the work, push the sts to the other end of the needle.
c K, pulling the yarn tight when working 1st st.
Repeat **b** and **c**. To end, work a double or multiple decrease.

Style secrets

Experiment by making cords with colours and textures. Try mixing several slightly different shades of the same colour, in three or four different textures.

Style secrets

Another way of making these cords is with bobbin (or French) knitting. If you can find a knitting mill, you can make yards and yards in next to no time, although you will be restricted to four stitches and medium-thick yarn.

Twisted cord

Everybody's idea of a cord (**Fig 5**).

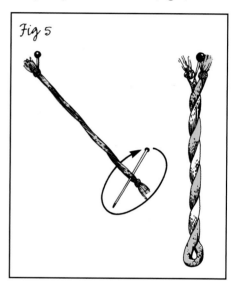

Fig 5

✿ *Knit it now...*

a Cut several strands of yarn, three times the desired length of cord.
b Knot the two ends, keeping the strands at an even tension.
c Hook or pin one end and insert a knitting needle through the other.
d Turn needle over and over, until the strands are well twisted.
e Fold in half, keeping the cord taut to avoid tangling.
f Knot the two ends together, let the cord twist, and even out the turns.

Plaited cords

Any cord, indeed any yarn or strip of knitting, can be plaited.

For an ordinary, three-strand plait (**Fig 6**):

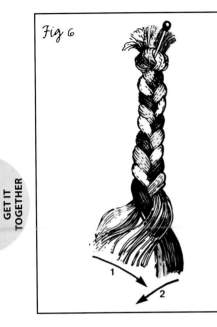

Fig 6

❀ Knit it now...

a Cut 3 strands, or bunches of strands, 1½ times desired length of cord.

b Knot them at one end, and hook or pin this end.

c Take, alternately, right strand over centre strand, then left strand over centre strand, until strands run out.

d Knot the strand ends.

More strands can be plaited in a number of ways. **Fig 7** shows an easy way with four strands.

Fig 7

Style secrets

Knitting makes a good base for embroidery because the stitches give you a grid – wonderful for counted-thread techniques.

Tassels

Easy to make (**Fig 8**).

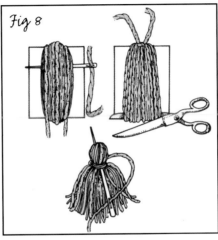

Fig 8

❀ Knit it now...

a Wrap yarn loosely around a book or piece of cardboard.

b Thread a strand (or more) of yarn through the top and tie firmly, with a square knot, leaving a long end for later winding and sewing.

c Cut the strands at the bottom.

d Hide the knot, and the short end left from tying it, under the folded strands.

e Wind the long strand a few times, to secure the folded end, then thread it through, so that it comes out at the top.

f Trim ends.

You could also attach the tassel directly to a cord by tying the tassel and the end of a cord together at **b**. Two or more strands would be best. The long strand should later be secured back and forth across the tied area, and trimmed.

Drawstring balls

They can be made in any pattern and any size. Stuffed, they make good buttons.

The instructions are for fourteen stitches and stockinette stitch (**Fig 9**). If you change the number of stitches, or the pattern, alter the rows accordingly.

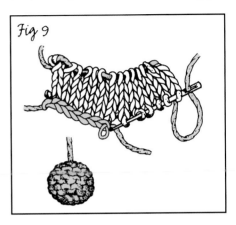

Fig 9

❀ Knit it now...

a Provisional cast-on 14 sts, leaving a 6–8in (15–20cm) tail. If looping cast-on, use 2 strands of the main yarn.

b Work 5 rows in st st.

c Provisional bind-off.

d Unpick contrast cast-on yarn, and thread the yarn tail through the free loops. (Omit if looping cast-on.)

e Thread yarn again through both cast-on and bound-off loops, in the same direction as before, closing the circle.

f Pull threads tight, stuff if desired, and seam the edges.

Follow me!

Many talented knitters design their own fabulous garments, but you will probably start off by following patterns. To the uninitiated, knitting patterns can seem quite mysterious. We'll explain all here.

Stitch pattern instructions

Patterns appear in two forms: row by row or charts and diagrams. Row-by-row instructions describe how to work every stitch of every row. Good instructions state whether the first row is a right-side or a wrong-side row. If nothing is said, it is likely to be a right-side row, but check it. In instructions for circular knitting, all rounds are right-side ones unless otherwise specified (wrong-side rounds are very rare, but not impossible).

Instructions assume that you have a needle full of stitches – if you are starting a fresh piece of work, cast them on. In any case, make sure that your total number of stitches is compatible with the pattern (see **Pattern repeats** and **Number of stitches**, below).

Some patterns include a selvedge stitch. If you do not want it, omit the first and last stitches of each row if you would like a different selvedge, and change the first and last stitches accordingly. Depending on the selvedge, more stitches may be required; patterns with selvedges often start and end each row with k1. If you want a selvedge and this is not included, add (an) extra stitch(es) at each end.

Lengthy instructions are not necessarily difficult. A simple k4, p4 arrangement travelling one stitch to right or left on alternate rows could be presented as an overwhelming 16-row pattern. From a chart, its simplicity would be obvious.

Pattern repeats

When the same action is repeated on every stitch of a row, the pattern can be worked on any number of stitches. Stockinette stitch is a good example. When the action keeps changing in a regular way, groups of stitches to be repeated will either appear in brackets () or have an asterisk (*) at the start, and possibly another one at the end.

Usually, the group of stitches forming a complete pattern repeat is pinpointed by asterisks. Smaller groups of stitches, within this large group, may appear in brackets if a working sequence is to be repeated two or three times. Example:

Row 1 (wrong side): p1; *ssk, (yo, slip 1) twice, k2 tog, p1*; repeat from * to * to last 2 sts; k2.

Classy clickers...
- **Place** *a fabric maker on right side, or make a note of whether the cast-on tail is on the right or the left edge when working a right-side row.*
- **Transcribe** *(or chart) instructions when they are difficult to read or use unfamiliar abbreviations.*
- **In** *lengthy instructions, use fabric markers every time you reach the last row.*
- **Use** *a row counter.*
- **Use** *a line finder.*
- **Develop** *a rhythm to sing – knit 1, slip 1, purl 2, would make a 1-2-3 beat.*

Number of stitches

Instructions for repeat patterns only work if the total number of stitches is a multiple of a certain figure, usually the number of stitches between asterisks. In flat knitting, a few extra stitches may need to be added to this figure to produce convenient edges. The example would need a stitch total multiple of 7 sts plus 3 sts (10, 17, 24, 31, 38, 45 … sts). Note that decreases count as one stitch only, and that overs and slip stitches count as worked stitches; in other words, what matters is the number of resulting loops, regardless of how they are achieved.

With the exception of some fairly rare patterns that change stitch total from row to row, the number of stitches between asterisks and the number of odd stitches will remain constant. Distribution, however, may vary: although the total of odd stitches does not change, the way they are split at either side of the asterisks can change. Sometimes, a whole pattern repeat is added to this number:

Row 4: k1, p4; *k2, p4, kl*; repeat from * to * to last 5sts; k2, p3.

The resulting multiple of 7 plus 10 sts, can obviously be taken as a multiple of 7 plus 3 sts. Knowing these rules, it is often possible to work out the pattern repeat figures when these are not given, as can happen in garment instructions. You can then use flat-knitting instructions for circular knitting.

Garment instructions

Commonly known as patterns, but not to be confused with stitch patterns, these are scaled, dimensioned garment diagrams of each piece to be knitted. Without diagrams it is difficult to measure and block accurately. Knitters should be wary of using the 'sleeve seam' measurement as the only indication of sleeve length. This varies so much from style to style that it becomes irrelevant (**Figs 1–3**). A pattern must indicate length at centre sleeve and width of back at shoulder level.

Fig 1

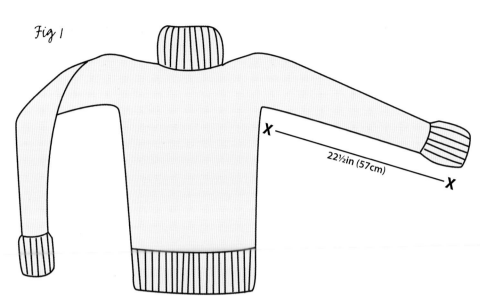

22½in (57cm)

Fig 2

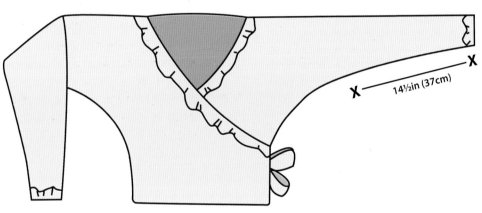

14½in (37cm)

Fig 3

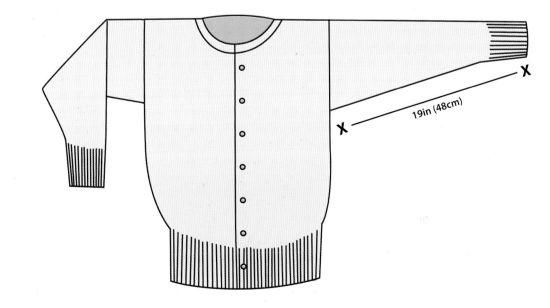

19in (48cm)

Format

Patterns describe how to knit a garment, piece by piece, and how to put it together. A photo, materials required, overall measurements, gauge, list of abbreviations, stitch pattern instructions plus special features are also included.

Double and treble asterisks (**, ***) may be used to pinpoint sections to be repeated, if single asterisks are being used for the stitch pattern. They could be used, say, for a sequence of raglan shapings on the back, when this is to be repeated on the sleeves.

Square brackets [] may be used in multi-size patterns when several options are given: cast on 85[91;97;105] sts.

Writing and checking patterns is tremendously complex. Despite all efforts, mistakes do sometimes escape attention. If you think you have found one, tell your retailer or inform the publisher.

Pitfalls

Beware of:

• Recommendations to change needles to obtain different sizes (see **Gauge**, below).

• Patterns that do not indicate 'actual width'. You should know exactly what to expect. Your idea of 'to fit size x' may not be the same as the designer's.

• One-size patterns 'to fit the average figure', either meaning 'to fit a designer's dream' or 'the design is awkward to adapt to other sizes, but fits nicely into this one – whatever this one happens to be'.

• 'Sleeve seam' measurements. Underarm seam length is inaccurate for fitting purposes. Length from shoulder to wrist (around slightly bent elbow) is best.

• 'Knit it tonight, wear it tomorrow' (and throw away the day after!) patterns based on an extremely loose gauge, without any tightening stitches or areas. Sweaters soon grow into tents.

Checklist

• Check your size. Do not rely on your dress size. Measure a similar garment.

• Use the recommended yarn. If that is impossible to find, use a substitution (see page 29).

• Note gauge warnings (see below).

• Insist on diagrams.

• Choose exciting designs that are not too difficult for your present abilities.

• Read the instructions carefully before you start, to get the general idea.

• As work progresses, read each step again with even greater care.

• Check whether selvedges for seams or free edges have been allowed for. If necessary, add them or alter them.

• Check whether the stitch pattern and the ribbings, if any, will flow continuously across seams, once the selvedges have been taken in (see **Planning for seams**, page 130). Alter the stitch total if not satisfied.

• Check whether the correct selvedge has been given to edges from which stitches are to be picked up.

• Check the look of the ribbings in the photograph. If they look too loose, cast on fewer stitches and adjust stitch total before starting main pattern, or work with finer needles. The section of ribbing directly under a cable always needs fewer stitches than the cable – otherwise it buckles.

• Measure work accurately and frequently.

• When working symmetrical pieces, remember to pair the increases and decreases. Bind off right-edge shapings from the right side, and left-edge shapings from the wrong side. Instructions for symmetrical pieces may be given as 'work as for first side, reversing all shapings', 'work to match' or 'work to correspond'. You could work the two pieces at the same time.

• Use needle and/or fabric markers as required.

• Highlight relevant information (such as the stitches for your own size) with a marker pen.

• Use a line finder.

Gauge

Instructions only give a needle size as guidance for you to work your first sample.

Your only guarantee that results will not be too small or too large, but just right, is to obtain the stated, compulsory gauge.

Remember that gauge samples must be measured away from the edges. If you need 28 sts in 4in (10cm), work a sample not smaller than 32 sts in the correct stitch pattern and with the yarn and colour you intend to use (see **Thickness**, page 29).

A tight gauge causes garments to matt and to stiffen. A loose gauge makes them grow and lose their shape. This is why you should NEVER change needle sizes to obtain larger or smaller garments.

Classy clickers... know that if you can't manage both the stated number of stitches and rows when knitting a gauge sample, you should concentrate on obtaining the correct number of stitches. Avoid patterns with complex shapings, and patterns where length is dictated by rows rather than by a measurement.

Charts and diagrams

Charts and diagrams have a number of advantages over row-by-row instructions:

- you can see at a glance what is to be done;
- you learn to think and judge;
- at the end of the day, your understanding is increased, and you feel more encouraged to continue knitting.

Classy clickers... *know that whole garment pieces can be shown in chart form, often combined with colour or stitch pattern charts. The charts clearly show all the shapings and exact position of pockets, buttonholes, etc.*

Be chart smart

- Charts are representations on graph paper of a piece of knitted fabric. Ideally, only ratio graph paper should be used, reflecting true stitch shape. When squared paper is used, allowance must be made for the knitted results probably being squatter than the chart.

- Each square or rectangle represents a stitch, and each horizontal line represents a row or round (in good charts these are numbered). Charts are usually read from the bottom up, normally starting at the lower right-hand corner. In flat knitting, right-side rows are read from right to left and wrong-side rows from left to right (**Fig 4**). In circular knitting, all rounds are read from right to left (**Fig 5**).

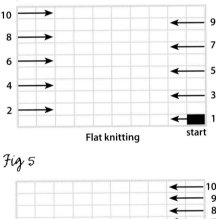

Fig 4

Flat knitting   start

Fig 5

Circular knitting   start

- Single motifs are usually shown in the centre of a chart. Repeat patterns are often shown from edge to edge. The repeat is highlighted by strong vertical lines – the chart equivalent to asterisks. In flat knitting only, there may be odd stitches at either side of the repeat. On right-side rows, work the stitches on the right edge once, then the repeat as many times as necessary, and finally the stitches on the left edge once. On wrong-side rows, do the same but in the opposite direction.

- Multi-size garment patterns may have more than one set of edge stitches (**Fig 6**). Read instructions carefully, and work the set intended for the size you are knitting. To save space, these patterns sometimes use the same chart for different purposes: one part of the garment is explained at the bottom, another at the top. In **Fig 6** the bottom instructions are for front and back, the top instructions are for the sleeves.

- Charts must allow empty squares for stitches to be increased, or for stitches that have been decreased. **Fig 7** shows such a chart for a round yoke. Paint the non-stitch squares in black if the chart has used another symbol. (Sometimes the missing stitches are put together at one edge, so as not to break the pattern – the chart then looks like a pyramid.)

- Reading a chart is not difficult, but requires concentration. A line finder is invaluable, even if you have to settle for an alternative. If using a proper one, place it just above the line you are knitting, so that you can see the area you have already worked. Mistakes will then be more easily spotted.

Fig 6

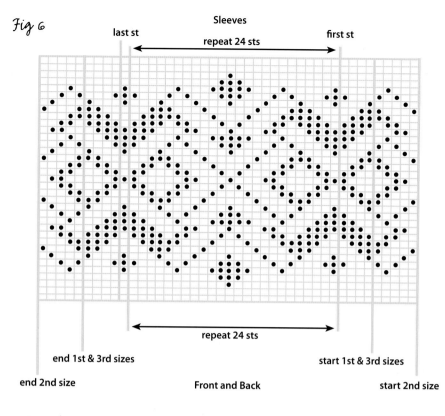

Sleeves

last st — repeat 24 sts — first st

repeat 24 sts

Front and Back

end 1st & 3rd sizes — start 1st & 3rd sizes

end 2nd size — start 2nd size

Garment diagrams

With garment diagrams (**Fig 8**), you have a perfectly clear idea of what each piece is going to look like, and a true guide for measuring and blocking. You can, if you want to, cut a full-size paper pattern against which to check work progress, or embark on alterations. The pieces used to make a knitted garment are very similar to those used in dressmaking.

GET IT TOGETHER

Fig 8

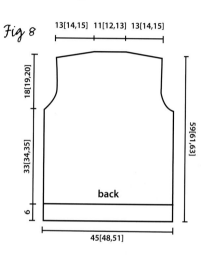

13[14,15] 11[12,13] 13[14,15]

18[19,20]

33[34,35]

59[61,63]

6

back

45[48,51]

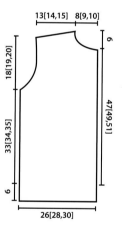

13[14,15] 8[9,10]

6

18[19,20]

33[34,35]

47[49,51]

6

26[28,30]

• To make small-square charts easier to read, get an enlarged photocopy, or transcribe onto large graph paper.

• Charts are very versatile. Damask, eyelet, two-strand, colour or bead knitting charts, and cross-stitch or other embroidery charts might be interchangeable. But with any adaptation, remember that each technique has its own rules. Not all charts will be good for everything.

• Most colour charts are intended for stockinette-stitch jacquard and show the right side of work. Bead knitting also uses this type of chart.

• Stitch pattern charts usually show the stitches from the right side, but occasionally charts for flat knitting show the wrong-side rows as they are worked. Damask and cable patterns translate extremely successfully into charts.

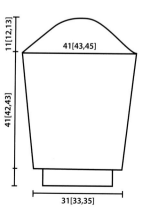

11[12,13]

41[43,45]

41[42,43]

31[33,35]

Fig 7

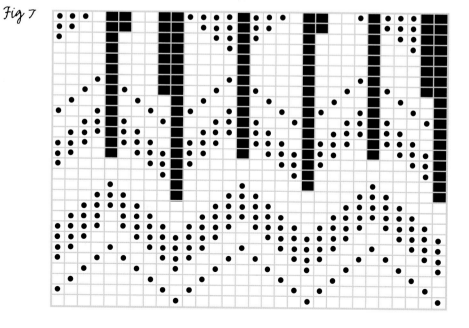

get it fixed!

If you find your work looks more like spaghetti than knitting, or the fetching little top you wanted ends up more like a kaftan, you might find yourself turning to this section. Don't worry; you certainly won't be alone. Everyone has the odd disaster, so don't think that you'll never be a fabulous knitter, and learn from your mistakes. If you can't turn an error into a 'design feature', then, whether you drop a single stitch, or knit a full-scale disaster, you'll find the solutions here.

Sort it out...

You may feel like chucking your needles out the window and swearing, but remember, errors and accidents happen to everyone. Even seasoned knitters drop their stitches, cross their cables the wrong way, and make gloves with two right thumbs. Keep a cool, clear head and you will almost certainly put things right.

GET IT FIXED

Dropped stitches

New knitters, slack knitters, and knitters not keeping a good grasp (see **Needle Know-how**, pages 18–21), tend to drop stitches. If you are working on your first project, or if your stitches drop like ripe apples in the wind, inspect every row before you start on the next.

If you spot the free loop a few rows later, rescuing it will make the fabric tighter. Highlight the area with fabric markers and correct it as well as you can when blocking.

> ***Classy clickers...***
> • ***Stop*** *free loop with right or left needle as soon as they spot it.*
> • ***Keep*** *safety pins at hand for catching dropped stitches immediately.*
> • ***Keep*** *stitches close together. Pulling them apart will cause more laddering.*
> • ***Relax.*** *Clutching the work may cause more stitches to drop.*

On row being worked

Unravel row back to free loop, if necessary.

• Put stitch back on left needle, making sure it is not twisted. If it is twisted, work it through the back. Or, insert right needle into it as if to knit-back (see **Fig 3**, page 48), take it off left needle and return to left needle in the correct position.

On row below

To correct a KNIT stitch:

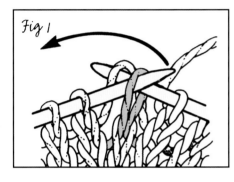

✿ Knit it now...

a Insert right needle into free loop and under strand above it, from the front. Notice that strand is behind st.
b Insert left needle into dropped st, from the back (**Fig 1**), and basic bind off the strand.
c Place new st on left needle.

> *Classy clickers...* if they drop several consecutive stitches, stop them all with one safety pin, then release them one by one and proceed as for single stitches.

To correct a PURL stitch:

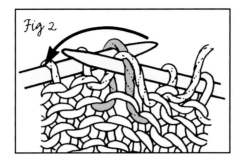

✿ Knit it now...

a Insert right needle into free loop and under strand above it, from the back. Notice that strand is in front of st.
b Insert left needle into dropped st, from the front (**Fig 2**), and basic bind off the strand.
c Place new st on left needle.

A few rows down

A ladder will have formed. Work up the rungs of the ladder in the correct order. Either follow the instructions just given for every row, or use a crochet hook finer than the knitting needles, and work as follows.

To correct a KNIT ladder:

✿ Knit it now...

a Insert hook into free loop, from the front.
b With hook pointing up, catch 1st strand of ladder, from below (**Fig 3**).
c Draw strand through loop.
Repeat **b** and **c**.

To correct a PURL ladder, turn work to obtain a KNIT ladder, or:

✿ Knit it now...

a Insert hook into free loop, from the back.
b With hook pointing down, catch 1st strand of ladder, from above (**Fig 4**).
c Draw strand through loop.
d The hook is now inserted into new st from the front. Remove it, and reinsert it from the back.
Repeat **b** to **d**.

On other fabrics, keep turning work to face always knit stitches, or alternate knit and purl actions as required. In complex fabrics, either unravel or try to find your way up the ladder keeping the pattern correct. Whether you succeed or not, your understanding of knitting will benefit no end. If forced to admit defeat, unravel.

> *Classy clickers...* if they discover a dropped stitch only after finishing, work the free loop up the ladder if it has run or secure it at back of work with matching thread.

Small errors

Extra stitches, split-yarn stitches, twisted stitches, and mistakes in pattern can all be corrected. If only one stitch is involved:

a Work to the st on the present row just above the error.

b Drop this st and ladder it down to the row below the error.

c Proceed as for dropped stitches a few rows down.

If you had a stitch too many, the new stitches will be larger than they should. Distribute the extra yarn on the adjoining stitches, either now or when blocking.

When several stitches are involved, you can drop them all, ladder them, put them on a safety pin or holder, and retrace the ladder up stitch by stitch. By clever use of safety pins and short, perhaps double-pointed, needle(s), plus a crochet hook, you can correct glaring mistakes this way.

GET IT FIXED

Classy clickers... as a safety measure, especially with silky, slippery yarns, thread a fine knitting needle or length of fine yarn through the first good row, before starting to unravel. No stitch will then drop beyond this row.

Major errors

When none of the previous methods work, or when you have actually missed one or more rows, there is only one possible remedy – unravelling, the most heartbreaking of all knitting techniques.

Unravelling a single row

Best done stitch by stitch. Keep the yarn in your usual hand. If this is the right hand, unravel from left to right. If it is the left hand, unravel from right to left. On knit:

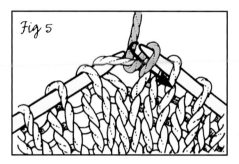

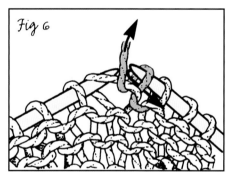

✿ *Knit it now...*

a Assuming st to be unravelled is on right needle, insert left needle into st below, from the front (**Fig 5**).

b Drop st off right needle.

c Pull yarn (**Fig 6**).
Repeat **a** to **c**.

On purl:
Proceed as for knit (**Fig 7**). The yarn is now in front, but the technique is otherwise unchanged.

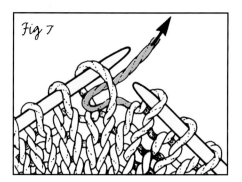

Unravelling several rows

The fast method is to take the work off the needles and pull the yarn. Keep the work gathered in the hand that is not pulling, to avoid laddering. Pull firmly, but with care; with hairy yarns or intricate stitch patterns you could create tight spots if you pulled too firmly.

Or, you could pull all the rows except the last one, and do this one slowly. Pull half a dozen stitches at a time, and thread the needle through them before pulling any more. A fine needle is easier to thread, but remember to change it back to the correct size after the first row.

When threading the needle, the stitches often seem easier to catch from the back, but this twists them. Catch them the easy way and work them through the back of the loop on the next row, or catch them through the front in the correct manner (**Figs 8** and **9**).

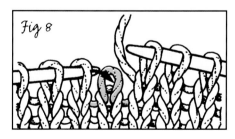

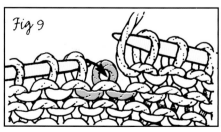

Recycling

Yarn need never be wasted. You may want to reuse yarn – perhaps because you are tired of seeing a brand new piece of knitting unworn!

Pull away

Unravelling needs some rather tedious preparation, but don't hurry or you could make the task much longer. Work in a quiet area, away from children and pets. Make a pile of yarn on the floor or inside a very large box. Left undisturbed, the yarn will not get tangled. Short lengths can be tied together, until you have roughly the equivalent of one of the original balls. Leave the last end clear of the pile. Make a skein, then continue pulling. Discard worn or very short lengths of yarn.

Unpick any seams, being careful not to snip the fabric. Loosen the stitches, one by one, with a blunt sewing needle. If you are not sure whether a loop belongs to the seam or to the fabric, pull it to see what other loops follow. Unpick any darning to free the yarn ends. Unfasten the last bound-off stitch. Gather fabric in one hand and, carefully, pull yarn with the other hand to the bitter end.

Classy clickers... don't pull hard at tight stitches (often caused by hairs getting tangled) – it makes them tighter. Tug gently to free them. Brushed and hairy yarns may be so tangled that unravelling becomes difficult.

Reconditioning

Because of blocking or washing, the unravelled yarn will be very crinkly. Recondition it in two stages: skeining and straightening.

Skeining

a Wind the yarn around a board, picture frame or chair back.
b Tie the two ends in an obvious knot.
c Tie the skein loosely with very strong yarn, tape or strips of fabric in three or four places (**Fig 1**). If the skeins are very thick, tie into a figure-of-eight loop so as to split the skein.

Fig 1

Classy clickers... know that unravelling from the cast-on end is impossible.

Straightening

Although wool and some other natural fibres can be steamed, washing is often preferable (check that the yarn is washable).

Fig 2

a Wash hanks as appropriate. Rinse well.
b Still soaking wet, hang them to dry away from direct heat and direct sun. Peg one of the ties, but not the yarn (**Fig 2**).
c Attach a small weight to the tie at the bottom of the hank for best results, especially if drying in the wind.

Put the dry yarn around the picture frame or chair back, and wind into loose balls.

Stitch and row tables

There is no great secret about calculating stitches and rows in order to knit exactly what you want, in the yarn you like, the stitch pattern you fancy and the tension that comes naturally to you. The basic procedure has been explained on page 15, but you might like to try one of the following tables. The first table is for those who work in inches, and the second for those who prefer centimetres.

GET IT FIXED

Imperial table (page 155)

Knit and measure a sample, to find out the number of stitches and rows in 4in – say, 19 sts and 24 rows.

Taking the stitches first, find the appropriate figure on the left-hand column of the table headed 'Gauge'. Place a ruler across the page, under that figure. In the 19 sts/4in example, you will see the figures 1, 3, 4, 5, 10... 114 and 171 immediately above the ruler.

Now look at the top line of figures giving measurements in inches, and find the width you require – say, 24in. Follow the column down until you reach the ruler, where it reads 114. This means that 114 stitches knitted at a gauge of 19 sts/4in will produce a piece of knitting 24in wide.

If you can't find the required width on the top line, break it down. For example, if your knitting has to be 30in wide, add up to 24in (114 sts) and 6in (29 sts). This will give you a total of 143 sts.

Rows are calculated in exactly the same way, placing the ruler under the corresponding figure on the Gauge column. In the 24 rows/4in example, the ruler highlights the figures 2, 3, 5, 6, 12... 144 and 216. For example, a project 50in long requires adding 36in (216 rows), 4in (24 rows) and l0in (60 rows) – which gives a total of 300 rows. A similar result is obtained by adding up twice 24in (2 x 144 rows) and 2in (12 rows), or five times l0in (5 x 60 rows).

Metric table (page 156)

Knit and measure a sample, to find out the number of stitches and rows in 10cm – say, 27 sts and 33 rows.

Taking the stitches first, find the appropriate figure on the left-hand column of the table headed 'Gauge'. Place a ruler across the page, under that figure. In the 27 sts/10cm example you will see the figures 3, 5, 8, 11, 14... 216 and 243 immediately above the ruler.

Now look at the top line of figures giving measurements in centimetres, and find the width you require – say, 50cm. Follow the column down until you reach the ruler, where it reads 135. This means that 135 stitches knitted at a gauge of 27 sts/10cm will produce a piece of knitting 50cm wide. If you can't find the required width on the top line, break it down. For example, if your knitting has to be 57cm wide, add up 50cm (135 sts) and 7cm (19 sts). This will give you a total of 154 sts.

Rows are calculated in exactly the same way, placing the ruler under the corresponding figure on the Gauge column. In the 33 rows/l0cm example, the ruler highlights the figures 3, 7, 10, 13, 17... 264 and 297. For example, a project 110cm long will require adding 90cm (297 rows) and 20cm (66 rows) – which gives a total of 363 rows. A similar result is obtained by adding up 30cm and 80cm, 40cm and 70cm, or 50cm and 60cm.

Number of stitches or rows in a given measurement, depending on tension of work (imperial)

Gauge (total number of stitches or rows in 4in)	¼in	½in	¾in	1in	2in	3in	4in	5in	6in	7in	8in	9in	10in	11in	12in	24in	36in
10	1	2	2	3	5	8	10	13	15	18	20	23	25	28	30	60	90
11	1	2	2	3	6	9	11	14	17	20	22	25	28	31	33	66	99
12	1	2	3	3	6	9	12	15	18	21	24	27	30	33	36	72	108
13	1	2	3	4	7	10	13	17	20	23	26	30	33	36	39	78	117
14	1	2	3	4	7	11	14	18	21	25	28	32	35	39	42	84	126
15	1	2	3	4	8	11	15	19	23	26	30	34	38	41	45	90	135
16	1	2	3	4	8	12	16	20	24	28	32	36	40	44	48	96	144
17	1	2	3	4	9	13	17	21	26	30	34	38	43	47	51	102	153
18	1	2	4	5	9	14	18	23	27	32	36	41	45	50	54	108	162
19	1	3	4	5	10	15	19	24	29	33	38	43	48	52	57	114	171
20	1	3	4	5	10	15	20	25	30	35	40	45	50	55	60	120	180
21	1	3	4	5	11	16	21	26	32	37	42	47	53	58	63	126	189
22	1	3	4	6	11	17	22	28	33	39	44	50	55	61	66	132	198
23	2	3	4	6	12	17	23	29	35	40	46	52	58	63	69	138	207
24	2	3	4	6	12	18	24	30	36	42	48	54	60	66	72	144	216
25	2	3	5	6	13	19	25	31	38	44	50	56	63	69	75	150	225
26	2	3	5	7	13	20	26	33	39	46	52	59	65	72	78	156	234
27	2	3	5	7	14	20	27	34	41	47	54	61	68	74	81	162	243
28	2	4	5	7	14	21	28	35	42	49	56	63	70	77	84	168	252
29	2	4	5	7	15	22	29	36	44	51	58	65	73	80	87	174	261
30	2	4	6	8	15	23	30	38	45	53	60	68	75	83	90	180	270
31	2	4	6	8	16	23	31	39	47	54	62	70	78	85	93	186	279
32	2	4	6	8	16	24	32	40	48	56	64	72	80	88	96	192	288
33	2	4	6	8	17	25	33	41	50	58	66	74	83	91	99	198	297
34	2	4	6	9	17	26	34	43	51	60	68	77	85	94	102	204	306
35	2	4	7	9	18	26	35	44	53	61	70	79	88	96	105	210	315
36	2	5	7	9	18	27	36	45	54	63	72	81	90	99	108	216	324
37	2	5	7	9	19	28	37	46	56	65	74	83	93	102	111	222	333
38	2	5	7	10	19	29	38	48	57	67	76	86	95	105	114	228	342
39	2	5	7	10	20	29	39	49	59	68	78	88	98	107	117	234	351
40	3	5	8	10	20	30	40	50	60	70	80	90	100	110	120	240	360
41	3	5	8	10	21	31	41	51	62	72	82	92	103	113	123	246	369
42	3	5	8	11	21	32	42	53	63	74	84	95	105	116	126	252	378
43	3	5	8	11	22	32	43	54	65	75	86	97	108	118	129	258	387
44	3	6	8	11	22	33	44	55	66	77	88	99	110	121	132	264	396
45	3	6	8	11	23	34	45	56	68	79	90	101	113	124	135	270	405
46	3	6	9	12	23	35	46	58	69	81	92	104	115	127	138	276	414
47	3	6	9	12	24	35	47	59	71	82	94	106	118	129	141	282	423
48	3	6	9	12	24	36	48	60	72	84	96	108	120	132	144	288	432
49	3	6	9	12	25	37	49	61	74	86	98	110	123	135	147	294	441
50	3	6	9	13	25	38	50	63	75	88	100	113	125	138	150	300	450
Tension	¼in	½in	¾in	1in	2in	3in	4in	5in	6in	7in	8in	9in	10in	11in	12in	24in	36in

Total number of stitches or rows

Number of stitches or rows in a given measurement, depending on tension of work (metric)

Gauge (total number of stitches or rows in 10cm)	1cm	2cm	3cm	4cm	5cm	6cm	7cm	8cm	9cm	10cm	20cm	30cm	40cm	50cm	60cm	70cm	80cm	90cm
10	1	2	3	4	5	6	7	8	9	10	20	30	40	50	60	70	80	90
11	1	3	4	5	6	7	8	9	10	11	22	33	44	55	66	77	88	99
12	2	3	4	5	6	8	9	10	11	12	24	36	48	60	72	84	96	108
13	2	3	4	6	7	8	9	11	12	13	26	39	52	65	78	91	104	117
14	2	3	5	6	7	9	10	12	13	14	28	42	56	70	84	98	112	126
15	2	3	5	6	8	9	11	12	14	15	30	45	60	75	90	105	120	135
16	2	3	5	7	8	10	11	13	15	16	32	48	64	80	96	112	128	144
17	2	4	5	7	9	10	12	14	16	17	34	51	68	85	102	119	136	153
18	2	4	6	7	9	11	13	15	16	18	36	54	72	90	108	126	144	162
19	2	4	6	8	10	12	14	15	17	19	38	57	76	95	114	133	152	171
20	2	4	6	8	10	12	14	16	18	20	40	60	80	100	120	140	160	180
21	2	4	6	9	11	13	15	17	19	21	42	63	84	105	126	147	168	189
22	2	5	7	9	11	13	16	18	20	22	44	66	88	110	132	154	176	198
23	2	5	7	9	12	14	16	19	21	23	46	69	92	115	138	161	184	207
24	3	5	7	10	12	15	17	19	22	24	48	72	96	120	144	168	192	216
25	3	5	8	10	13	15	18	20	23	25	50	75	100	125	150	175	200	225
26	3	5	8	10	13	16	18	21	23	26	52	78	104	130	156	182	208	234
27	3	5	8	11	14	16	19	22	24	27	54	81	108	135	162	189	216	243
28	3	6	8	11	14	17	20	22	25	28	56	84	112	140	168	196	224	252
29	3	6	9	12	15	17	20	23	26	29	58	87	116	145	174	203	232	261
30	3	6	9	12	15	18	21	24	27	30	60	90	120	150	180	210	240	270
31	3	6	9	12	16	19	22	25	28	31	62	93	124	155	186	217	248	279
32	3	6	10	13	16	19	22	26	29	32	64	96	128	160	192	224	256	288
33	3	7	10	13	17	20	23	26	30	33	66	99	132	165	198	231	264	297
34	3	7	10	14	17	20	24	27	30	34	68	102	136	170	204	238	272	306
35	4	7	11	14	18	21	25	28	32	35	70	105	140	175	210	245	280	315
36	4	7	11	14	18	22	25	29	32	36	72	108	144	180	216	252	288	324
37	4	7	11	15	19	22	26	30	33	37	74	111	148	185	222	259	296	333
38	4	8	11	15	19	23	27	30	34	38	76	114	152	190	228	266	304	342
39	4	8	12	16	20	23	27	31	35	39	78	117	156	195	234	273	312	351
40	4	8	12	16	20	24	28	32	36	40	80	120	160	200	240	280	320	360
41	4	8	12	16	21	25	29	33	37	41	82	123	164	205	246	287	328	369
42	4	8	13	17	21	25	29	34	38	42	84	126	168	210	252	294	336	378
43	4	9	13	17	22	26	30	34	39	43	86	129	172	215	258	301	344	387
44	4	9	13	18	22	26	31	35	40	44	88	132	176	220	264	308	352	396
45	5	9	14	18	23	27	32	36	41	45	90	135	180	225	270	315	360	405
46	5	9	14	18	23	28	32	37	41	46	92	138	184	230	276	322	368	414
47	5	9	14	19	24	28	33	38	42	47	94	141	188	235	282	329	376	423
48	5	10	14	19	24	29	34	38	43	48	96	144	192	240	288	336	384	432
49	5	10	15	20	25	29	34	39	44	49	98	147	196	245	294	343	392	441
50	5	10	15	20	25	30	35	40	45	50	100	150	200	250	300	350	400	450

Tension   1cm   2cm   3cm   4cm   5cm   6cm   7cm   8cm   9cm   10cm   20cm   30cm   40cm   50cm   60cm   70cm   80cm   90cm

Make contact

Once you've fallen in love with the world of knitting, you will want to keep up to date with the latest developments in designs, patterns, yarns and knitting networks. Here are some starting points on where to look when you go online or into your local book store to find great resources for your new craft.

Books

If you want to expand your library with further books, check out the internet and your local book and craft stores for a great selection. Some of our favourites include:

Stitch 'n Bitch: The Knitter's Handbook
Debbie Stoller (Workman Publishing, 2003)

Stitch 'n Bitch Nation
Debbie Stoller (Workman Publishing, 2005)
Check out these hip guides to knitting from one of the foremost US knit chicks. Techniques, projects and attitude are all included.

The Knitter's Bible
Claire Crompton (David & Charles, 2004)
Another great guide to knitting that includes gorgeous projects for you to try out your skills straight away.

200 Knitted Blocks
Jan Eaton (David & Charles, 2005)
A library of 200 patterns, colours and textures to create blocks for throws, ponchos, scarves, hangings – just use your imagination…

Magazines

Keep up with the latest trends, yarns and knit-happenings with regular magazines – buy them at the craft store or newsagent, or ask for them at your local library.

Simply Knitting
simplyknitting@futurenet.co.uk

Vogue Knitting
www.vogueknitting.com

Interweave Knits
www.interweave.com

Rowan
www.knitrowan.com

Rebecca
www.rebecca-online.de/cont_en/

Classy clickers... share their books and magazines with their fellow knit chicks. It's a great way to swap ideas, and of course save money to spend on more yummy yarns!

Style secrets
Websites and magazines are a great way to stay in touch with the latest yarn suppliers – new yarns are available all the time, so keep an eye out for suppliers and outlets.

Websites

Get online – the fastest way for knitters to spread and word and much else besides!

www.stitchnbitch.co.uk
www.stitchnbitch.org
Join the knitting revolution and get into knitting networks.

www.castoff.info/
A great UK site with plenty of links to other knitting sites, plus other useful information.

www.knitty.com
A US site containing funky free patterns and loads of fab articles and contacts.

www.bhkc.co.uk
The British Hand Knitting Confederation is dedicated to promoting the craft of hand knitting. This site will keep you up to date with shows, courses and competitions, plus a feast of contacts.

Index

Sitting pretty

Knitting tends to be thought of as a stay-at-home hobby; a craft for people who either don't get out much or can't get out much. This is not to be sneered at; on a cold winter's night, there is something very comforting and cosy about sitting at home immersed in wool. But one of the joys of knitting is that it is a very portable craft. All you need are two sticks and a ball of yarn. Most of us spend a lot of time hanging around waiting for things – buses, trains, planes, friends, children – and knitting is just the thing to put that dead time to creative use. Knitting is the ideal occupation if you're facing long train journeys, short bus trips, or an arduous commuter haul. You can knit while idling in the park or sunning yourself on a beach. Once you've started knitting in public, you won't stop.

Have knitting, will travel!

Making on the move

If you're a knitter on the go, you will have to think about how to tote your equipment and projects around with you. An extra-chunky aran sweater might not be the ideal project to transport if you intend to be knitting on a sardine-packed subway train, for example. So go for something smaller and more manageable, like a beanie hat or the panel of a bag. A lot of travelling knitters swear by socks as the ideal knitting-in-transit item. You will also become the object of fascination for your fellow voyagers; socks need at least four double-pointed needles, so you will look as if you are tussling with a hedgehog.

Take to the skies

Knitters tend to be ingenious people and will use whatever they have to hand in emergency situations to get their knitting fix. In the post-9/11 days when a lot of airlines banned knitting needles from hand luggage (some still do, so find out if you're intending to do some mile-high stitching), some unstoppable knitters made do with biros (for a chunky knit) and cocktail sticks (for a finer gauge). The security situation is a little more relaxed now, so you should be able to knit to your heart's content until you touch down.

The knitty kit

If you intend to knit on the move regularly, you might want to kit yourself out with the essential accessories. You will need a roomy bag with lots of compartments and pockets to keep your needles, yarn and gadgets (see pages 25–27) separate from all the rest of your stuff. If you're working from a pattern, photocopy it and keep it in a plastic envelope to save lugging round the magazine or book it came from. Rather than taking large-sized dressmakers' scissors, take a pair of nail clippers, or, at a pinch, use the metal cutter you find on a box of dental floss. To keep your yarn clean and untangled, put it in an empty baby-wipes carton – you can feed the end of the yarn through the hole in the lid.

There's no stopping you

Knitters find it hard to stop, sometimes. They've even been known to knit on rollercoaster rides, in breaks between surfing, and while skydiving. Then again, you could just knit in the bath…Try taking up the needles, and see where it takes you.

knitting

Finding your own way

You will soon find out what sort of knitting most fires your creativity and imagination. Once you know the basic stitches and processes, you're free to explore all sorts of paths. You might be drawn to making stylish, ornamental beaded purses and bags. You might want to see your children dressed in fun, colourful rainbow-striped jumpers. Maybe you'll fall in love with the beautiful intricacies of lace knitting, and make your own featherlight heirloom shawl. You might want to brighten up your home with a few lushly textured chenille cushions. Maybe you just want to keep out the winter chill with a satisfyingly chunky woolly hat and scarf. There are no limits.

The new knitting circles

Once you've made knitting a part of your life, you will want to share it with other people. Generations ago, knitting circles were a traditional way for women to come together to work and bond. Modern knitters (and not just women) are revitalizing this tradition. Lively, convivial knitting groups are being set up in cafés, bars, pubs and members' homes for people to come together to eat, drink, stitch, socialize, and to learn from and inspire each other. If you're a newbie uncertain of your technique, there'll be someone you can ask for advice. The Internet has been a real spur in the creation of the new knitting community, with yarn enthusiasts publishing their own blogs, the availability of online yarn stores, and bustling knitting forums. It's all out there – go and join in!

Make fabulous friends

Simply fabulous

Knitting is fun, fabulous and creative. It's a craft that's being rediscovered by a new generation. Pick up your sticks and join the yarn revolution…

Shop till you drop!

Who's knitting now?

Knitting has long suffered an interminably unfashionable image. It's been associated with everything grannyish, unhip and unsexy. But if you start exploring the current world of knitting, you could have your preconceptions seriously challenged. A whole new generation of knitters has taken up the needles – kids, students, young people, old people, women and, yes, even men. And they're not just knitting afghans and baby bootees; they're creating seriously desirable and stylish accessories, garments and beautiful things for their homes. So what's the appeal?

Why knit?

In a world that is increasingly dominated by mass production, high-street consumerism and homogeneity, there is something hugely satisfying about making something unique by hand. A few generations ago, knitting was functional and utilitarian. People made their own clothes because they had to. There is still a strong practical element to knitting – there are plenty of people around churning out socks and sweaters for their families – but many modern knitters get a buzz from the creativity of wielding sticks and yarn. They don't necessarily need to knit, but they love it.

There are some truly beautiful yarns around in a huge range of alluring colours. You can use the traditional, tried-and-tested materials of wool and cotton, the more upmarket luxury fibres like cashmere, angora, silk and linen, or the more experimental yarns. There are yarns available made from bamboo; a silk-like fibre can be made from soya protein; and there are funky synthetic yarns around that knit up like fake fur.

Knitting in fashion

So, once you've been dazzled by the array of yarns available, what are you going to make? Again, there's been a total revolution in the handknitting world. Most people's idea of a handknitted garment is probably very far removed from anything you might see on a catwalk. Even if you never had an elderly female relative knit you a horrendously garish Christmas sweater, we can all picture what sort of monstrosities might once have been inflicted on us. But if you're looking for inspiration, there are some brilliant patterns around now by some very talented designers. Whether your taste is chic, classic, funky, casual, punky or quirky, you'll find things that are inspiring and enjoyable to make and that make you look fantastic when you wear them. And then you can always start designing your own items…

Contents...

A DAVID & CHARLES BOOK
Copyright © David & Charles Limited 2006

David & Charles is an F+W Publications Inc. company
4700 East Galbraith Road
Cincinnati, OH 45236

First published in the UK in 2006

Text copyright © University of Southampton

Montse Stanley's estate asserts their right to be
identified as author of this work in accordance with
the Copyright, Designs and Patents Act, 1988.

A catalogue record for this book is available from the
British Library.

ISBN-13: 978-0-7153-2177-5 paperback
ISBN-10: 0-7153-2177-3 paperback

Printed in China by SNP Leefung
for David & Charles
Brunel House   Newton Abbot   Devon

Commissioning Editor Vivienne Wells
Editor Jennifer Proverbs
Head of Design and Illustrations Prudence Rogers
Production Controller Roger Lane
Project Editor Nicola Hodgson

Visit our website at www.davidandcharles.co.uk

David & Charles books are available from all
good bookshops; alternatively you can contact
our Orderline on 0870 9908222 or write to us at
FREEPOST EX2 110, D&C Direct, Newton Abbot,
TQ12 4ZZ (no stamp required UK only);
US customers call 800-289-0963 and
Canadian customers call 800-840-5220.

Acknowledgments

The publishers would like to thank the Montse
Stanley's Estate and the Winchester School of Art
for their permission to use Montse Stanley's material
in this work.

Simply Fabulous
knitting

based on the work of
MONTSE STANLEY

D&C
David and Charles